The Quest for Utopia in
Twentieth-Century America

TIMOTHY MILLER

The Quest for

UTOPIA

in Twentieth-Century America

VOLUME I: 1900–1960

Syracuse University Press

The paper used in this publication meets the minimum requirements of American
National Standard for Information Sciences—Permanence of Paper for Printed Library
Materials, ANSI Z39.48-1984. ∞ ™

Permission to reprint or adapt the following is gratefully acknowledged:
Timothy Miller, "Artists' Colonies as Communal Societies in the Arts and Crafts Era,"
Communal Societies 16 (1996), 43–70.

LIBRARY OF CONGRESS CATALOGING-IN-PUBLICATION DATA
Miller, Timothy, 1944–
    The quest for utopia in twentieth century America / Timothy Miller.
      p.   cm.
    Includes bibliographical references and index.
    Contents: Vol 1. 1900–1960
    ISBN 0-8156-2775-0 (v. 1 : alk. paper)
    1. Collective settlements—United States—History—20th century.
    2. Utopias—History—20th century.   I. Title.
    HX653.M55   1998
    335'.12'09730904—dc21   97-48903

Manufactured in the United States of America

For Jesse
Let all things be done decently and in order.

TIMOTHY MILLER is associate professor of religious studies at the University of Kansas. He is the author of *American Communes, 1860–1960: A Bibliography* and *The Hippies and American Values* and the editor of *When Prophets Die: The Postcharismatic Fate of New Religious Movements* and *America's Alternative Religions.*

Contents

Acknowledgments

This survey of a diverse and often obscure set of American historical phenomena could not have been conducted without extensive assistance from dozens of persons. At the hazard of omitting mention of important contributors to the effort, I want to thank several students, scholars, and others whose roles in making this work as comprehensive as possible were critical.

As a group the members of the Communal Studies Association provided valuable information and reflection on dozens of occasions. Specific contributions from CSA members have ranged from single perceptive comments to long episodes of spadework. No other academic organization equals the CSA in collegiality or congeniality. A version of chapter 2 appeared as an article in the CSA's journal *Communal Societies,* and I appreciate permission to republish it here.[1]

My students have always been among my best teachers and research associates, and their contribution to the work at hand has been very considerable. They have often traveled and worked long hours to do valuable fieldwork and have regularly turned up new groups with which I had been unfamiliar. I would single out for special appreciation Eva Garcia, whose clear insights helped me refine my ideas about definitions of intentional community, and Elly Wynia, who started with a simple term paper assignment and ultimately wrote the definitive study of the previously obscure Church of God and Saints of Christ.[2] A complete list of students who provided valuable assistance would be pages long.

Several persons provided me with essential materials I could not obtain independently, and at the risk of omitting some important ones I will name a few of them. Daryl Ann Dutton Cody put considerable effort into retrieving materials about Trabuco College from the UCLA library system. My brother Jeffrey Miller supplied accounts of Utah fundamentalist LDS communal life. Marion Goldman found essential contemporary accounts of Franz Creffield. Ernest Green and Sally Kitch provided primary materials on the Woman's Commonwealth. Lyman Tower Sargent sent a steady stream of references to a wide variety of primary and secondary source materials. Brad Whitsel alerted me to small apocalyptic communities I would otherwise have missed. Robert Fogarty helped me sort out the extensive archives of Community Service, now housed at Antioch College. Deborah Altus, my closest research associate for the last several years, has embodied scholarly competence, hard work, and good cheer in unrivaled proportions.

Archivists and librarians at many institutions ranging from large university libraries to small local institutions have been research partners in all my work, and the diligence and competence of library professionals is steady and unmatched. My colleagues in the library system at the University of Kansas have always cheerfully met my every research need, and Gina Walker of the University of Southern Indiana has always been most helpful in finding materials in the archives of the Center for Communal Studies. J. Gordon Melton has given me access to his vast research collections at the Institute for the Study of American Religion in Santa Barbara, and without his resources this study would have been greatly impoverished. Mark Weimer and his staff at the Syracuse University library provided essential documents and handled my inquiries most agreeably.

In my research travels I have visited dozens of active intentional communities, and their members have always been supportive of my work, even though they have other things to do than help scholars ferret out obscure information. Their hospitality and assistance are outstanding and much appreciated.

My family has been remarkably tolerant of trips to distant libraries, communal sites, and other information sources for more than a decade. My appreciation of the support of Tamara, Jesse, and Abraham is beyond expression in words.

Introduction
The Persistence of Community

Many students of communalism in American history, including some of the most distinguished of them, have declared the twentieth century—or at least the first two-thirds of it—virtually devoid of intentional communities. One widely repeated thesis has it that communal societies, exemplified by such prominent cases as the Shakers, the Harmony Society, and the Oneida Community, had a historic heyday in the early nineteenth century but were on their way down, if not out, by the last third of that century, doomed by the rise of modern transportation, industry, and social mores—as well as, in several cases, their commitment to celibacy. Everett Webber, in his *Escape to Utopia* (1959), argued that although sectarian religious communes had once been among the principal loci of social reform activity, reformism eventually moved from the religious arena to the political, and the communes lost an essential part of their reason for being. Private health insurance and pension systems, along with government social-assistance programs and other "innovations and leveling contrivances," made the security blanket once offered by communes unnecessary. Webber's flat conclusion was that communitarianism was "surely done."[1] In those remarks Webber echoed the noted historian of American communitarianism Arthur Bestor, who a few years earlier had argued that by the late nineteenth century communal settlements could not achieve the technological sophistication needed to compete in the industrializing world, and that in any event reformers were approaching social problems in new and noncommunal ways: "For most American reformers in an industrial age, communitarianism was a tool that had lost its edge, probably for ever."[2] If a few communities might have defied the inevitability of oblivion, they were insignificant; the last refrain of the American communal song had been sung by about the 1860s, and only faint echoes remained thereafter.

That sweeping generalization does not stand close scrutiny. Robert

Fogarty has done more than any other scholar to date to refute it by publishing a book-length survey of American communes from 1865 to 1914, and his work serves to some extent as a predecessor to the present volume.[3] Fogarty argues that communitarianism has survived in part because its forms and characteristics have not been unchanging, because communalism has evolved in step with the larger history of the culture. The fact is that at no point since the early eighteenth century, when Ephrata was established in Pennsylvania and brought rigor to the communal form of organization that had been experimented with earlier, has America been without communes. The period of supposed communal declension, from about the 1860s onward, has had a full complement of functioning communities. Indeed, it is entirely possible that communitarianism has grown rather than dwindled with the passage of years both in numbers of communal sites and in membership. The explosive growth of the Hutterites since their arrival on these shores in 1874 has alone created a communal boom economy; thousands of Latter Day Saints (in the main Mormon church and in several smaller LDS denominations) have lived in geographic and economic communities since founder Joseph Smith Jr. announced in the 1830s that it was the will of God that a theocratic communitarianism called the United Order of Enoch be a part of the LDS way of life; and in pursuit of their diverse visions of a better world any number of socialists, religious visionaries, and secular idealists have repeatedly gathered into small colonies, hundreds of which were founded in, and many more of which had been founded earlier and were still operating in, the first half of the twentieth century alone.[4] Although firm statistics are impossibly elusive, it is just possible that more people are now living in community than ever before in American history, save for the incredible outburst of the late 1960s and early 1970s, by far the largest episode of commune building in American history. Certainly the death of the communal ideal is much exaggerated.

If the 1860s represented a communal watershed, it was as a marker of an accelerating move toward a diversity of communal forms. Earlier communities tended to be somewhat ghettoized; they were largely self-sufficient, and members did not spend much time away from the communal premises, in large part, undoubtedly, because for communal groups as for society as a whole modern technology had not yet made travel and communication commonplace.[5] Some communities, notably the Hutterites, maintain that kind of isolation today. But with the rise of separation of la-

bor and diversified economies in the nineteenth century, communes tended to expand their interrelationships with the rest of the world. Just as individuals and families now tend not to be subsistence farmers but wage
earners who are inextricably imbedded in a vast social fabric, most intentional communities interact daily with the outside world. Some communities eagerly sought widespread publicity, often because they were
demonstration projects for various social theories: the single-tax movement of the late nineteenth century, for example, eventually built more
than half a dozen "enclaves," villages where the economic theories of Henry George could be tried out in microcosm. Several groups of socialists
had similar motivations in their construction of communities. The idea
was that they would function as lighthouses to the world, beaming the
message of the single tax (or socialism) far and wide. The single-tax enclaves in particular helped pave the way for a new model of intentional
community consisting, spatially, of clustered private homes of like-think-
ing individuals and families. Historical circumstances, then, mandate new
understandings of the basic dimensions and nature of the communitarian
enterprise.

This book is the first installment of a larger effort that seeks to provide
a historical survey of American communal history in the twentieth century. Because so much of the story here is known to a few specialists at best,
this work has a cataloglike character; the emphasis has been on getting basic names and dates and facts, previously obscure, on the historical table.
In significant part this volume and its forthcoming sequel that will cover
the latter portion of the century seek to provide hitherto elusive basic data
to those who will interpret and place within the larger culture that special
type of applied idealism that is communal living. In an era in which individualism is enshrined, in which retreat from commitment to a common
good in favor of devotion to selfish interests seems to dominate the American outlook, this work argues that community has remained and does
remain a viable alternative way of life. It also seeks to demonstrate that
contrary to some assertions, intentional community is not so much an
episodic series of isolated occurrences as it is a continuous, if small, ongoing theme in American life.[6]

The Genesis of the Project

I did not at first undertake to survey the whole of communal history of
the twentieth century. In the mid-1980s I became interested in finding the

roots and causes of the tidal wave of thousands of communes, notably the countercultural ones, that appeared in the Western world in the 1960s and early 1970s, and set out to write a short book on the origins of that communal explosion that would focus on Drop City, a commune of bohemian artists founded in 1965 in Colorado that was just about the first of the genre. After I had written more than half of my draft text I began to work on an introduction.

The introduction to the work sought to place the communes of the 1960s era in their historical context, and that meant that a brief survey of intentional communities operating in the earlier twentieth century would be necessary, because I had become convinced that 1960s-era communes were not a sui generis phenomenon unrelated to the larger American communal tradition but largely a piece of a continuous, if not utterly seamless, communal fabric that stretches back for more than three centuries. Soon the brief survey itself was approaching the length of a book, and it became clear that what I was really about was the writing of the survey of recent and contemporary communitarianism that is by now long overdue.

Drop City and the other communes of the 1960s era and after will get their due, but they are now framed as only part of a much larger drama. This volume begins with the new century and chronicles the lives and projects of a remarkably dedicated and idealistic cadre of communitarians who kept a vision of human cooperation alive against sometimes formidable odds.

The Evolution of Communal Forms

Communal living has been an evolving phenomenon in American history. The genre has always been characterized by diversity and as a whole has undergone changes that are related to its slipping into relative obscurity in the past century. It may be that those seeking (but not finding) evidence of an ongoing communitarian tradition looked for dozens of large, orderly Shaker villages flooding the land with familiar images and lovely furniture, or for flamboyant, charismatic leaders such as Robert Owen or John Humphrey Noyes whose controversial philosophies kept them in the public spotlight, or for legions of people living from a common purse. Those patterns receded in the latter nineteenth century, and more recent communes have tended to be smaller than their predecessors, more democratically (or at least less flamboyantly) governed, and less rigid in structure, including economic structure. The changes in the pattern of community can be summarized in several categories:

Smaller size. Large individual communities with many hundreds of adherents living at one site became rare in the new century, and except for the Hutterites large networks of communal settlements were rare as well. The newer communes were mostly smaller than at least the more prominent of the earlier ones; where once hundreds or thousands had banded together, now a dozen or two might make a pleasing communal congregation. Smaller communities, incidentally, tended to have fewer assets, less wealth, than some of the larger, prosperous nineteenth-century societies had enjoyed, and America's long fascination with monetary success was not fed by the communes that in the twentieth century came to characterize the genre.

Leadership. Charismatic leaders headed several of the prominent nineteenth-century communes; such figures as George Rapp of the Harmony Society and John Humphrey Noyes of the Oneida Community were both unquestioned leaders of their flocks and well-known public figures of their respective epochs. Leaders with some charisma did continue to surface from time to time in the twentieth century, as in the case of Job Harrison, the founder of Llano del Rio Colony outside Los Angeles, and Katherine Tingley, the "Purple Lady" who oversaw the great Theosophical community of Point Loma in San Diego. They did not, however, reach the national stature of some of their more prominent nineteenth-century predecessors. That decline of personal, centralized leadership reflects in part the shift of many communities to new systems of organization.

New structures. Strong organizational hierarchies and benevolent autocrats belonged more to the nineteenth century than to the twentieth. The new communities were not likely to have powerful individual leaders on the order of Christian Metz in nineteenth-century Amana, or the centralized power that the various elders did among the Shakers. Twentieth-century communities were much more likely than their predecessors to be democratically governed and to allow substantial individual liberties to their members. Indeed, in the turn-of-the-century era a whole new type of community previously unimaginable surfaced—the community of anarchists, one with virtually no rules or leadership at all. As odd as it might seem, such anarchist communities as Home (Washington state) and Ferrer (New Jersey) became visible and durable contributors to the communitarian tradition.

New economic patterns. In many cases the completely communal economy popular in many nineteenth-century and earlier communities went by the wayside; although some economic commonality is inherent to the definition of "intentional community," many communities now demanded less than totally unitary financial arrangements. New systems evolved in which members, after they had arranged to provide appropriate support for the group as a whole, could retain some private assets instead of contributing all to the common fund.

New patterns of land ownership. Hand in hand with financial decentralization came changes in ways of holding property. A single tract of land held by the community for the benefit and use of all eventually ceased to be the normative pattern; in its place came a new system of small, adjacent tracts to which their occupants had certain specific rights—either outright ownership or at least leasehold rights. The first inklings of such a system came with the single-tax movement, which in about ten so-called enclaves in the United States developed private leaseholds within cooperative villages, most famously at Fairhope, Alabama, and Arden, Delaware (both of which, incidentally, are still in operation at this writing). In the new century many new groups—the Fellowship Farms and Little Landers, for example—experimented further with new ways of possessing and using land in community. By the 1930s what came to be known as land trust communities, in which residents leased tracts of land for personal homes while sharing common land and facilities as well, were becoming well established. An early example of that pattern was the Celo community, now more than half a century old and thriving, in North Carolina. The land trust arrangement is more prominent among intentional communities today than ever before.

Lower demands for commitment by members. Communities once typically asked their members for lifelong commitment, even though frequent defections in many cases belied that goal. In the twentieth century some communities continued to seek total commitment, but many more, adjusting to reality, did not. Membership may or may not have been more fluid than it had been in earlier times, but turnover in many communities was accepted as a normal part of the landscape. Mechanisms for the transfer of property in land trust and similar communities were developed to ease the comings and goings of members. In the secular communities, especially, where no threat of burning in hell kept marginal members in the fold, membership turnover, as a percentage of total numbers, was often well into double digits annually.

Lowered profiles. Certainly communities operating in the century after 1865 were less prominent, less publicly visible, than their illustrious predecessors had been. No communal situation in the twentieth century (at least before the 1960s) was as flamboyant as that of the hundreds of Oneidans living in complex marriage or the thousands of Shakers living celibately in a score of tidy, quaint villages had been. The decline in distinctiveness and size caused public interest in communal living to diminish. What now would attract a swarm of Sunday feature writers? Who would care?

Moreover, outside pressure led many twentieth-century communities to keep their profiles deliberately low. After 1917 the United States went through a major Red scare, one that would persist in various episodes until the last decade of the century. Intentional communities were taunted and harassed by their neighbors in some places, and they were occasionally berated by demogogic public officials.[7] Simply put, the rise of the Bolsheviks in Russia made all collectivist tendencies, all common enterprise, suspect. The early Palmer raids of the 1920s communicated to small-*c* communists that what they were trying to do was un-American. In the 1930s the government-sponsored cooperative colonies that New Dealers had started to help displaced farmers and workers get back on their feet met their demise on the floor of an angry Congress, some of whose more vocal members engaged in egregious Red-baiting to stifle collective approaches to dealing with the deprivations of the depression. In the 1950s Sen. Joseph McCarthy again created an atmosphere in which anything dedicated to the common good rather than private gain smelled subversive. Marx and Engels may have sneered at the socialism of intentional communities as "utopian" and utterly to be avoided in favor of "scientific" socialism, but such fine distinctions were lost on the Red-baiters. A solid core of committed communitarians survived throughout these hard times, but one can hardly blame them for keeping their ideals and aspirations largely to themselves.

As one might suspect, on sober reflection, not many actual Reds lived in American communes during the century. There were a few, notably at Commonwealth College in Arkansas and perhaps a handful at Newllano, but the Red scare never had much contact with reality. What mattered was that the heat was on the communes just as surely as it would have been had they truly been Communist indoctrination camps. The Red scare was compounded, moreover, by the fact that several twentieth-century communities were composed largely of pacifists; during World War II, particularly, pacifists were generally unpopular, to say the least, and sometimes, as at the Macedonia Cooperative Community in Georgia, local tensions ran high over the pacifists' unwillingness to support the war effort as well as their definitely suspect (i.e., communal) living arrangements.

Reflecting the larger culture. Finally, the intentional communities of the twentieth century may have been noticed less than their predecessors had been because they were in many ways reflections of the larger society, not necessarily challenges to it. Communal patterns evolved, reflecting larger social themes: socialism was in its American heyday in the late nineteenth and early twentieth centuries, and several avowedly secular socialist communes (Equality and Llano, for example) became leading communal centers of their times. When the social gospel movement swept through American churches, a communal embodiment of it emerged in such enclaves as the Christian Commonwealth Colony and the Straight Edge Community. A prominent new current in the visual arts at the turn of the century, the arts and crafts movement, spawned perhaps a dozen artists' communes. Intentional communities may have had distinctive ideologies and residential and economic systems, but they also reflected what was going on in the larger society around them.

What Is an Intentional Community?

If communes became smaller, less wealthy, less visible, and less distinct from the larger culture than they had been in earlier days, were they still communes at all? Might it not be true that communitarianism, properly speaking, had died out and that some pale imitation not worthy of stepping into its historical line had simply managed to steal its name and reputation?

It all depends on one's definition of terms. Some communes had grand goals that amounted to an enshrinement of the hubris that began with the Puritans, the belief that mortal humans could create heaven on earth.[8] More circumscribedly, however, the historical fact is that intentional communities have always been a diverse lot, usually with fairly modest goals, and communal forms have always been evolving. Groups one could logically consider communal can vary widely in ideological or religious outlook, organizational structure, spatial arrangements, internal cohesiveness, architectural preferences, and any of a hundred other ways. Allen Butcher and Albert Bates, trying to create categories in which to group the wide array of organizational systems found in contemporary intentional communities, came up with four forms of communitarian organization, which they called collective, cooperative, communal, and diverse. That last category, moreover, is simply a catchall for any number of different arrangements.[9] Comprehension of the whole phenomenon of communal living, broadly defined, necessitates the casting of a wide net. If we were to restrict the scope of this volume to deal only with groups with fully common economies (the Hutterites, for example), we would be left with only a narrow slice of the otherwise large and diverse communal pie, for many of those who have pursued the common life in the twentieth century have not given up individual title to all their assets and possessions. Instead, the groups surveyed here occupied a variety of points on the spectrum of community. My inclination has been to minimize definitional requirements to broaden the range of groups in the study, the better to understand the wide variety of ideas and systems found under the general rubric of residentially based cooperation.

To put the matter differently, it makes sense to define communitarianism not so much in terms of form as in terms of impulse, of motivation. When people choose to live together and share at least some of their resources for the common good or for the betterment of the world, something communal has happened. Once the prime impulse has proceeded to be embodied in a particular outward form, we are talking details, not essence.

On the other hand, the kinds of communitarianism discussed in this volume are not without limits. Not included, for example, will be a difficult borderline case, the Amish. These people whose lives focus on their religious/ethnic common life certainly meet most of the standards laid out in the definition of intentional community offered below; they do live in largely contiguous neighborhoods, and they do engage in substantial economic sharing, at least in times of duress. Their homes are typically well separated, however, and they hold their property privately. The Amish represent a shade of gray, but the noncommunal central features of their otherwise close-knit life cause them to be excluded here.

One category of community that clearly qualifies for inclusion has not been examined here mainly to help keep the study from being much larger than it already is. The religious communities, or orders, of the Catholic Church and a few other denominations fit the model covered here in every regard. However, they are so many, so pervasive, so long-lived that giving them full attention would easily double the length of this work. Because a large literature on the religious communities already exists and most such communities preserve their own history well, I have not included them in this otherwise broad survey.

Trying to balance comprehensive coverage with a need for limits, I have included groups other than the Catholic and similar religious communities in this study if they have met all of the following fairly inclusive criteria:

1. *A sense of common purpose and of separation from the dominant society.* Common purpose can be found in a detailed and exclusive religious ideology, or it can simply be a desire to get together with other like-minded folks and live communally. A rejection of or at least commitment to separation from the dominant society is involved in that sense of purpose; some dissatisfaction with the way things as a whole are going is fundamental fuel for communitarianism. A living situation in which a common residence is only incidental to the lives of the group's members and does not involve any real critique of the larger society (as in the case of college students living in group housing, for example) does not provide an articulated intent by members to live communally and to some extent apart from the cultural mainstream; thus it does not qualify.

2. *Some form and level of self-denial, of voluntary suppression of individual choice for the good of the group.* Communitarianism is predicated upon some degree of suppression of individualism and the pursuit of the common, not just the individual, good. Many twentieth-century communities have been broadly tolerant of individual will, but all included here have put limits on what one can choose for oneself, as in the case of the land trust communities that meddle little in one's life most of the time but require that one sell one's property only to a buyer approved by the group as a whole. It is critical that limitations on individual choice be voluntary, because attitude is essential. Involuntary suppression of the will is imprisonment, not community.

3. *Geographic proximity.* Members of the community can all live in one dormitory, or in rooms in one or more common buildings, or in separate houses on commonly owned ground, or even in separately owned houses on clustered small landholdings. Somehow a geographic closeness and a clear spatial focus must be involved.

4. *Personal interaction.* Those living closely together cannot simply be neighbors who commute to jobs and shut their doors to the rest when they return home. Intentional communities always have a good bit of gemeinschaft about them; their members have regular, personal interactions at a level deeper than that of, say, a street in suburbia.

5. *Economic sharing.* The range of options here is enormous. Some groups have total community of goods; the Hutterites, for example, individually own virtually nothing, preferring instead that the community supply the needs of all from the common stores. Most modern communities, however, have allowed a fair degree of personal property ownership. Thus the threshold for this study is low. A group qualifies if it holds land in common, even if it allows members to have privately owned plots as well. If members maintain private finances but pay dues to a pool for common purposes, the group qualifies for inclusion here. As long as there is some mingling of finances or property ownership the standard will be considered met.

6. *Real existence.* The world of utopian communities is largely a world of dreams, including many that never reach any kind of actuality. Many a would-be founder of a commune has written a tract, issued a prospectus, mailed letters to inquirers, published a utopian novel, given a speech, or otherwise proclaimed in good faith that some commune or other is in the works. One might guess that for every community begun, a hundred have remained on the drawing board. In many cases an individual or a family has proclaimed the establishment of a community, only to see few, if any, rally to the call.[10] Thus it is important to specify that the communities surveyed here are those that managed to get off the drawing board and into real existence, although their populations were in many cases small or their life spans short or both. Although a study of communities projected but never started would be valuable in its own right, this book seeks to avoid projects built only of rhetoric.

Historical actuality is frequently hard to determine, given the paucity of information on some groups and the boosterish tone of most of the literature on certain others. The literature of intentional community is packed with manifestos and calls to community, some of which resulted in concrete projects and many of which undoubtedly did not. I have tried in this volume to include only actual groups, but inconclusive evidence may have led me into error in both inclusion and exclusion.

7. *Critical mass.* Although I hesitate to establish a rigid size threshold here, I am not regarding a family, or a single person interested in having

others move in, or a pair of roommates, as a community, even if those involved are magnanimous, community-minded souls. Generally, it seems reasonable to think that an intentional community should include at least five individuals, some of whom must be unrelated by biology or exclusive intimate relationship. Determining size is often problematic, however; the limited literature on many of the more obscure communities discussed in this volume never mentions the size of the population of the group in question, and I have often had to make hazardous guesses about size to include or exclude a group.

Here endeth the definition. Others have defined communes in other ways—as groups deliberately withdrawing from the larger society, as structured, private subsocieties, as value-oriented social systems, or as groups demanding the absolute eschewal of private holdings or personal free will, for example. Some have seen work relations or rigid restrictions on membership or a sense of withdrawal from the larger society as definitive.[11] Others have tried to exclude from qualification certain "cults" on the grounds that they are authoritarian rather than cooperative or patriarchal rather than egalitarian. However, drawing a line around such categories, especially the more value-laden ones, is difficult, and runs the risk of excluding a group that really is communal but does not conform to one's personal preferences about, say, democracy in communal government. By avoiding such tests I hope to avoid eliminating from this study many groups more logically included than excluded.

Communal Terminology

No generally accepted system of terms describing communalism exists. What to one author is "communal" is to another perhaps "cooperative" or "collective." This book is not theoretical in nature, and thus I have avoided the thorny problem of creating a terminologically precise language for dealing with my subject. Such terms as "commune," "community," "colony," and "enclave" are used interchangeably.

Types of Communities

Recounting the stories of dozens of diverse communal societies in something resembling systematic fashion requires that some kind of categorization of communities be established. Here as in the case of terminology no standard has ever been established as normative among communal studies scholars. One might group communities by date of founding, or longevity, or public renown, or organizational structure, or ideology, or any one or more of dozens of similarly identifiable characteristics. After more than a decade of research in communal history, I have found no entirely satisfactory system of categorization, and thus in this book the categories that are employed are not offered as definitive. This work is historical in nature, and chronological categories are therefore primary here; communities are broadly grouped by date of founding in chapters that cover one or two decades. Next it has seemed to me that religious and secular communities can be readily distinguished, and I have generally used those broad groupings in each of the book's chapters. Further subcategorization becomes progressively more difficult, and I have thus simply created ad hoc categories that are not consistent from chapter to chapter, letting the historical data drive the categorization process rather than trying to shoehorn a multifaceted phenomenon into a predetermined analytical structure. One of the central arguments of this book is that communal patterns have varied considerably as communitarian ideas and forms have evolved over the years, and I have tried to establish categories that fit circumstances as required, recognizing that some inconsistencies are unavoidable and that most readers conversant with American communal history would probably have organized things differently.

The exception to that scheme occurs with the special phenomenon of artists' colonies. Most of them were active in the early years of the century, but a few were later, and their distinctive nature seemed to dictate that they be considered as a whole. Thus they have their own chapter at a point in the volume that reflects their chronological heyday.

The Limitations of the Study

This study has sought to be as comprehensive as possible a chronicle of communal living in the first six decades of the twentieth century. Inevitably, however, it has gaps and limitations. Several such shortcomings should be enumerated to let the reader know just where this investigation most clearly falls short of its goal of inclusiveness:

Paucity of data. Some communal groups have not been included because not enough credible evidence on them has surfaced. Various observers of the communal scene, both contemporaries writing of their own time and place and historians writing retrospectively, have presented lists of intentional communities that seem reliable enough—most of the groups on the lists, after all, demonstrably existed, and the authors of the lists seem to know what they are talking about—but simply do not provide enough information to support discussion of certain groups here and do not contain references that would lead a researcher to further information. Daniel Greenberg, for example, in his dissertation research on children and education in intentional communities compiled a list of modern communities that included Aloe Community (founded 1916), Circle Pines Center (1938), Grailville (1944), Meeting School (1957), and Pumpkin Hollow Farm (1937), along with many more familiar communities. Those dates would place all of those groups squarely within the purview of this volume, and the thoroughness and care of Greenberg's scholarship is such that one can be fairly confident that each of them did exist. If further information about them has survived, however, I have not been able to find it.[12]

The paucity of data about many communes reflects the marginal status to which intentional communities have been relegated in American life. We have records about every pitch thrown and every fly ball caught in every professional baseball game played over the past century, and every bit of gossip about the life of every hack actor ever to grace the silver screen, but about many a group of people who set out to save the world by constructing a new society from the ground up we know virtually nothing. Such are our collective priorities for knowing our past.

Indeterminate dates. Here we have a subset of the previous shortcoming. Historical work by definition pays attention to dates, but in some cases reliable chronological information on certain communes is unobtainable. Even after considerable investigation, I found it impossible to date certain communities firmly, particularly in regard to their dissolution, and in a few cases that problem meant that I could not determine whether or not a given group properly fit within the chronological scope of this book. I could not, for example, figure out just when the New Jerusalem community of Cyrus Spragg ended (or when it began, for that matter)—if it existed at all.[13] The odds are strong that if it did exist it was over before 1900, for we are told that Spragg had been married for five years in 1840; but he is said to have lived to be an old man, and seems to have had the kind of charismatic presence that attracted followers through thick and thin, despite his thoroughly unconventional behavior and ideas. Given the factual shakiness and chronological vagueness of the story, it seems prudent to omit it in a work of history, intriguing yarn that it is. In this and several other cases communal chronology and even certain existence seem destined to remain beyond our grasp.

The problem of indeterminate dates is abetted by the fact that many American intentional communities never exactly disbanded, but gradually dropped their communitarian features and became neighborhoods or towns. Commune members sometimes lived in the area for years afterward. Norvelt, Pennsylvania, for example, now appears on state maps as a small town, which it is today; it was founded as one of the depression-era subsistence-homestead communities, and evolved into a village of private homes, its cooperative features evaporating slowly over years or even decades. Most of the New Jersey Jewish colonies underwent the same kind of transformation, and picking a date at which an enclave ceased being recognizably communal is at best difficult. Thus I have had to make judgment calls in compiling my lists of communities within the scope of this study, and recognize that some will find that I have wrongly included or excluded certain communities.

We are dealing here only with groups that had important communal features in 1900 or thereafter. Many movements, most of them religious, had early communal periods but by the dawn of the twentieth century had abandoned those arrangements completely, although they continued to exist as religious organizations. For example, the small group of Latter Day Saint believers who followed James Strang to Beaver Island, Michigan, and lived communally there for several years gave up intentional community early on, but their descendants still exist as a small LDS denomination today. Their communalism and that of other similarly situated groups belongs to an earlier era, not that covered by this tome.

The Continuing Tradition

The venerable American institution of communal living was alive and well at the dawn of the twentieth century. Dozens, at least, of communities imported or founded in earlier years were still active. The most prominent communitarian movements active were then, as has typically been the case throughout American history, religious in nature: Hutterites, Shakers, and some of the smaller Latter Day Saints groups. All were active players on the communal scene, as were many other groups, ranging from several of the various Theosophical organizations to such small and isolated groups as the Esoteric Fraternity. In the following pages we will examine the historical contours of the communal enterprise as the century opened, surveying not only the more prominent groups but also several heretofore unheralded ones.

The Giants of the Communal Past

The first two-thirds of the nineteenth century, the era long regarded as the golden age of American communitarianism, saw the flourishing of the Shakers, the Harmony Society, the Oneida Community, the Amana Society, and other long-lived religious movements, along with such major secular groups and movements as the Icarians, who founded seven colonies in five states and in all spanned half a century, from 1848 to 1898, and the diverse Fourierists, whose ordered concept of utopia was the centerpiece of dozens of fairly short-lived experiments. By the opening of the new century many of the Grand Old Communes had folded, but others, including several of the largest and most famous of them, were still functioning with varying degrees of vigor.

THE SHAKERS

Second only to the Hutterites, arguably, in longevity and influence among American communitarians was the United Society of Believers in Christ's Second Appearing, or Shakers, who arrived in America in 1774 and still cling tenuously to existence more than two centuries later. In the early twentieth century these celibate idealists were in sharp numerical decline, their villages closing at a pace that alarmed the remaining believers. But they were well known, and their tidy settlements continued to be beacons for communitarians. In their earlier years the Shakers had been somewhat cloistered against the "world" and worldly luxuries, but in the latter decades of the nineteenth century they increasingly relaxed some of their stringent rules, allowing more and more pleasures and modern conveniences to creep into their lives. Decoration increasingly crept into architecture and landscaping, a deviation from the early Northeastern Shaker tradition of plain simplicity. The believers also became more public in their social activism. Eldress Anna White embodied the new outlook well, joining such outside organizations as the Women's Suffrage Association, lecturing publicly on social activism, and even, in 1905, spearheading a universal peace conference at the Mount Lebanon, New York, Shaker headquarters that brought in delegates from around the world. Although Shakerism was not destined to recapture its status as the preeminent American communal movement, at the dawn of the twentieth century it continued to be a visible embodiment of the communitarian ideal.

The decline in numbers had begun about the middle of the nineteenth century and continued unabated for much of the twentieth. By 1960 only two societies remained, both with few members, and the following year the last of the old-line brothers died, leaving a handful of sisters to carry on. About that time the leadership decided to close membership to newcomers, fearing, among other things, the plundering of the assets of the society along the lines of what had taken place at the hands of John Duss in the late years of the Harmony Society, about which more later.

But the Shakers at Sabbathday Lake, Maine, whose community had a history of accepting long-term visitors and who in the early 1960s were accepting, at least informally, one new male member, resisted the closure of membership, which was decreed by the Shaker leadership housed at the other functioning village, Canterbury, New Hampshire. A rift between the two small colonies continued until the last of the Canterbury leaders, Bertha Lindsay, died in 1990. At this writing Sabbathday Lake continues with eight members of varying ages, two of them males, and others have recently expressed interest in entering the novitiate. The Shaker flame promises to burn for some time to come.[1]

AMANA

One of the longest-lived and largest American communal groups, the Amana Society, was operating with stable prosperity as the twentieth century opened. Amana had its roots nearly two centuries earlier in Germany as a part of the Pietist movement, whose adherents found the state Lutheran church cold and spiritless and sought a warm, heartfelt, zealous faith. Many groups of Pietists eventually separated from the Lutheran church and created their own intimate fellowships, sometimes under local charismatic leadership. The distinctive principle of the Society of True Inspiration, as the group that founded Amana was formally known, was the belief that God could communicate with human beings through special persons, or prophets, as surely in the present as had been the case in biblical times. Attracted like many other groups and individuals to the promise of the new American nation (and burdened by economic and social difficulties at home), the Inspirationists began their migration across the Atlantic in 1842. They purchased the five thousand-acre Seneca Indian Reservation just outside Buffalo and with great industriousness built a settlement they called Ebenezer. In 1843 the group of about eight hundred members adopted, at the behest of its inspired leader Christian Metz, community of property, an arrangement that would prevail for eighty-nine years. Problems in New York state (notably the growth of Buffalo, which soon threatened the geographic isolation the Believers sought) eventually prompted a relocation, and in 1854 the Amana Society, as it became known in its new home, began moving to eastern Iowa.[2]

By the dawn of the new century the Inspirationists appeared to be thriving, but omens of future economic problems had already appeared. The agricultural depression of the late nineteenth century had taken a toll on the Amanans, who had, among other industries, extensive farming operations. Economic stagnation marked the first years of the new century;

although the society had some good years, the general trend was downward, and a catastrophic fire in 1923 dealt the community a sharp blow.[3] At least as important as the economic decline, however, was a decline of communal commitment. Members of the society increasingly disdained demanding work assignments and created opportunities for the individual accumulation of money and possessions. The arrival of the Great Depression brought economic and social problems to a head, and in 1932 the society ended its eighty-nine-year experiment in community of property, turning its industries into private enterprises and transferring homes and other property to individual ownership. In effect the once-communal villages that constituted Amana became small towns of persons more or less bound together by religion and heritage but otherwise not terribly unlike the rest of rural America, except that they have become swamped by tourists. A communal society that looked unchanging as the century opened had major transformations looming.

THE HARMONY SOCIETY

The Harmony Society was one of the grandest and oldest communal organizations still functioning as the twentieth century began, but it was by then feeble. Like the Amana Society, it had its roots in the Pietist movement that arose out of German Lutheranism in the sixteenth and seventeenth centuries.

Among the Pietist teachers who gathered groups of believers about themselves was George Rapp of Iptingen, Württemberg, Germany, whose followers gathered into a separate movement in the mid-1780s. Like other Pietists the Rappites experienced persecution, and by the early 1800s decided to move across the Atlantic. The first large group of immigrants arrived in 1804, and they formally organized themselves into the Harmony Society the following year. Their new home, Harmony, was a tract of forty-five hundred acres (later expanded to seven thousand) in western Pennsylvania; there they built homes and workshops for the population that grew until it reached more than eight hundred by about 1810.

Growth from immigration ceased by 1819, and the society never attracted the numbers of German-speaking American converts it would have taken to hold the population steady. Thus Harmony's demise was written as early as 1807, when a rule of celibacy was adopted. Many good years remained, however, even though the community twice pulled up stakes and moved hundreds of miles, first to New Harmony, in southwestern Indiana, in 1814, and then, a decade later, back to Pennsylvania. The last move was cushioned financially, because the society was able to sell the beautiful and well-constructed New Harmony in a single transaction—to the Scottish industrialist Robert Owen, who in the 1820s had journeyed to the United States to found an intentional community in which to put into practice his secular utopian theories. The Rappites purchased land just a few miles from the original Harmony and built yet another new town, this time known as Economy. There they prospered like no other communal society before or since, amassing a huge fortune largely from their highly successful business enterprises.

Slow decline, however, crept inevitably in and became ever more apparent after the death of Father Rapp in 1847. As the new century dawned, the few remaining members made the society a shadow of its former self. The situation was abetted by the work of John Duss, who had grown up in Economy after having been taken there by his mother as a young child in 1862 and who, after several years away, returned to the community in 1890 and soon thereafter became trustee with authority over the still-extensive assets of the society. With little opposition from the few aging Harmonists, Duss used much of the money to satisfy various of his personal whims, perhaps most notable among them the financing of a summer tour of the Metropolitan Opera orchestra in 1903, with Duss himself as nominal conductor. With much of the money thus dissipated, the few surviving members finally agreed to dissolve the commune in 1905.[4] The Harmony Society survived into the new century, but its great contribution to the American communitarian tradition was long over.

THE ONEIDA COMMUNITY

By most reckonings of communal life and death, the Oneida Community in upstate New York ended when it gave up complex marriage and privatized its industries in the early 1880s. By the inclusive definitions of community we are using in this volume, however, the major reorganization of the Oneida lifestyle and devolution of the communal enterprises do not represent a termination of communal life. In fact many of the Oneida communitarians stayed on after the "breakup," living under one roof in the cavernous Mansion House and sharing meals and other parts of life as before. At this writing some forty Oneidans, including many descended from the original community, are still carrying on the tradition today in the same historic location.

The contemporary Oneidans, to be sure, are less publicly visible and vastly less controversial than their renowned ancestors. The original community was undoubtedly best known—and most reviled by many "proper" Americans—for its practice of complex marriage, a free-love system in which every man and every woman of the community were considered spouses and open to (hetero)sexual contact with each other. The Oneidans were Christian Perfectionists, devout believers who, having overcome the moral limitations of normal human life, could install in the place of conventional family relations a system they considered heavenly. But what was to them Christian Perfection was sin and scandal to most Americans in the Victorian era, and public outrage against this life of "sin" had much to do with the community's downfall. Today complex marriage is memory, not practice.

Similarly, the businesses are no longer directly related to community life. When the community dissolved its common holdings of property, stock was issued to each member, and Oneida, Ltd., became a public corporation—one that over time has prospered. Oneida Community Silverplate and Stainless are brands of tableware now distributed worldwide. The corporation has done well financially for many who inherited its stock, and for many years it continued to own the Mansion House property, the huge (more than three hundred rooms) common dwelling that for decades housed the original community. Lately, however, the Mansion House has been severed from Oneida, Ltd., and now under the auspices of a historical society it functions as a museum as well as a home.

Significant community remains in the Mansion House. Several of the current residents bear the surname Noyes, being direct (or in a few cases collateral) descendants of the community's charismatic leader, John Humphrey Noyes. The building and expansive grounds are held in common, meals are taken in a common dining room, and various programs and activities continue to keep a fair degree of community alive where once hundreds lived in one of the best-known intentional communities of the nineteenth century.[5]

The Giant of the Communal Future: The Hutterites

Several of the largest and most prominent of America's historic communal movements may have been declining by the turn of the twentieth century, but one that would eclipse them all in size, economic vigor, and longevity was just gathering steam. Although they were unknown even to most students of communitarianism, the Hutterites in 1900 had centuries of history under their belt and were poised for the greatest expansion in American communal history. The Hutterites, a movement of Anabaptists who trace their origins to the Tirol in 1528, arrived in the United States in a series of migrations in the 1870s after the revocation by the Russian government of the special privileges—notably the freedom to operate their own schools and exemption from military duty—they had enjoyed during a century in the Ukraine. At first they established three colonies in South Dakota, and from those colonies developed three subgroups known as *leuts,* each of which has prospered and branched out into more than 90 new colonies, for a total of more than 350 active colonies in North America.[6] Much of the growth of the Hutterites has been due to the movement's amazing fertility (at the peak of fertility the average family had more than ten children), but powerful commitment mechanisms have been at work as well, keeping defection as low as 2 percent.[7] Today Hutterites are scattered from Minnesota to Washington in the northern United States and across the prairie provinces of Canada.

The Hutterites have had some interaction with other communitarians over the years. In their early years in the New World they received aid from the Harmony Society, then prosperous but declining in Pennsylvania; some Hutterites lived for a time on Harmonist property near the main settlement of Economy. They have returned the favor by helping other communitarians in need, notably an enclave of Japanese Christians who independently started their own version of Hutterism. As successful as the Hutterites are today, however, they were not prominent early in this century. Keeping largely to themselves in geographically isolated colonies, they stayed out of sight of much of the world. Apparently, there were fewer than a dozen colonies before 1918; most of the movement's extraordinary expansion has come since 1930. Thus these most successful of communitarians did not, by example or direct action, do much to promote other communal activity in the early twentieth century. Until the 1920s the various historians of American communalism do not list them, surely out of ignorance of their existence. One of the first hints that any outsider had heard of them came in 1924, when Ernest Wooster, in his *Communities of the Past and Present,* gave them two paragraphs in a survey of "Smaller or Short-Lived Communities," but regretted that "efforts to get in touch with them to learn of development during the last 20 years were not successful, and it may be that they are no longer in existence," even though "they had a total of more than 30,000 acres of land and several hundred members during the first years of the present century." The shakiness of Wooster's knowledge is underscored by his misdating their arrival in the United States by more than a decade, placing it in 1862 instead of 1874, and placing their first colony on the James River instead of the Missouri.[8]

So obscure were these sturdy communitarians that when a group of Germans, reading Anabaptist history, decided to emulate the example of the original Hutterites and formed the Bruderhof, or Society of Brothers, they lived in Hutteritelike community for a decade before they even learned that the original movement was still alive! Once these neo-Hutterites learned that their traditional forebears had survived, they established contact; their founder, Eberhard Arnold, spent a year visiting the North American colonies, and was ordained a Hutterite minister.

The Hutterites' obscurity seems to have served them well, however, poising them for their explosive expansion in the twentieth century. Such a juggernaut did they appear to become that several states and provinces, notably Alberta, took steps to limit their land purchases on the grounds that they were, in their rapid expansion and their economically efficient operations, squeezing out traditional farmers. No opposition, however, has managed to do much damage to the communal movement that has been larger and longer-lived than any other in the Western world save the religious communities of the Catholic Church. At the opening of the new century the Hutterites themselves could hardly have realized what a spectacular future lay just ahead.

Evangelical Christian and Social Gospel Communities

The Hutterites were not the only committed Christians living communally in 1900. Perhaps a dozen other groups, typically fairly small and not noticed greatly by the general public, were also living out creeds ranging from born-again conservatism to the temperance crusade to Christlike service to humanity.

SOCIAL GOSPEL EXPERIMENTS
IN COMMUNITY

In the latter third of the nineteenth century the social gospel movement swept through American Protestantism (and to a lesser extent other religions, including Catholicism and Judaism) and among other things spawned several intentional communities. The social gospel arose at a time of high immigration and rapid industrialization, seeking to meet real social needs of society's underclass—decent housing, safe and humane working conditions, and education, for example—by providing dedicated service that ultimately, the more optimistic of the movement's prophets proclaimed, would usher in the Kingdom of God on earth.[9] The tools of the movement were many and as varied as the movement itself, ranging from direct provision of social services (as through settlement houses) to temperance crusades to agitation on behalf of labor unions. In a few cases committed social gospelers, in their search for ways of working out their vision, banded together into communal settlements.

The preeminent social gospel community: The Christian Commonwealth Colony. The most prominent such experiment was the Christian Commonwealth Colony, a commune that lived a hand-to-mouth existence in Georgia from 1896 to 1900 and whose periodical, *The Social Gospel,* gave the definitive name to the movement that thereto had most commonly been known as "social Christianity" or "applied Christianity." The project arose out of articles and letters published in the Minneapolis-based social gospel periodical *The Kingdom* in which several committed social Christians inquired about ways in which they might live their radical convictions fully. Finally, a principal in the correspondence, the Congregational minister Ralph Albertson, led the group in purchasing a played-out cotton plantation near Columbus, Georgia. The thousand acres of swamp and unproductive upland cost $4,000. About 350 persons eventually moved to Commonwealth, although high turnover meant that many fewer than that were present at any one time.

The economic communism of the Commonwealth was, at least ideally, total. "I will not withhold for any selfish ends aught that I have from the fullest service that love inspires," read the group's covenant. As for membership, the constitution specified that "membership in this body shall be open to all, and never denied to any who come to us in the spirit of love, unselfishness and true fellowship."[10] Broad idealism, however, did not lead to economic prosperity; some cash farm crops were raised and sold each year, but other enterprises—notably a cotton-weaving business that produced towels to sell by mail to subscribers to *The Social Gospel*—were unproductive. The Commonwealth's standard of living was abysmal.

So elemental was the living and so sparse were the rations that serious suffering was always lurking nearby. One winter Ralph and Irene Albertson's seven-year-old son died "of cold and starvation."[11] The presence of several freeloaders—the combination of open membership, noncoercion, and absolute sharing was too much for some miscreants to resist—aggravated the poverty. The members might have struggled on, especially because the promising orchard they had planted was nearly ready to bear, but a typhoid epidemic that killed several members and laid others low applied the coup de grace. At the cusp of the new century the property was sold and most of the proceeds used to satisfy debts.[12]

The Straight Edge Industrial Settlement. Stories of hard times at the Christian Commonwealth in Georgia apparently did not discourage other social gospelers from starting their own colonies. Probably the most successful of them was the Straight Edge Industrial Settlement, which was founded in 1899 and for several years thereafter provided jobs to the unemployed, turning, as the founder put it, "the waste labor of the world into useful, self-supporting industries."[13] It was dually sited: the industrial operations were in lower Manhattan, and the workers' residence (which incorporated a children's school) was at Alpine, New Jersey. Wilbur F. Copeland and his wife, whose given name unfortunately does not appear in any of the published accounts of the community, conceived the Straight Edge as a vehicle for providing jobs for the unemployed in cooperative industries such as baking, dressmaking, and printing. To find members they placed an advertisement in the New York *Herald:* "Wanted—Men and Women who take the teachings of Jesus Christ seriously, and want to go to work in a co-operative enterprise founded upon the Golden Rule. . . ."[14] A hundred responded, and the colony was off and running. Its constitution was the briefest on record: "All things whatsoever ye would that men should do to you, do ye even so to them."[15] Copeland reported that during the community's first seven years, more than two hundred persons had participated, with an average membership of eighteen at any given time.[16] Copeland's periodical, *The Straight Edge,* remained in publication until 1921, but operations seem to have ceased after 1918, when financial problems were encountered.[17]

The Southern Co-operative Association of Apalachicola. At least one colony was a direct descendant of the Christian Commonwealth, largely populated by former members of the Commonwealth and dedicated to the same kinds of social Christian goals of transforming society that the Georgia settlers had embraced. The Southern Co-operative Association of Apalachicola, or Co-operative Association of America, was established in 1900, about the time of the Christian Commonwealth's demise, in Franklin County, Florida. There, under the leadership of Harry C. Vrooman, its members, several of whom were Swedenborgians, acquired seventeen hundred acres. Little information on the colony survives, however; it apparently endured until 1904, when Vrooman departed, but then vanished from the record.[18]

The Salvation Army farm colonies. The two decades or so on either side of the turn of the century era saw a great surge of back-to-the-land sentiment that resulted in dozens, if not hundreds, of cooperative communities that featured intensive farming on small acreages. Some of the Jewish immigrant colonies of the 1880s exemplified the genre; several other notable experiments in that vein, including the Fellowship Farms and the Little Landers, would surface in the early twentieth century.

One part of that larger tide integrated the prevalent back-to-the-land romanticism with social, evangelical Christian conviction when the Salvation Army set out to establish farm colonies to provide a constructive future for the urban poor. The Army had always sought concrete solutions to difficult social problems, and by the end of the nineteenth century it had aid facilities—rescue missions, soup kitchens, homeless shelters—in place in cities throughout the country. By the end of the century the organization also owned a number of tracts of rural land. Into this situation strode Frederick Booth-Tucker, son-in-law of Salvation Army founder William Booth, who set to work raising money for rural settlements for the urban poor.[19] Various refinements of the scheme were promoted; finally it was proposed that in a typical settlement of a thousand acres, each family would be allotted five acres for its own production and a core site would be reserved for the common good—a townsite plus grazing land.

The logic of it all seemed inescapable. As Albert Shaw, a contemporary observer of communal living, observed in an enthusiastic magazine article on the Fort Amity colony,

> It is an obvious fact that there are, in the aggregate, millions of people in our cities and towns who would be better off if established in the country; and, on the other hand, there are tens of millions of acres of land,—still cheap or wholly uncultivated,—upon which a vast, self-sustaining population might well be located. The difficult questions have been how to bring the people to the land, and how to tide them over the first few years.
>
> Evidently, the ideal plan must be some form of systematic colonization.[20]

In 1897 the first land for colonizing was purchased in California, near Soledad, from Charles T. Romie. It was eventually dubbed Fort Romie, in line with typical Salvation Army military nomenclature. Soon a second colony was sited as well, this time in eastern Colorado; it was named Fort Amity. In 1898 the third and final tract was acquired in Ohio, to be called Fort Herrick, again after the incumbent owner of the property, who, like Romie, had sold his land at a low price and on good terms.

A sort of presettlement phase of the Romie experiment began in 1897, when the first caravan of settlers from the San Francisco area left for the new colony grounds. Problems set in almost immediately, however; a financial shortfall quickly appeared, the colonists could not make the mortgage payments due in 1898, and the crucial irrigation system proved woefully inadequate for its task. By 1901 the prototype colony appeared doomed.

But much more was yet to come. The Army regrouped, solidified its financial arrangements, and purchased more water rights and irrigation equipment. In 1900 and 1901, even as the earlier group of settlers was disbanding, a new wave was arriving, and here the story of the Salvation Army colonies as a substantial phenomenon properly begins. The now-adequate irrigation system was set up as a cooperative owned by the colonists, and the land became productive. Modest cottages housed twenty-four families by October 1904, and the successful settlers began making steady progress toward paying off the debts the Army had incurred in buying the land.

Once Fort Romie was successfully under way, the Army turned its attention to Fort Amity, west of the small town of Holly in the expansive plains of southeastern Colorado. The requisite land was purchased in the fall of 1897 and the Army moved to prepare the site and to select settlers, mostly urban-based "worthy poor" who would have the initiative to succeed in life once they had escaped the fetid cities and who would work the land until they had paid back the Army's purchase price (about $20 per acre), thus becoming free agricultural entrepreneurs. An Army crew built minimal dwellings for the settlers, and by the end of 1898 Fort Amity was a flourishing colony with a school, a post office, stores, and an assembly hall. More land was added to the original 640 acres, and the population soon exceeded a hundred. Other businesses, including a bank, a newspaper, and more stores would soon follow.

Amity's first principal cash crop, melons, proved an unreliable economic base for the new farmers, given to huge gyrations in market price and subject to the vagaries of the weather (the 1903 crop was virtually destroyed by hail). Sugar beets, however, were experiencing a boom in the region, and colonists willing to do the extensive manual work that crop requires did well with their cultivation. Some colonists established small industries (a broom factory using locally grown broomcorn was an early one), and the Army gave the colony another economic injection with its establishment there of an orphanage housed in what was, by colony standards, a palatial building.

However, by about 1905 serious problems confronted the burgeoning colony. Salt buildup, a by-product of irrigation, caused crop yields to drop and even began to erode building foundations. Despite efforts to solve the problem by the colonists and the Army, by 1907 many colonists were exiting and Fort Amity was clearly in dire straits. Between 1907 and 1909 the property was sold and the experiment was over.

The third of the Salvation Army colonies was located near Willoughby, Ohio, outside Cleveland. Fort Herrick was founded in 1898 after a fundraising campaign spearheaded by the consummate political insider of the day, Mark Hanna. As at the other colonies, Army crews built cottages, and small acreages were parceled out to the settlers—in this case five to ten acres to farmers, and smaller plots to artisans. By the end of the year, the colony had ten families who were mainly engaged in small-scale market gardening, and its facilities included a post office, a schoolhouse, and a store.

Problems came quickly. Poor drainage interfered with agriculture and damaged some of the homes. Some colonists left, and few new ones arrived. By 1903 the Army gave up on the original plan and reorganized Fort Herrick as an "industrial colony," specifically a home for the drying out of alcoholics. Later much of the property became a fresh-air summer camp for Cleveland children, a use that continued until the property was finally sold in 1974.

Thus was the ambitious Salvation Army colonization plan concluded. Although none of the colonies survived for many years, the model of community they represented did endure, popping up again a few years later in other small-acreage settlement projects and in the depression-era colonies sponsored by the federal government. The Salvation Army itself went on to further successes that were almost entirely urban.[21]

The Christian Cooperative Colony. Some colonies emphasized only selected parts of the larger social gospel agenda, notably prohibition. Several such enclaves were started up in the late nineteenth century, some of
which (such as the Willard Colony in North Carolina[22]) did not outlast
the century, but at least one of which survived into the early twentieth: the
Christian Cooperative Colony of Sunnyside, Washington. Three members
of the Progressive Brethren Church purchased a defunct townsite with a
hotel and moved their families there in 1898. A forfeiture clause was written into every real estate deed in the town: any violation of the ban on
alcohol, gambling, and prostitution would result in the perpetrator's
property's reverting to the townsite company.

Irrigation made Sunnyside a prosperous agricultural area. People
moved in and the town thrived. Gradually, the colony departed from its
cooperative founding ideals, and eventually the moral regulations were
abandoned as well. The cooperative prohibition colony became a conventional American town.[23]

And how many more? How many social gospel colonies operated at one
time or another will never be known. Many were short-lived and noticed
only locally. There was apparently a Christian Social Association somewhere in Wisconsin, but the sole reference to it provides only its dates of
operation (1899 to 1904), a head count at some unspecified point in its
history (forty-eight), and its reason for closing, "withdrawal of members."[24] Beyond that we are left to wonder.

EVANGELICAL PROTESTANT COLONIES

For two thousand years a steadfast few devout Christian believers, often inspired by the example of the early church as depicted in Acts 2:44–45
and 4:32–5:11, have wanted to live in close company and cooperation with
others of like mettle. For much of that time the need was met by religious
orders in the Catholic and Eastern Orthodox Churches, but the closure of
that option for Protestants propelled the communal impulse in new directions. Hundreds of conservative Protestant groups have founded intentional communities in America since European settlement; at the turn of
the century several such enclaves were operating in various places in the
country.

The Olive Branch. Among those in operation at the onset of the twentieth century, the one with the longest history was the Olive Branch, found-

ed in Chicago in 1876 by Rachel Bradley. Originally simply running an evangelistic outreach program, in 1883 Bradley and some fellow Free Methodists began to provide social services to the poor. As of 1984 fourteen adults and three children were living communally, in an atmosphere of an extended family, at the inner-city mission, serving the skid-row neighborhood of West Madison Avenue. Individual families have their own sleeping quarters, but the group eats, worships, and serves its clientele in common. The services are not unlike those provided by other urban missions: temporary housing is provided for the homeless; food and clothing are made available, as are opportunities for counseling; worship and Bible studies are provided for those interested in such things. Special programs for children, including a summer day camp, are also part of the offerings of this community whose evangelical Christian commitment undergirds all the service activities. Service to others is often a goal of communities, but few have achieved it as well or as long as the members of the Olive Branch.[25]

The Commonwealth of Israel. Other evangelical colonies took the opposite tack on social involvement, establishing themselves in isolated areas far from the corrupting influence of the cities. An example here, one about which relatively little is known, was the Commonwealth of Israel, founded in 1899 in Mason County, Texas. A group of some one hundred fifty communally inclined Baptists purchased nine hundred acres and led an apparently amicable life for three years before dissolution.[26]

The New House of Israel. Another group established in Texas, but one with a distinctly different theological orientation, was the New House of Israel, which settled on 144 acres in Polk County in 1895. According to the scanty information available, these Israelites, as they liked to be known, were from the Flying Roll, one of the several branches of the adventist movement that traced its origins to the late-eighteenth/early-nineteenth-century English visionary Joanna Southcott, another branch of which was the House of David, a prominent religious commune in Benton Harbor, Michigan (about which more in a later chapter). Like their Michigan brethren, the Israelites were vegetarians whose members did not cut their hair or beards. The colony had an apparently quiet existence for some years until a leadership vacuum developed and families gradually moved away, leaving a ghost town by the early 1920s.[27]

Shiloh: Church of the Living God. On the other hand, some remotely located Christian colonies received much publicity. A prime example is the
Church of the Living God, perhaps better known as Shiloh, after its headquarters complex, which achieved fame ("infamy" might be closer to the
mark) for its early belief in faith healing that contributed to the deaths of
members and more spectacularly for a bizarre nautical misadventure that
cost a number of believers their lives. Shiloh was the creation of Frank W.
Sandford, who had become an ardent Protestant believer as a college student in the 1880s and thereafter labored variously as a pastor, a missionary,
and an itinerant revivalist who fervently believed that God had picked him
to evangelize the entire world. In 1893 he began to build a nondenomina-
tional Bible school in rural Maine, between Lewiston and Brunswick, that
would serve as a base for foreign missions. Other believers and converts
joined him and supported the building of a fabulous complex of ornate
Victorian buildings. Eventually, the school had a substantial communal
component, as whole families moved in and donated all they had to the
common work. As with many other Christian communes, the example of
the early church depicted in the Acts of the Apostles was emulated.

The first round of tragedy came when six members died, medically un-
treated for smallpox, during the black winter, as Shiloh called it, of
1902–3. Shiloh received a good dose of bad press from the episode, and in
early 1904 Sandford was charged with cruelty and manslaughter. He was
convicted of cruelty and fined, but the manslaughter charge eventually
ended with a hung jury unable to resolve Sandford's culpability in his
aversion to modern medicine.

The most incredible and tragic phase of the Shiloh story began in 1905,
when Shiloh acquired a fine 133-foot schooner, the *Coronet,* to use to transport workers to missionary fields abroad. At first the voyages were unre-
markable, but in the last days of December 1910, a goodly group set sail
from the United States to the Canary Islands and the African coast. Off
Gambia a companion ship, the *Kingdom,* foundered, and its crew and passengers had to be taken onto the *Coronet.* The rescue quite overloaded the
Coronet; sixty-six persons were now on board a ship designed to carry thirty. In May, after several crowded but uneventful weeks, Sandford decided
to head across the Atlantic to Greenland, the next missionary destination,
despite a serious shortage of rations and water and a deteriorating vessel
that had started leaking substantially. Adverse winds dictated a change of
route, toward the West Indies. In June the travelers sighted Trinidad, but

did not put in to mend their vessel and its ill and hungry occupants; instead they headed north. But approaching the United States they still would not land: Sandford, apparently worried about what port authorities would think about conditions on board as well as about what a few "traitors" on board would tell the authorities about what had happened already, declared that God had forbidden them to visit any country for which they had prayed during the previous year. Onward the increasingly battered ship headed, avoiding the Coast Guard by Sandford's refusal to allow the party to land, bound for Greenland. Eventually, pressure from a few of the more forceful passengers made Sandford back down, turn around, and head for home in Maine, but contrary winds and a series of gales thwarted them. By the time the ravaged ship limped into Portland, nine had died and many others were severely ill with scurvy and malnutrition, among other maladies.

Sandford was indicted on six counts of manslaughter, convicted, and sentenced to ten years in the Atlanta penitentiary. He served nearly seven, and upon release in 1918 returned to Shiloh, which a cohort of true believers had struggled to keep afloat during the prison years, at times undergoing privations at least mildly reminiscent of those suffered by the hapless sailors of 1911. But prosperity did not materialize. Shiloh had always lived "on faith," its members not holding outside jobs and always dependent on timely charity. Now it was not forthcoming. Although hundreds remained at Shiloh when Sandford returned, the spirit of the place collapsed in early 1920 and the members scattered. Sandford lived obscurely until his death in 1948 at age eighty-five. The glory days of Shiloh, with its spectacular physical plant and hundreds of members, had long since become just a memory. Today remnants of the physical complex of the former intentional community survive as a country church.[28]

The Woman's Commonwealth. Another colony founded on evangelical—in this case, holiness—principles made a much larger impact on communal history than it would have for its members' faith alone because of its outstanding example of empowerment for women. The long-lived and colorful Woman's Commonwealth was organized in 1879, a decade after Martha McWhirter began to organize an ecumenical Sunday school in Belton, Texas. McWhirter, a devout Methodist, experienced, in classic Wesleyan fashion, entire sanctification and concluded that the sanctified life implied, among other things, celibacy. In theory, and to a limited extent in fact, men could join the sanctified band, for, as a scholar of the movement has written,

In embracing celibacy, the sisters discarded old models of humanity, including those that distinguish between the worth and rights of males and females. Their standard of celibate sanctification was designed to eradicate all other distinctions among persons except those of religious conversion. In their experience, however, only women were willing or able to accept the rigors of celibate sanctification.[29]

A few men did join the community. Six men were members in the Texas days, including the Dow brothers, Matthew and David, who joined in 1879. But the brothers, at least, suffered the wrath of a hostile outside populace for their choice; as an early account put it,

The intensity of feeling against them was increased by false reports, until in February, 1880, they were taken from their houses at midnight by a number of men, and were whipped most severely and ordered to leave the country. . . . The brothers declined to leave, whereupon they were adjudged lunatics and sent to the State asylum at Austin in order to protect them. The authorities there declared them to be sane and refused to keep them, and they were immediately discharged upon their promise not to return to Bell County.[30]

The commune began to emerge after many of the celibate women had become divorced or separated from their husbands. At first it boomed, quickly reaching fifty members, and although it later dwindled in numbers, it was a brilliant economic success throughout most of its history. It was not without controversy, however; a good many of the men of Belton were dismayed at the radicalism and celibacy of their wives and sisters, and repeated confrontations—sometimes laced with violence—marked the Belton years.

Nevertheless, the sanctified sisters, as they were often called, managed to develop solid businesses. Their Central Hotel in Belton became a major success by offering excellent food and pleasant rooms. Several other businesses in Belton, on surrounding farms, and even as far away as Waco were similarly successful. The sisters did so well at their businesses that by 1898 they had amassed a fortune in six figures, and proceeded to use it to remove themselves from Belton. They purchased, from Willard A. Saxton, a community-minded man who had once lived at Brook Farm, a large house in a northern district of Washington, D.C., known as Mount Pleasant, and a farm of more than a hundred acres in nearby Maryland. They built a thriving communal society in the house, where the sisters lived comfortably for several years. The strict holiness commitment became more casual, and in Washington the community gave up its own religious services, its members attending whatever churches they pleased. Some attrition set in when McWhirter died in 1904, the membership declining from about thirty to seventeen (split between the two locations) by 1907. At that point the urban house was sold and the remaining sisters retired to the farm, where they operated a nursing home and later a popular restaurant. Although one source says that prospective members frequently asked to join, few were accepted, and so the Commonwealth, apparently never concerned about its institutional future, inevitably declined throughout the twentieth century.[31] By 1946 only two members remained; the last surviving sister died at the farm (by then a part of the suburbs) in 1983 at the ripe age of 101.[32]

COMMUNITARIAN SWEDENBORGIANS
AT BRYN ATHYN

A different kind of Christian communitarianism was developed by the Swedenborgians, whose General Church of the New Jerusalem, one of the three American branches of the larger Swedenborgian movement, has operated an important community at Bryn Athyn, Pennsylvania, for nearly a century. Emmanuel Swedenborg, the eighteenth-century scientist and mystic whose writings inspired the church, proposed a new system of interpreting the Christian message in the light of his purported revelations, and his followers came to adopt a theology of realized eschatology: their cornerstone belief is that the Second Coming of Christ has already occurred in Swedenborg's theological writings. Like members of other realized-eschatology groups (including the Shakers and the Oneida Community), Swedenborgians have come to see themselves as a people apart from the rest of the world, as citizens of the new heaven and new earth, ones of whom a certain lifestyle, as well as a particular faith, is demanded. Given such an outlook, the development of intentional communities has been a natural part of the movement. In the United States, that took place most importantly at Bryn Athyn, outside Philadelphia, after 1889, when Swedenborgian industrialist John Pitcairn began buying property in the area. Eventually, more than a thousand Swedenborgians, as many as a third of the worldwide members of the General Church, took up residence at Bryn Athyn. Although they lived economically private lives in private homes, Bryn Athyn was very much a religious colony. Its residents effectively restricted property ownership to church members, stressed endogamy, and educated their children in parochial schools. The colony, still an important center of American Swedenborgianism, is perhaps best known for its large, impressive cathedral and its respected schools and libraries.[33]

Jewish Communities

Listing Jewish intentional communities functioning at the turn of the century is problematic, because many of them were evolving from focused communities into conventional towns, and it is impossible to identify a precise date at which a given colony gave up its communal or cooperative status. Most of the colonies were created in the wave of Jewish immigration that poured into the United States after 1880, when persecutions in eastern Europe made life impossible for the many Jews there. The Jews already established in America, struggling to deal with the overwhelming numbers of immigrants with whom they shared a heritage of Jewishness but not necessarily much else, found colonization appealing, a means of providing the immigrants with agricultural and light industrial work and, not incidentally, sweeping them out of the way. However, many of the immigrants were not farmers and were not much interested in living in remote colonies, and their unsuitedness for the situation along with various agricultural and climatological disasters brought most of the colonies to quick and ungracious ends.

THE SOUTH JERSEY COLONIES

Exceptions to that pattern did occur, however. Several of the colonies in southern New Jersey, the biggest single site of colony settlement, became relatively prosperous, and with prosperity communal solidarity gave way to individual enterprise and homesteads. At the turn of the century several of the colonies—Vineland, Alliance, Carmel, Rosenhayn, and Woodbine—were still formally in existence, but were losing their cooperative features.[34] A good example of the process can be seen in the Alliance colony, founded in 1882 to house immigrating Russian Jews with financial assistance from the Alliance Israelite Universelle, a French organization dedicated to helping persecuted Jews, whence the colony's name. Some of the colony farmers did have modest success with crops and poultry, but early in the colony's life industry began to be introduced—a sewing shop and a cigar factory, and then other enterprises. Prosperity gradually ensued, and although the lively social life of the colony continued for many years, individualism gradually supplanted the spirit of cooperation. About 1908 the evolving privatization was formalized; the communal landholdings were parceled out to individual owners, and Alliance was thenceforth simply a country town.[35]

One other Jewish colony, far from New Jersey, was also alive, barely, at the beginning of 1900, although it was formally closed that year: the Palestine colony in Michigan. It had been established in 1891 by a group of immigrant Russian Jews who had been living in Bay City, Michigan, and surviving by peddling. Reading of the other colonization projects, Hyman Lewenberg organized a dozen or so of his comrades to buy, on credit, a section of land near the village of Bad Axe. By all accounts the farmers were industrious, but lack of farming experience and economic problems in the larger society (notably the Panic of 1893) took their toll, and more than once the settlers defaulted on their land payments. As 1900 dawned, only eight families remained, and those left (or at least abandoned farming) that year.[36]

Other Religious Communities

THE THEOSOPHICAL EXPERIMENTS IN COMMUNITY

In 1875 Helena Petrovna Blavatsky and others founded the Theosophical Society, dedicated to the propagation of occult wisdom and esoteric religiosity as well as free inquiry into science and other departments of human knowledge, and before many decades had passed the movement had spawned several collective settlements, some of which are still alive in some form nearly a century later.

Point Loma. The largest and best-known Theosophical communal outpost, probably, was Point Loma, which was founded on a peninsula near San Diego (today a part of the city) in 1897 by Katherine Tingley, leader of one of the factions into which the movement splintered after Blavatsky's death in 1891. Tingley oversaw the erection of several exotic buildings with intricate, mystical decorations—buildings of substantial and unusual beauty. A Greek theater on a hillside overlooking the Pacific was the scene of Shakespearean and classical dramas, and in 1902 a theater building was purchased in San Diego proper where the Point Loma residents staged major productions for the cultured citizens of San Diego. The community worked hard at achieving self-sufficiency, with an extensive garden and a tailor shop that met most of the members' food and clothing needs. A publishing house produced magazines and books, many of them by Tingley. Central to it all, in Tingley's view, was the Raja Yoga school, which taught meditation and Tingley's version of Theosophy. During the founder's lifetime the community functioned well, but after her death from an automobile accident in 1929, her successor, Gottfried de Purucker, found major financial problems to deal with and finally gave up on trying to keep the eroding community together when World War II began and military activity at the adjacent Point Loma naval base threatened the whole area. The property was sold in 1942 and the headquarters moved on to a noncommunal location in greater Los Angeles, where today the organization continues to maintain a library and a publishing house.[37]

Krotona. Another branch of the Theosophical movement, headed by Annie Besant, who was widely regarded as Blavatsky's designated successor, developed a small commune known as Krotona in Hollywood in the early twentieth century. Besant's follower A. P. Warrington was the chief activist for this experiment in Theosophical community, which by 1913 had forty-five members, various buildings, a press, and a variety of educational and spiritual programs. Financial problems pressed the community continuously, however, and in 1924 most of the land was sold to meet various obligations. New land was purchased in Ojai, California, at least in part because it was the residence of Jiddu Krishnamurti, the Indian man whom Besant had earlier identified as the World Teacher who would initiate a new age. Krotona eventually developed a library, a bookstore, a retirement community, and a broad array of educational programs, most of which continue today.[38]

The Temple of the People. Meanwhile, in 1903 the Syracuse local of the splintered Theosophical movement had moved en masse to California, buying land near the coast south of Pismo Beach and founding a community called Halcyon. Like the other branches of the movement, the Temple of the People, as the adherents came to call their group, saw itself as a headquarters of a larger movement and encouraged the founding of local groups across the country. Halcyon would operate on cooperative principles, it was agreed, and it began several businesses, including farming and a construction enterprise. Financial pressure led to the abandonment of cooperative economics in 1912, but the community's members developed independent businesses and the movement as a whole prospered. By the 1920s finances were available for the erection of a temple building, a classical-revival edifice with an unusual rounded triangular shape. The temple has served as the headquarters of the small but worldwide movement ever since; Halcyon remains a community of a few dozen believers, some of whom claim still to receive messages from the Ascended Masters central to Theosophical theology.[39]

The Aquarian Foundation. Another mysterious Theosophical offshoot, the Aquarian Foundation, operated a community with some two hundred members from 1927 to 1933. The community was located in Canada, but many Americans were among its members. Edward Arthur Wilson, known to his followers as Brother XII, announced in 1926 that he had encountered eleven Masters of Wisdom who thenceforth directed his actions. He began to gather followers in England, and by early 1927, when he departed for Canada to establish the community, more than a hundred Theosophists had joined him. Several of them were persons of means, and they made large gifts that enabled the group to buy property near Cedar-by-the-Sea on Vancouver Island. Wilson's appeal to Theosophists was enhanced by his vocal "back to Blavatsky" ideology that resonated well with those who thought that the second generation of Theosophical leaders, especially Annie Besant and Charles Leadbeater, had introduced undesirable corruptions into the pristine work of Theosophy's founder.

Wilson, whom many outside observers regarded as an utter fraud, demanded that his followers, including the wealthy ones, give him all their worldly possessions; conflicts over his use of money and his abuse of his followers, among other things, followed. In 1933, three followers sued to regain the money they had donated, and when they prevailed in court, Wilson responded by doing extensive damage to the physical facilities of the colony and sailing away on his yacht with his female companion, Mabel Skottowe, known within the group as Madame Zee, as well as the group's large treasury. The two seem to have ended up in Switzerland, but their trail soon vanished. The colony and its charismatic leader were history.[40]

The Camphill movement. The most extensive network of intentional communities with Theosophical roots is the Camphill movement, which has moved in a direction different from that of the groups just discussed. Rudolf Steiner, the important European Theosophical leader whose wing of the movement came to be called Anthroposophy, had, among many other innovative ideas, approaches to the education of the handicapped that attracted much attention in the 1930s. In 1939 Karl Koenig established the first Camphill community in Scotland to put Steiner's ideas into practice, and the movement spread to the United States in 1961, when Carlo Pietzner and others established a similar community at Copake, New York, whose reason for existence was assisting and educating handicapped and retarded children. The movement has spread worldwide, reporting, in 1993, some eighty-five communities in sixteen countries. The North American movement has seven communities, all therapeutic in mission but with slightly varying specific purposes and clienteles, involving some six hundred persons living on more than two thousand acres of "biodynamically" farmed land.[41]

Other Theosophical communities. Communitarianism has been a persistent theme among Theosophists, and several communities have been established over the years with little public fanfare. The Brotherhood of the White Temple, for example, under the leadership of Maurice Doreal, founded its Shamballa Ashrama outside Sedalia, Colorado, in 1946 in a canyon whose thick rock walls were believed to be high in lead content and thus would protect settlers from an atomic holocaust expected to occur in 1953. Doreal died in 1963, but the movement and the village continue, disseminating the founder's courses he said were rooted in the teachings of Tibetan masters.[42]

Other such idiosyncratic variants on the multifaceted Theosophical tradition have undoubtedly waxed and waned as well.

THE KORESHAN UNITY

One of the more exotic communal groups, at least in its philosophy, was the Koreshan Unity, a celibate community that moved from Chicago to Estero, Florida, in the 1890s. Its founder, Cyrus Teed, called "Koresh," the Hebrew version of his first name, preached that the earth was hollow and that its inhabitants live on the inside of the sphere. That insight had been communicated to Teed, he said, through a visionary experience in 1869, and he tried earnestly to prove its truth experimentally. In Florida the group built hollow globes to illustrate their view of the cosmos and eventually constructed a "rectilineator," a structure that supposedly described, when installed on a Gulf coast beach, a four-mile-long horizontal line that was truly straight rather than bending with the curvature of the earth. On a convex sphere the ocean would be farther from the straight line at its ends than at its middle, but the Koreshan experimenters found just the opposite—that the ocean curved upward from the middle to each end—and thus proclaimed that their central hypothesis had been proved true.

The Koreshans grew in number to more than two hundred—for a time the population of the colony was greater than that of Fort Myers, the area's largest city—and the fact that they voted as a bloc was disturbing to the local Democratic machine, whose entrenched rule they came to oppose. In 1906 Teed was beaten by a local marshal in Fort Myers and suffered injuries that the Koreshans believed led to his death two years later. Given Teed's teaching of immortality of the body, many followers kept vigil around his remains, expecting his resurrection. Reluctantly, the group finally entombed their leader at the direction of county health officials.

Teed's death was certainly discouraging, but the Koreshans managed to stay active for several decades thereafter. Although disciplined and celibate, the hollow-earthers were not dour, and continued to pursue an active social life and a wide range of musical and artistic activities, eventually becoming best known for their work in tropical horticulture. The lush gardens they developed on their property were donated to the state of Florida when the commune had declined to nonviability in the 1960s, and the tract is now known as Koreshan State Park. Several of the Koreshans' buildings, including the commodious Art Hall, remain at the park and house a number of artifacts, including hollow globes and a model of the rectilineator. At this writing efforts at restoration of some of the buildings are under way, and in time the Koreshan site should be one of the country's fine museum villages.[43]

SPIRITUALIST COLONIES

Spiritualism, a movement based on belief in unusual psychic phenomena and communication with worlds beyond the one we experience in waking consciousness, developed a large American following in the middle and late nineteenth century after Kate and Margaret Fox announced in 1848 that they could communicate with dead persons, and it had a communal side almost from its inception. Several spiritualist communities were started in the nineteenth century (the Harmonial Vegetarian Society of Benton County, Arkansas, for example, which had as many as fifty-four members in the early 1860s[44]), although many spiritualist gatherings took place at summer camps, not permanent settlements, and most of them did not survive the general decline in the popularity of spiritualism later in the century. A few colonies bucked that trend, however.

Lily Dale and Cassadaga. Lily Dale, founded in southwestern New York in 1879, was a summer camp that eventually attracted year-round residents and remains an important, and communal, center of spiritualism today, with many practicing mediums, various churches, and a reference library, as well as the ongoing summer assembly grounds. The upstate New York winters at Lily Dale impelled some of its spiritualists to found the colony-town of Cassadaga, Florida, which developed quickly after its founding in 1895. Cassadaga was developed on land donated for the project by spiritualist medium George Colby, who claimed to be steered in his decisions by his spirit guide, an Indian named Seneca. During the first half of the twentieth century, Cassadaga flourished as a pilgrimage center for wealthy northeastern spiritualists who found the Cassadaga Hotel a perfect place to take a winter vacation and explore the spiritual world. It has declined in the second half of the century, despite (or perhaps because of) the enormous growth of the nearby Orlando area, but still retains a substantial spiritualist population and has a number of psychics who give readings for the visitors who manage to find their way to this important outpost of one of America's less conventional religions.[45]

Preston. Other spiritualist colonies did develop, although none were as substantial or permanent as Cassadaga. One example of a smaller encampment was Preston, which was established two miles north of Cloverdale, California, by Emily Preston, a spiritual healer in San Francisco, who moved to the site with her husband, H. L. Preston, in 1869. People began to journey to Mrs. Preston's home for healing, and eventually more than a hundred of them settled there, building simple dwellings on the fifteen hundred acres owned by the Prestons or on other nearby properties. The community provided running water, a school, and other amenities for all who lived there, and Preston preached her "Religion of Inspiration" in a church built there for her. In 1909, at age ninety, she died, and the colony, sometimes called "Free Pilgrims Covenant," soon largely dissolved. A few faithful, however, were still having meditation services in the church in the 1940s. Later an artists' colony developed on the site and remained until a disastrous fire consumed most of the colony buildings in 1988.[46]

The Societas Fraternia. A twist on the spiritualist theme came with the Societas Fraternia, which added to the psychic phenomena at the heart of spiritualism such elements as group marriage and a commitment to eating only raw food. The Societas began with the purchase by immigrant English businessman George Hinde of twenty-four acres of land near Fullerton, California, in 1876. On his new property Hinde erected a fourteen-room house with a tall octagonal tower. The spiritualist and communal activity on the property began in 1878 with the arrival of Dr. Louis Schlesinger, who moved into the Hinde household and began announcing a series of commands from spirit guides that mandated communal living, including communal sharing of sexual partners (although intercourse was to take place only for procreation), and a diet limited to raw fruits and vegetables. Neighborhood pressure—Schlesinger was accused of endangering the lives of children with his unusual diet and of fabricating bogus spiritual manifestations, such as "balls of fire" and a ghost rider—eventually forced Schlesinger to leave the little colony, and leadership, after reverting briefly to Hinde, soon passed to a new member, Walter Lockwood, a retired Methodist minister, who became widely known for his development of the Placentia Perfection Walnut. Lockwood led the colony until his death in 1921, whereupon the enterprise disbanded.[47]

The Land of Shalam. John B. Newbrough, a physician and dentist in New York, was the prime mover behind a colony that combined a distinctive spiritualism with charitable works—an orphanage, notably—in the late nineteenth century. Through an episode of spiritualistic automatic writing on that new-fangled device known as a typewriter, Dr. Newbrough produced *Oahspe,* a "New Bible" that reinterpreted traditional biblical teachings and presented a new cosmology and sacred history. Published in 1882, the work still has a devoted following.[48]

The "Faithists," as the *Oahspe* believers were called, exhibited communal tendencies from the first, quickly starting an unsuccessful colony in New Jersey and then another in New York state. These efforts were eclipsed in 1884, however, when Newbrough reported another spiritual communication that commanded the Faithists to found an orphanage in the West. The precise location was mystically determined and turned out to be a tract of some 1,490 acres near Dona Ana, New Mexico, about fifty miles north of El Paso. The Faithists soon moved to the site to operate the orphanage and incorporated their religious society as the "First Church of Tae" in 1885. Most of the money for the venture, including its large main building, the forty-two-room "Fraternum," and the round Temple of Tae, seems to have been provided by Andrew M. Howland, a wealthy coffee importer.

Some success greeted the colony's early years. Children were brought in as planned and were provided good, healthy accommodations. An irrigation system was built to allow cultivation of the harsh New Mexican desert. For a time Shalam, in its remote location, had dozens of colonists besides the residents of the orphanage. But problems eventually emerged. The internal dissent so familiar to students of communal history reared its head, leading to substantial depopulation, and worse, perhaps, various bouts with epidemic disease sapped the colony's morale as well as its health. Newbrough died during an influenza epidemic during the winter of 1890–91. Howland thereupon became the colony administrator, and in 1893 married Newbrough's widow, Frances.

By dint of Howland's ongoing generosity, the colony survived and even prospered for several more years, but in 1900 his fortune ran out. Most of the other colonists left. Howland supported his family for seven years by selling milk from the Shalam dairy herd door to door in nearby Las Cruces. In 1907, the orphans by now having largely grown up and departed, the Howlands moved to El Paso.

Oahspe-based communitarianism was not yet over, however. The most important of the later ventures was led by Wing Anderson, who became interested in the *Oahspe* teachings in Los Angeles and added his visionary literature to the Faithist canon.[49] In 1942 he purchased land in Utah for an intentional community of believers, where he and other followers again undertook agricultural operations and laid plans for operating another orphanage. Eventually they purchased land near Montrose, Colorado, for the orphanage, and soon a colony there was adhering fairly closely to the principles enunciated more than half a century earlier by Newbrough. At last report some followers were still in the Montrose area; meanwhile, many cells of Faithist believers still operate worldwide, some of them more or less communally.[50]

THE SPIRIT FRUIT SOCIETY

One of the longer-lived communities among those active at the turn of the century was the Spirit Fruit Society, which one of its historians, H. Roger Grant, has called a "gentle utopia." Its founder, Jacob Beilhart, was born in 1867 and as a young adult converted from the Lutheranism of his

German upbringing to Adventism. At Battle Creek, Michigan, the world center of Adventism at the time, he worked for a time at both the Battle Creek Sanitarium of Dr. John H. Kellogg and the La Vita Inn of C. W. Post, whose names would later become renowned because of their breakfast-food empires. However, Jacob, as he always preferred to be called, with his wife, Lou, and children (who left Jacob and the nascent community soon afterward) moved in 1898 or 1899 to Lisbon, Ohio, where individuals attracted to Jacob's teaching of selfless giving moved into a growing communal home. The Spirit Fruiters had more freedom than did many communards of their era; they were allowed to retain private property and were not asked to subscribe to any very specific doctrinal precepts. Moreover, their basic attitude of tolerance embraced a kind of sexual freedom in which some members were conventionally married, some changed mates occasionally, and others were celibate.

In 1904 Jacob moved his community to Chicago, and within two years the Spirit Fruiters had moved on to a farm near Ingleside, Illinois, in the Chicago exurbs. There they built their grandest communal dwelling, a "Temple House" with at least eighteen bedrooms and ample public spaces, and a similarly massive barn. But there Jacob died suddenly of complications of appendicitis. The community proved resilient, lasting for decades after the departure of its leader, boosted in no small degree by the spiritual communications from Jacob that Charlena "Ma" Young announced daily after lunch. The biggest change came in 1914, when the still-solid believers packed up and headed for America's seductive western utopia, California, ending up on a hilltop ranch near Santa Cruz. There they remained for fourteen years, supporting themselves with a dairy herd and other agricultural operations. Only the aging of the members and the death of Virginia Moore, the group's latter-day leader, ended one of America's longest-lived yet oddly obscure communal experiments.[51]

THE ESOTERIC FRATERNITY

The Spirit Fruit Society was not the only relatively long-lived community to receive little publicity and thus remain obscure in the annals of communal history. The Esoteric Fraternity presents another example of the genre. Founded in the 1870s in Boston by Hiram Erastus Butler, the Fraternity purchased five hundred acres near Applegate, California, in the late 1880s and developed a successful headquarters commune there. The movement, which had both male and female members, was celibate and promised believers immortality, or at least resurrection after death. Butler and his successor, Enoch Penn, developed and published voluminously in books and magazines a complicated cosmology and metaphysics that embraced, among other things, a doctrine of reincarnation and a belief that the Esoteric Fraternity would eventually grow to a millennial 144,000 members who would thereafter rule the world. By the time of Butler's death (or at least departure from the physical plane) in 1916, the communal property had eleven buildings, including a twenty-six-room main house, and operated various successful businesses, including a good-sized publishing operation. Decline set in, but at last report the group was still holding on and even making a very occasional younger convert.[52]

A religious commune of a decidedly different kind was founded in New Jersey in 1889. Mason T. Huntsman, who took the name Paul Blaudin Mnason after his Christian conversion experience, became a revival preacher in the 1880s who stirred up such controversy that he served a jail term for, among other things, impersonating the Savior. Upon his release, the "New Christ," as his followers deemed him, moved in with a family of supporters and gradually turned their farm in Woodcliff, New Jersey, into a religious commune. Mnason's Christianity centered on the Sermon on the Mount, but he imposed no doctrinal—or any other—test on members. Consequently the Lord's Farm was reported to be a freewheeling place, with no private property and an open-door policy toward visitors and new members. The communards were known to their neighbors as the Angel Dancers, after the nude group dances they were widely believed to hold from time to time. The commune's economy, such as it was, was agricultural, specializing in the growing of fruit on the farm's modest acreage.

Not surprisingly, before too long a variety of problems dogged the settlement. The open-door policy meant, here as elsewhere, that freeloaders, cranks, and even outright criminals were attracted in some numbers, burdening the colony's productive members. The unstructured community was regarded as scandalous by its neighbors, and disapproving local authorities repeatedly intervened in community life until the farm was dissolved in 1910. Given its tumultuous community relations, the community was surprisingly long-lived and populous; in 1906, seventeen years after its founding, by one account it housed forty members. Mnason, never forsaking his distinctive Christian convictions, apparently lived out the rest of his life noncommunally in New York City.

The long-standing, repeated rumors of nudity, sexual promiscuity, and other wanton behavior that sparked enormous opposition to Mnason and his followers seem to have had virtually no basis in fact. David Steven Cohen, a historian of the community, reminds us that wildly excessive rumors about events in communes are perhaps the norm, not the exception, and should be regarded with considerable skepticism. As he concludes, "By showing the lack of foundation for the rumors about one sect, it calls into question the truthfulness of the rumors about the other sects."[53]

Political, Economic, and Anarchist Communities

The previous pages have focused on the diverse world of religious communities, but religious believers were not the only founders of cooperative colonies. Secular visionaries of many differing stripes have long been involved in the larger communitarian movement in America, and several of the communities they founded in the nineteenth century were still operating as the twentieth opened.

SINGLE-TAX ENCLAVES

Socialists and anarchists have long provided the impetus for most secular communes. However, other radical and reformist schools of thought have spawned communes as well; repeatedly in American history groups of persons dissatisfied with the course of society for whatever reason have turned to communitarianism, in one form or another, to prove a variety of social theories. A case in point is the single-tax movement. Disciples of Henry George campaigned for years for an unorthodox taxation system in which the only tax would be levied against the value of unimproved land; his crusade became so widespread and well publicized that eventually George even undertook an unsuccessful race for mayor of New York City.

After years of promoting their ideas through books, periodicals, and political organizations, some single-taxers began to despair of ever winning in the political arena and decided to test their theories in collective settlements. The idea was that within the enclaves, as the settlements came to be called, the residents, who legally held their land communally but who rented and lived on separate lots, would redivide the tax bill for the settlement according to Georgist theory, in effect assessing land and not homes.

The most successful and prominent of the single-tax enclaves was Fairhope, across the bay from Mobile, Alabama. Founded in 1895 under the leadership of Ernest B. Gaston, and financed by radical millionaire Joseph

Fels, Fairhope continues to operate in modified form today, having weathered the attempts of some nonbelieving newcomers—usually persons frustrated at their inability to buy land in the town—to abolish the system of unorthodox assessments. Another enclave was Arden, in northern Delaware about twenty miles from Philadelphia, which was founded in 1900 by Frank Stephens in concert with, among others, William Lightfoot Price, who would later start the art colony known as Rose Valley in Pennsylvania, a few miles north of Arden. Like Fairhope, Arden, which at one time had Upton Sinclair, Scott Nearing, and many other radicals among its members, continues to operate largely along its original lines. Yet another single-tax experiment was Free Acres, in New Jersey, which was founded and promoted by Bolton Hall, a vigorous proponent of small-scale cooperative farming whose writings influenced William Smythe, the founder of the Little Landers colonies.[54] Altogether, about ten of the enclaves were founded, along with several independent experiments that used different versions of the single-tax system. The concept remained in vogue for a surprisingly long time; the last recognized enclave to be founded was Wall Hill, in Mississippi, in 1932. Given that the single tax still has advocates today, it is conceivable that more such communities could be founded in the future.[55]

THE COLONIES OF WASHINGTON

Washington state was an unusually powerful magnet for the communal impulse in the years shortly before and after the turn of the twentieth century. Something of a last frontier in the lower forty-eight states, Washington in its early years attracted a remarkable assortment of freethinkers, social innovators, religious and political radicals, and commune-builders. The two earliest communities, the Puget Sound Cooperative Colony and the Glennis Cooperative Industrial Company, founded in 1887 and 1894 respectively, had already folded their tents by 1900. Others were in their heyday, or at least still alive, as the new century opened.[56]

Home. The best-known of the Washington communities was thriving at the turn of the century. Home, or more formally the Mutual Home Association, was an anarchist colony founded by Oliver Verity, George H. Allen, and B. F. Odell on a remote branch of Puget Sound in 1897. Repelled by the restrictiveness they had experienced in the short-lived Glennis colony (1894–97), Verity and his comrades decided to establish a community with as few rules as possible. They purchased twenty-six acres fronting Von Geldern Cove, more popularly known as Joe's Bay, and then in piecemeal fashion expanded colony property to more than two hundred acres by 1901. Each member was allowed to occupy two acres of ground, and most managed to eke subsistence livings from their plots.[57] Home was not economically fully communal, but it always had much neighborly cooperation and was cherished by most of its members. Some stores were cooperatives. Cooperatively, the residents built Liberty Hall, which housed the school and social activities. They routinely helped one another build houses and sheds. Various kinds of eccentricity, from vegetarianism to prohibitionism, were tolerated, although nude swimming proved too much for some residents to take (they filed criminal complaints against the nudists, creating a deep rift in the colony).

The Home folks might have lived in the peaceful obscurity they sought had they not started up an anarchist paper, *Discontent: Mother of Progress,* in 1898. The well-edited monthly received enough notice to draw a steady stream of newcomers to the colony.[58] Among those who found the place congenial were a number of Russian Jewish socialists who secured, had it ever been in doubt, Home's status as a radical enclave. *Discontent* also brought notoriety to the colony in 1901 when, after its printer had been fined for publishing an obscene article, a Tacoma newspaper vigorously denounced the colony as a nest of free lovers. Conflicts involving the colony's radicalism in various ways punctuated Home's history thereafter. Later publications, including periodicals called the *Demonstrator* and the *Agitator,* continued to keep Home at the center of controversy.[59]

Although the colony was formally dissolved in 1919, quite a few of the members lived at the site for several decades afterward. As a successful colony of anarchists it became something of a pilgrimage site among radicals. Emma Goldman was perhaps the best known of many leftist visitors.[60]

Equality. No colony was founded with a grander vision than Equality. Named after the latest opus of the utopian novelist Edward Bellamy,[61] this colony was designed as the first of a series of colonies that would usher socialism into Washington and eventually the whole nation.

Equality grew out of the work of an organization known as the Brotherhood of the Cooperative Commonwealth.[62] The BCC in turn had emerged from frustrations socialists and populists had experienced in the American political arena; unable to promote their social agenda effectively, a small group of them, including, briefly, Eugene V. Debs, the labor leader who would become the foremost socialist of his day, decided to demonstrate the superiority of socialism by establishing it in model colonies that would spread until the entire nation had been engulfed by it.[63] Under the leadership of Norman Wallace Lermond, a Maine populist, the BCC raised enough money to inaugurate its first colony and went forward with its plan under the leadership of Lermond's associate, Ed Pelton. Pelton bought 280 acres on Puget Sound north of Seattle, and work began in the fall of 1897.

The first building, called Fort Bellamy, was soon completed, and several others were started the following spring. The future looked bright; BCC membership nationally was swelling, and with it the organization's treasury. But internal dissension arose, leading to Lermond's departure in the summer of 1898, and progress slowed. Other eager believers started other colonies even though no support was forthcoming from either Equality or the BCC, but they came to little, and indeed the plan to socialize the whole state made no real headway. Equality certainly appealed to American socialists,[64] and attracted enough of them to grow in membership for a time, reaching 300 in late 1898, but by the summer of 1900 the number had dropped to 120, and a count taken late in 1903 found only 38 residents.[65]

During its heyday the colony had some modest prosperity. Many residents worked long hours and built up an array of business enterprises including lumbering, milling, and a tailor shop as well as agriculture. The colony newspaper *Industrial Freedom*, founded in 1898, became a leading radical periodical of the day. Members had an active common social life. With its reduced population the colony seemed fairly stable—until 1905, when a group of newcomers arrived under the leadership of Alexander Horr, who had been deeply influenced by Theodor Hertzka's utopian novel *Freeland*.[66] Equality quickly became divided into pro-Horr and anti-Horr factions; Horr emerged victorious and soon had renamed the colony Freeland, but the old guard of Equality was not happy with the new state of affairs. Capping increasingly acrimonious disputes was a disastrous fire (of unknown origin, although each faction accused the other of arson) in February 1906. The colony soon began to close itself down, and by 1907 all its assets had been liquidated.[67]

Burley. The impetus behind the establishment of the Burley Colony was similar to that for Equality. The Social Democracy of America, an organization with affinities and organizational ties to the Brotherhood of the Cooperative Commonwealth, provided for a colonization department in its founding constitution in 1897,[68] and a movement to find a colony location soon went forward under the leadership of, among others, Cyrus Field Willard, a Boston aristocrat who had previously been an active Theosophist and proponent of the ideas of Edward Bellamy. In 1898 the colonization commission spun itself off into a relatively independent organization, the Co-operative Brotherhood, and opened a settlement at Burley, on the south end of Puget Sound and just a few miles northeast of Home, in October of that year. The colony was officially named "Brotherhood," but "Burley" was the name by which it was generally known.[69]

Progress was promising in the colony's first months, during which houses were built and a time-check ersatz money system and a newspaper, the *Co-operator*, were established. But divisions soon appeared in the group, notably between the genteel Willard and his wife, Bessie, and the rougher crowd who did most of the colony's physical work. Before long, the Willards left for the Theosophical community at Point Loma. Membership at Burley, however, continued to increase slowly, peaking at about 150 in the summer of 1901. As was the case at most other Washington communities, the logging and sawmill operations were the pillars on which the colony's economy rested. Colonists ate good common meals, enjoyed an active social life, operated a school for their children, and even (remarkably for the time and place) had several religious organizations.

Burley's decline was gradual. Its industries, never lucrative, eventually stagnated, especially as many residents began to run private cottage businesses.[70] With the passage of time the heady optimism that had characterized the early years of the colony dissipated. Unhappy members finally filed suit asking for Burley's dissolution late in 1912, and a judge approved the request in January of the following year. The colony's assets were sold and Burley became simply a pleasant agricultural community.[71]

Freeland. The last of the Washington colonies to be founded in the nineteenth century was Freeland, or rather the first Freeland (Equality would not take that name until several years later). George Washington Daniels and two associates bought land on Whidbey Island in Puget Sound from Seattle entrepreneur James P. Gleason and organized the Free Land Association in late 1899. At the heart of the association was a cooperative store that would pay dividends to members; because members could pay for most of their land with those dividends, in effect they would get "Free Land."

Many settlers at the new colony were discontented emigrants from Equality, including several who had been officers there. They held their small tracts—five acres was a typical size—independently, but were joined by the store, a community boat (necessary for travel to the mainland from their isolated outpost), and the spirit of common purpose and solidarity that permeated progressive thought at the turn of the century. An unofficial newspaper, the *Whidby Islander,* also helped provide a focus for the island colony.[72] Various social and educational organizations, and eventually a colony school, provided cohesion as well. From time to time various socialist and other radical lecturers visited Freeland and thus buttressed the community's sense of leadership in the radical cause.

Freeland, like Home, was decentralized; its status as a colony depended on common location and radical spirit rather than common ownership of all assets. As an enclave of socialists it persisted for many years, evolving gradually into a "normal" isolated village on Puget Sound.[73]

RUSKIN

The single-tax enclaves and the various Washington colonies accounted for most of the radical political communities at the opening of the century, but a few others in that vein were quietly functioning in scattered locations as well. The largest and best-known of those others was Ruskin, which operated in Tennessee and then briefly in Georgia as yet another model of what a socialized country might look like.

Ruskin was the brainchild of J. A. Wayland, the most influential socialist editor in American history. Wayland, who had earlier become prosperous speculating in real estate, gradually became convinced that capitalism was not providing social justice to all, and eventually became a dedicated convert to socialism. In short order he founded *The Coming Nation* in 1893 and watched it grow, in only a few months, into the nation's most widely circulated radical periodical. In the meantime Wayland had become enamored of the utopian socialists—Robert Owen, Charles Fourier, and especially John Ruskin among them—and began to have visions of founding a socialist communal settlement, one that would demonstrate to all the superiority of socialism over capitalism. The colony would provide "every convenience that the rich enjoy, permanent employment at wages higher than ever dreamed of by laborers, with all the advantages of good schools, free libraries, natatoriums, gymnasiums, lecture halls and pleasure grounds."[74] How would such a colony be financed? By the profits from *The Coming Nation,* which was doing very well indeed. Beginning in 1894 he challenged his readers to send in masses of subscriptions; those who sent in two hundred or more would become charter members of the new colony. A circulation of one hundred thousand would do the trick, he announced.

Although that lofty circulation goal was never quite reached, Wayland had become so devoted to his dream that he pressed ahead with his colonization plan anyway. He found a thousand suitable acres in Tennessee west of Nashville, and in the summer of 1894 called the charter members to join him at the site. The first wave consisted of a few dozen stalwarts who braved primitive facilities and oppressive summer weather to begin the construction of Ruskin colony. Within a few weeks a printing press had been installed and *The Coming Nation* began to be issued from the colony. Development occurred quickly; membership reached nearly a hundred by fall, and several small industries were soon operating.

It did not take long for Wayland to get into disputes with a fair number of his fellow colonists. He insisted on retaining editorial control of his newspaper, and some accused him of retaining some of its profits as well—not a trivial matter, given that the paper provided most of the colony's income. Things came to a head and Wayland finally resigned in the summer of 1895, only about a year after the colony's founding. Because the paper belonged to the colony, Wayland had to leave it behind, but he quickly founded a new incarnation of it called the *Appeal to Reason*. It would later eclipse the impressive record of *The Coming Nation* and become the country's leading socialist periodical, finally achieving a circulation of 750,000 and becoming perhaps the single most potent element in socialism's rise to political viability in the early twentieth century.[75]

Ruskin colony did not fall apart without its founder. *The Coming Nation* continued to do well, at least for the time being, and new colonists arrived steadily. In fact, the colony was solid enough to undertake the major venture of moving a few miles; the old site was simply hopeless agriculturally, whereas the new one not only had much fertile farmland but also had timber and other resources, including two large caves that soon housed community industries. The move lived up to its promise, and by 1897 the colony had eighteen hundred acres of land, an array of successful businesses, including the thriving newspaper and printing operations, several dozen buildings, and some 250 members. The population was marked by high turnover; over five years, about five hundred persons lived at Ruskin. Turnover at that level has never been uncommon in intentional communities, and it did not impede Ruskin's progress.[76] Even relations with the nearby outside world, typically a problem for young intentional communities, were relatively good. The popular press featured Ruskin repeatedly in warmly sympathetic articles.[77]

It was not to last. Internal disputes simmered almost from the first, and before long they brought the colony to its knees. Factional disputes flared and spilled over into the Tennessee court system. Fierce battles were fought over religion, schools, and monogamy. Dissatisfaction with the generally low standard of living at the colony grew. Dissolution came in 1899, and the extensive assets of the community were sold at auction for fire sale prices.[78] The bidders were mainly representatives of two groups, those who wanted the colony to continue and those who wanted to leave and wanted their fair share of the assets.

However, the Ruskin story was not over. Most of the colonists who constituted the faction for continuation remained true believers. They pooled their limited resources to buy *The Coming Nation* (now less valuable than previously, for its circulation had slipped precipitously) and moved to join a like-minded small band of socialists known as the American Settlers Association, who a year earlier had moved from Dayton, Ohio, to found their Duke Colony at a former lumber mill site on the edge of the Okefenokee Swamp near Waycross, Georgia.[79] Renamed Ruskin, the merged colony had early glimmers of success, but internal dissension arose again, and weather, disease, and bleak poverty added to its toll. In 1901 the colony was forced to sell its printing equipment as well as its land and buildings to cover debts. The circle was later closed: Wayland, hearing that *The Coming Nation* had been shut down and was for sale, bought it and merged it with his *Appeal to Reason,* which remained successful until his death at his own hand in 1912.[80] The colony staggered on for a few more months, finally closing in 1902.[81]

Ruskin seems to have inspired two additional offshoot colonies, Niksur and Kinderlou, both of which may not have reached viability. The name was also preserved elsewhere as the colonists scattered; Ruskin, Florida, for example, just across Tampa Bay from St. Petersburg, was founded in 1906 by devotees of John Ruskin, some of whom had lived at the Tennessee and Georgia colonies, and featured a Ruskin College (sponsored by the Christian Socialist Guild) and a Ruskin Commongood Society that financed community improvements and survived into the 1960s.[82]

Niksur. In 1899, after two years of preparation, a few persons founded the Niksur Cooperative Association (Niksur is Ruskin spelled backward) near Mille Lacs Lake, Minnesota. Two tailors were in their number, and they advertised trousers as available from their community business. Ralph Albertson, mentioning the community briefly in a survey article, wrote that it had fifty members and lasted three years, although it seems highly doubtful that most "members" could have been residents.[83] The community likely was both small and short-lived.[84]

Kinderlou. Finally, in 1900 eleven families at the new Ruskin colony in Georgia left that enclave, by then in the throes of crises that would soon lead to its dissolution, and moved some sixty miles southwest to Kinderlou, near Valdosta. There they tried again to establish a communal way of life. But serious intentional community seems not to have lasted long at the Kinderlou colony; participants took local jobs and commonality slipped away.[85]

FREEDOM

Another colony in several respects like Ruskin was Freedom Colony, which operated at Fulton, Kansas, from 1898 to 1905. It had its origins in a work-bartering project called the Labor Exchange, several of whose members became interested in colonization and left the exchange to found Freedom. The colony encompassed sixty acres with several residential and industrial buildings and rented additional adjacent farmland. The colony's industries included farming and a sawmill; an attempt to mine coal never was successful. Two years after its founding, Freedom had grown from an original dozen founders to more than thirty members. The best-known of them was Carl Browne, an artist from Berkeley, California, who had been a leader of the Coxey's Army march on Washington (and whose wife, Mame, was Jacob Coxey's daughter) and who arrived at Freedom in 1900. There he constructed a meditation platform in a tree and, after considerable observation of crows, conceived, before the Wright brothers, a plan for an airplane. Grandiosely, he announced that his airplane factory would employ everyone in the Midwest who needed a job and would turn out airplanes so cheaply "as to soon supersede the bicycle for [home] use."[86] Several models were built and exhibited in the area, but no full-size prototype emerged.[87] Browne also ran for Congress as a Populist while at the colony. Although Freedom was said to have attracted more than its share of loafers, it experienced several good years, despite slowly declining membership, until 1905, when a mysterious arson fire destroyed most of the buildings and with them the morale of the settlement.

And There Were Others. . .

Still more communities were operating at the opening of the twentieth century, experiments that either do not fit very conveniently into the previous categories or are not terribly well known or documented. This chapter ends with brief notes on five more intentional communities.

Colorado Co-Operative Company. Like several communities discussed previously, the Colorado Co-Operative Company could be considered a successor to an earlier cooperative colony, in this case the Topolobampo Colony in Sinaloa, Mexico, on the Gulf of California. Topolobampo was founded with the grandiose goal of becoming North America's principal Pacific Ocean port, located significantly closer to eastern U.S. manufacturers than the West Coast ports of the United States are; thus shippers could save on train transport and reach the Pacific docks more easily by using a planned new railroad to Topolobampo. However, problems were many for Topolobampo, and the railroad was never finished, even though some limited progress was made on the city-colony itself.

Several veterans of the project regrouped in Denver after Topolobampo's demise. After some searching they found a good new community site in Tabeguache Park in southwestern Colorado. They moved in during the autumn of 1894, filed homestead claims, and began to build what became the town of Piñon. The success of the project hinged on the digging of a thirteen-mile-long irrigation ditch, and although it took ten years, the ditch was indeed completed. The colonists, who had been living in primitive structures while they poured their energy into the ditch, then turned toward building better facilities, and thus grew up the town of Nucla. Gradually, Nucla turned into a noncommunal small town, and most of the company's common holdings were transferred to private ownership in 1906. The Colorado Co-Operative Company was thereafter no longer an intentional community but a cooperative of water users who owned a common canal.[88]

Home Employment Co-operative Company. The Home Employment Company, like many others, derived from earlier communal experiences. Its founder, William H. Bennett, had been a member of the Friendship Community, one of the string of communes founded in the nineteenth century by the indefatigable Alcander Longley, who later in life sought to start his own community patterned after the then-new Ruskin Colony.

The Home Employment Co-operative Company, founded in 1894, had several cottage industries, including a broom factory, a flour mill, a barbershop, a blacksmith shop, a shingle mill, and a cannery, plus a farm. The population of the community never exceeded thirty. Its end came about gradually; no exact closing date has been ascertained, but it was probably between 1904 and 1906.[89]

Winters Island. The colony at Winters Island, in Suisun Bay (in the upper reaches of San Francisco Bay), is relatively little known and little documented, even though the colony was sturdily enough established to publish a periodical, *The Co-operator,* from 1895 to 1897. In 1893 Erastus Kelly, who owned the island and had been inspired by glowing reports about Kaweah Colony in the socialist press,[90] enlisted Kate Lockwood Nevins, a Populist activist, to help him organize the colony. By 1893 the fledgling Co-operative Brotherhood of Winters Island reportedly had a hundred members, not all of whom lived at the site. That initial vitality did not last long; the depression of the 1890s made it hard for many members to pay their dues. Gradually, colony operations were scaled back. The record does not show how long a group of colonists remained on the island, but Nevins, at least, carried on and was reported present in the 1930s.[91]

Lystra and Friedheim. Very little is known about either of these two communities. Ralph Albertson reports that Lystra existed in Virginia between 1899 and 1902 and had twenty-five members, and that Friedheim, also in Virginia, had fifty-two members and lasted from 1899 to 1900.[92] Albertson seems to have obtained his information from a 1905 survey by Frederick A. Bushee, who reports the same information, only adding the enigmatic note that Friedheim closed because of "human weakness [and] lack of intelligence."[93] A more recent scholar, Otohiko Okugawa, looked for local information on the two colonies and could find nothing.[94]

Even at this length the foregoing chronicle is abbreviated, but it should make it clear that the ongoing communal tradition was still active early in the twentieth century. Meanwhile, as at virtually any other time in the past three hundred years, the new communes that were being founded complemented the longer-established ones. These new communities will be the subject of the balance of this volume.

2

Art Colonies

During the two decades between 1890 and 1910, many artists in the United States and abroad banded together in colonies in which they could pursue their muses in the company of other artists. While artists' colonies in the sense of locales with high concentrations of working artists and some sharing of studio and gallery space are of ancient vintage (and have long been well represented by such American enclaves as Provincetown, Taos, and Old Lyme), the turn-of-the-century colonies, products of the then-popular arts and crafts movement, were a new breed. Their diverse economic systems often involved some kind of sharing of money (ranging from pooling of financial resources to helping peers in need to living off the charity of wealthy patrons), the artists usually lived on commonly owned property rather than simply in a neighborhood, and the colonies embodied a sense of common purpose among the participating artists, a conviction that art could be a powerful instrument of social change.[1]

The arts and crafts colonies numbered a dozen or so, although because art colonies represented a spectrum of organizational patterns, any count of the ones that could be considered more or less communal is arbitrary.[2] They were typically in rural areas or small towns, reflecting the "back to the land" sentiment that about the same time was spawning other communities, including those underwritten by the Salvation Army rural colonization program, some of the Jewish agricultural colonies, and various cooperative enclaves of one-acre microfarms.

Earlier intentional communities—Brook Farm was a notable example—had been havens for artists, but as a movement encompassing hundreds, if not thousands, of artists in several widely dispersed locations, the arts and crafts colonies represented a new twist on the venerable theme of intentional community and stood as a key historical link between the prominent communes and communal movements of the nineteenth century (the Shakers, the Harmony Society, and the Fourierists, for example) and the great revival of communitarianism that was to emerge in the last third of the twentieth century.

The model that beckoned the new colonists was European; for the better part of a century colonies of artists had prospered there, most notably, perhaps, at Barbizon, the French village that first began to draw artists as early as the 1820s and that by midcentury had among its inhabitants such distinguished painters as Camille Corot, Jean François Millet, and Théodore Rousseau.[3] In the latter part of the century, the model spread, particularly to England and the United States, its dispersion coinciding with the rise of the arts and crafts movement, which emerged in England in the late 1850s and 1860s under the inspiration of John Ruskin and William Morris—both of whom, not incidentally, were founders of arts-oriented communities in their homeland.

The impact of Ruskin and Morris must not be underestimated, but in the United States several domestic social and cultural currents contributed to the colony impulse as well. One was the popularity of culturally oriented summer camps in latter-nineteenth-century America, where educated vacationers, disproportionate numbers of them fairly prosperous, attended Chautauqua presentations, Bible studies, and a wide variety of aesthetic endeavors—lectures, performances, and workshops in visual arts, music, philosophy, and so forth—at any of hundreds of campgrounds. Another was the tide of social-reform activity—populism, the social gospel, progressivism, and single-tax agitation, not to mention the more radical advocacy of socialism, anarchism, and free love—that surged in the latter years of the century and embodied the kind of idealism typically congenial to the founding of intentional communities. Yet another was the movement to establish garden cities, pleasant semirural towns not defiled by sooty factories. Still another was the work of feminist reformers, among them Charlotte Perkins Gilman, who were outlining new models of home life that would relieve women from exclusively domestic duties, models that meshed well with cooperative endeavors. In this milieu a good many artists, both prominent and obscure, were drawn to participate in reform-minded social experiments while enjoying the cultural richness of villages of artists and the patronage of prosperous visitors.

The arts and crafts movement, the heart and soul of the art colony movement, from its beginning had goals beyond the mere creation of works of art by individual artists. It sought to revolutionize the organization of workshops, eliminating the distinctions among designers, crafts-persons, and managers, and, in the age of laissez-faire capitalism, subscribed to a labor theory of value.[4] Importantly for communal studies, the movement tried, notably through the creation of cooperatives patterned after medieval craft guilds, to engender a sense of cooperative endeavor and an atmosphere of equality among its artists.[5] It championed handwork, and although machines inevitably crept into many arts and crafts studios, the movement had a strong sense of making sure that they were the servants, not masters, of the workers: "The Arts and Crafts [movement] is a soul-reaction from under the feet of corporations and the wheels of machines," declaimed Edward Pearson Pressey, the founder of the New Clairvaux art colony.[6] Although Gustav Stickley, one of the most successful marketers of arts and crafts works, could allow that a "machine is simply a tool in the hands of the skilled worker, and in no way detracts from the quality of his work," he also observed,

The trouble is that we have allowed the machine to master us. The possibility of quick, easy and cheap production has so intoxicated us that we have gone on producing in a sort of insane prolificness, and our imaginary needs have grown with it. Originally intended to make simpler and easier the doing of necessary things, the introduction of machinery with its train of attendant evils has so complicated and befuddled our standards of living that we have less and less time for enjoyment and for growth, and nervous prostration is the characteristic disease of the age.[7]

Like many in other communitarian movements, the arts and crafts colonists had a strong sense of profoundly reforming society as a whole through their efforts. In that they failed, inevitably, but they did succeed in communicating a reformist message to a wide segment of the educated public, and in any event they embodied a minigolden age of the arts. As one contemporary observer concluded, "It cannot be said that they have done very much as yet toward curing the numerous ills that society is heir to, but they have at least provided congenial quarters in beautiful spots for some of the most gifted of our craftsmen and have thus contributed to the production of not a little work of a very high order; and this in itself suffices to justify their existence."[8]

Roycroft

The earliest of the more or less communal art colonies was that of the Roycrofters at East Aurora, New York. Its founder and ubiquitous leader, Elbert Hubbard, made a small fortune early in life as a soap salesman. Looking for more satisfaction than the conventional business world offered, he sold his half interest in the Larkin Soap Company and turned to study and writing. In 1892, on a trip abroad to collect materials for a major writing project, he visited—possibly in the company of George Bernard Shaw—William Morris's Kelmscott arts and crafts colony at Merton Abbey, outside London, and deliberately imitated it in building his own community, which began to take shape the following year.[9] The earliest ventures focused on hand printing and hand illuminating elegant (some would say pseudoelegant[10]) books; the publishing operation turned out to be a commercial success, largely because of Hubbard's tireless and corny but canny promotion of it. Indeed, the consummate salesman used his promotional genius to make all of the Roycroft product lines profitable—so much so that his detractors saw him as more a carnival barker than an artist or communitarian. Although the ceaseless hoopla did have its distasteful side, it is useful to remember, as Leslie Greene Bowman has observed, that though Hubbard's gaudy promotion of Roycroft wares, including ideas, may have turned the campus into a "kind of arts and crafts amusement park," the promotion did sell the products and kept the venture alive while the less commercially oriented colonies had shorter life spans.[11] Years earlier Hubbard had written, "To refer to me as 'commercial' does not hurt my feelings. The World of Commerce is just as honorable as the World of Art and a trifle more necessary. Art exists on the surplus that Business Men accumulate."[12] In any event, for two decades Hubbard reigned as the P. T. Barnum of the arts and crafts movement.

About the time the books began to come off the presses, in 1895, Hubbard also founded the *Philistine,* a little magazine of aphorisms and miscellany. The tone was mildly iconoclastic; Hubbard took frequent slaps at monogamy, for example (it later became known that he had had a lengthy affair, which led to a divorce from his first wife).[13] The magazine found an immediate niche and quickly developed a healthy circulation; seven years after its founding, riding Hubbard's own increasing renown, it reached an incredible 110,000.[14] Eileen Boris has characterized its appeal thus:

While it appears juvenile and hackneyed today, the *Philistine* opened new worlds of art and thought to young people in small towns where parochialism and religiosity circumscribed their lives. Hubbard achieved this impact only by borrowing liberally from classic authors. Nor was he beyond outright distortion or fabrication; he ran articles under the pen name of "Clavigera" to make them seem from the pen of Ruskin.[15]

Eventually a second magazine, *The Fra* (Hubbard frequently styled himself "Fra Elbertus"), appeared as well, and all the while the books continued to pour forth—largely Hubbard's works, some of which found a wide audience. The centerpiece of the books was a long series called *Little Journeys to the Homes of Good Men and Great*.

Curious visitors began to drop in at East Aurora; eventually, the Roycrofters built a hotel to house the inquisitive, and in furnishing the hotel they hit upon what became a mainstay industry, Morris-style furniture. (The hotel, in fact, became a showplace of Roycroft crafts, and it had the calculated whimsy so characteristic of Hubbard: the rooms, for example, were not numbered, but named for such persons as Aristotle, Charles Darwin, William Morris, Elizabeth Cady Stanton, Walt Whitman, and Rosa Bonheur.) Eventually, the line of craft products included copperware, leather, stained glass, wrought iron, and other such things; the mail-order business even carried food specialties. Although most of the Roycrofters built artifacts of standard pattern, several artists of distinction provided excellent designs and prototypes (Dard Hunter, who produced fine metalworks and later produced exquisite handmade paper and other works, was probably the most prominent of them).[16] Roycroft also had a bank and a farm. By the turn of the century the whole thing was a thriving business.

Hubbard on a number of occasions claimed that the Roycrofters lived and worked in a true commune that included a common treasury, organized as a corporation for legal purposes but operating in the interest of its employees, who owned much of its stock.[17] The claim seemed to be fairly widely accepted at the time, and various socialists applauded the seeming progressivism of the Roycroft Shops.[18] Hubbard's biographer, Freeman Champney, calls the setup "quasi-communal," emphasizing the sense of freewheeling camaraderie and the little fragments of classless democracy, such as the fact that the Roycroft workers and their paying hotel guests all ate together in one dining hall.[19] Champney concludes:

In the early years, Roycroft had much in common with the utopian communities that had dotted the country earlier in the century. Not economically, since the property was Hubbard's. But Roycroft had common meals, meetings, sports, studies, and a library. Cash wages were small, but there wasn't much need or opportunity to spend money. The work was still work, but there was an effort to make it humanly satisfying. There was a real—if informal and basically paternalistic—feeling of shared values, adventure, responsibility.[20]

Certainly working conditions in the Roycroft shops were enlightened for the time. The Roycroft Creed began by affirming "a belief in working with the Head, Hand and Heart, and mixing enough Play with the Work so that every task is pleasurable and makes for Health and Happiness."[21] Roycroft in effect became one of the "welfare capitalist" industries of the turn-of-the-century era, resembling in some respects, for example, Leclaire, Illinois, the company town built by plumbing-fixture entrepreneur Nelson O. Nelson where workers enjoyed such amenities as a library, a kindergarten, schools, community buildings, a cooperative store, and an easy payment plan for home ownership.[22] Workplaces at Roycroft were comfortable and well lighted; the workday was only eight hours long; workers tiring of one task could take up another.[23] Roycrofters had recreational and cultural activities unusual for businesses in their day—a baseball team, for example, and a Roycroft band. Boris argues that Roycroft combined "symbolic medievalism with communitarianism and benevolent capitalism," even though it was less a utopian community than a laboratory for Hubbard's ideas.[24] Hubbard's system was benevolent, if paternalistic, and it worked in the marketplace. By 1906 the workforce exceeded four hundred.[25]

The Roycrofters' communitarian image was enhanced in a variety of ways. Hints of collective endeavor were scattered about the "campus"; for example, Hubbard nicknamed the Roycroft Inn the Phalanstery, evoking the Fourierists, famous nineteenth-century communitarians.[26] Progressive causes and fads were often endorsed; for example, a sign in the dining room recommended Fletcherism, or slow chewing of food, which was believed by adherents to insure perfect health as well as to cause the eater to consume less.[27] The community presented itself as committed to left-of-center social causes, as evidenced by its inviting as visiting lecturers such progressive lights as Eugene V. Debs, Clarence Darrow, Booker T. Washington, and Margaret Sanger. Moreover, the Roycrofters periodically sponsored conferences on socialism and other progressive topics. An announcement for a Roycroft conference scheduled for June 1909 opened by intoning, "Socialism is coming. The question is in what form, when, and how?" On the other hand, the Roycrofters sponsored several conferences annually on a variety of topics (after 1903 they had a hotel to fill, after all), and they did not hesitate to use their appeal to socialists and other reformers to sell advertising for their periodicals.[28] Eileen Boris, a perceptive historian of the arts and crafts movement in America, has concluded that "more than any other self-proclaimed follower of Morris, Hubbard manipulated antiestablishment symbols to support the existing culture."[29]

Hubbard swore that he was egalitarian through and through. "All the money I make by my pen, all that I get from my lectures and books, goes to the fund of the Roycroft—the benefit goes to all."[30] "I want no better clothing, no better food, no more comforts and conveniences than my helpers and fellow-workers have. . . . The Roycroft Shop is for the Roycrofters, and each is limited only by his capacity to absorb."[31] But he has had a fair number of detractors who have argued that he, like some other charismatic leaders of intentional communities, was more equal than his fellows, that he was a skillful publicist, an opportunist, and a seeming bohemian who served the American ruling class well and skillfully.[32] A Hubbard associate, Felix Shay, tried to dismiss such criticisms by arguing that some Roycrofters refused to work and, when they were fired, "paraded their tales."[33] But disgruntled former employees were not the only ones carping at Hubbard. "By 1914," notes Frank Luther Mott sardonically, "the Fra was playing golf with John D. Rockefeller." In his last years, "Hubbard rode two horses—socialism and big business."[34] Certainly some shift in his outlook had occurred over time. In 1903 Hubbard had been able to write, "The Superior Class is a burden. No nation ever survived it long, none ever can." But by 1913 he had become what would now be called a neoconservative: "Trust-busting attorneys, intent on barratry, working under protection of an obsolete law, have wrought havoc and worked a dire wrong to the working people. The endeavor to destroy our Captains of Industry—our creators of wealth—has been a blunder, vast and far-reaching in its malevolent effect."[35]

One of the more vitriolic attacks came, after Hubbard's death, from Upton Sinclair, who denounced Hubbard for having tried to sell large quantities of an antilabor motivational tract to John D. Rockefeller and thus help the archcapitalist head off worker unrest.[36] Hubbard's most fa-

mous literary creation, by far, was "A Message to Garcia," a paean to devotion to duty that was purchased in bulk by many industrialists and distributed to their employees, eventually reaching a circulation in the millions.[37]
The tract eulogized self-reliance and teamwork, and as such it meshed well
with the interests of corporate managers, even though those virtues are
not far from ones dear to socialists and cooperators. In any event, Hubbard adroitly promoted the profitable proliferation of the piece, and the
whole thing raised, understandably, serious doubts about Hubbard's status as a reformer among those devoted to social change.

But Hubbard's reputation as a progressive and communitarian had defenders as well. One sympathizer wrote in 1905 that because of "Garcia,"
Hubbard was condemned by progressives, but that conservatives also dis-
trusted him "because he insists on work for the idle rich and work for the
idle poor; because he does not stand pat on the present system and is trying to replace competition with co-operation . . . . because he has identified himself with street gamins, monists, heretics, cowboys, mothers,
lovers, babes and sages."[38] J. Wade Caruthers has argued that the depiction
of Hubbard as an apologist for big business seems to derive from posthu-
mous publications of his selected works, pieces that do not constitute a
balanced sample of his thought. The whole Hubbard corpus, Caruthers
maintains, discloses a reformer who promoted socialist ideas and criti-
cized orthodox religion, the wealthy who lived off the work of others,
government oppression, imperialism, and child labor, among other
things. Caruthers concludes that Hubbard was on the whole quite progressive—indeed, was a dreamer who had tried to implement his vision of
a better society.[39] One would have to overlook quite a few important
Hubbard writings to conclude that his only agenda was the promotion of
himself and corporate America.[40]

Whatever communitarianism the Roycrofters may have achieved, and
whatever the purity of Fra Elbertus's thought, the enterprise was prosperous for many years, producing and successfully marketing elegant books,
arts and crafts furniture, and other items. Moreover, Hubbard was, as
Robert Koch has noted, "the first to promote Morris' ideas in this country" and therefore to be credited as a notable precipitator of the flowering
of the arts and crafts movement. Roycroft was undeniably a major force—
perhaps *the* major force—in placing arts and crafts furniture, books, copperware, and the like in middle-class American homes, and foreshadowed
the success of other arts and crafts ventures, such as some of Gustav Stickley's work, which, as Koch has observed, "could never have had such a

widespread vogue had not Hubbard paved the way with the printed word."[41] He had at least a modicum of influence on later artists and architects as well. Wayne Andrews suggests that Hubbard influenced Frank Lloyd Wright in style and self-promotion, if not architecture:

> It is just possible that it was Hubbard who taught Wright there was no easier way of attracting attention than wearing one's hair long and sporting flowing ties. After all, the nation listened when the editor of *The Philistine* preached: "Wear thy hair long: it is a sign that thou art free." Wright may have listened more attentively than anyone else, for he and Hubbard were one in their admiration for the teachings of William Morris.
>
> Possibly, too, the architect might never have dreamed of ending his days as a patriarch surrounded by young admirers if he had not been aware of what the founder of the Roycroft Press accomplished at East Aurora. The Taliesin Fellowship of future architects come to learn the secrets of the profession from the master has more than a little in common with the Roycrofters—in Spring Green as at East Aurora, young people are obliged to recognize that, as Hubbard put it, "all work is respectable, including the dirty work."[42]

Roycroft served as something of a beacon to those who would combine art, community, social reform, and, to some extent, radical politics. It rapidly slipped into obscurity, however, after Hubbard's death. Hubbard, ever the master of the flamboyant gesture, and his second wife, Alice, went down with the *Lusitania* in 1915.[43] Such commonality as there was at the Roycroft shops did not long outlast Hubbard, although the business survived under the management of his son, Elbert II, until 1938. Thereafter several of the Roycroft campus buildings became public facilities, one of them the East Aurora town hall. In the 1980s a Roycroft renaissance arose along with a general renewal of interest in the arts and crafts movement; once again artists worked in East Aurora, and galleries flourished anew. The Roycroft Inn underwent a major renovation, and at this writing the artistic, if not the communal, spirit of the Roycrofters lives on.

Rose Valley

The most fully communal and certainly the most democratic of the major art colonies was Rose Valley, founded outside Philadelphia in 1901. Its participants represented the fusion of two groups, a radical circle of intellectuals and professionals that included the respected Quaker architect William Lightfoot Price and a bohemian scene whose most prominent figure was Horace Traubel. Price was an architect of some renown; among his better-known projects were several extravagant mansions—one of them, Woodmont, on the Main Line outside Philadelphia, later became the headquarters of Father Divine's Peace Mission Movement—and two grand hotels in Atlantic City. Price and Traubel had met in the 1890s, and Traubel had introduced Price to the radical thinking of William Morris, Henry George, and Walt Whitman. Since then, Price had become involved with, among other radicals, the Fels brothers, Samuel and Joseph, single-tax devotees and heirs to a considerable fortune who devoted much of their money to fighting the system that had provided it, and Edward Bok, the influential editor of the *Ladies' Home Journal,* who used his mass-circulation pulpit to promote such causes as sex education, pure food and drug laws, and wilderness preservation.[44] At the end of the century Price and his friends began to focus their efforts on colonization projects, which they saw as helping the epic arts and crafts struggle for a revival of craftsmanship in an industrial age. The first colony, founded in 1900 by Price, Frank Stephens, and Joseph Fels, was the single-tax enclave of Arden, Delaware, just a few miles from their suburban Philadelphia base.

Once Arden was under way Price and his associates—this time his business partner, Hawley McLanahan, was the other principal participant—turned their attention to a pair of aged and empty mill buildings at Rose Valley that would house what they intended to be not only a work space for artists but a community that, at its ambitious best, might become the nucleus of the new social order they so fervently sought.[45] Half a century earlier Rose Valley had been occupied by several houses and water-powered mills; its main industry had been the manufacture of snuff. The decline of snuff taking in society had turned the mills and homes into a ghost town that to Price and McLanahan seemed made to order for a colony of the arts.[46] Price purchased the site in April 1901, incorporated his organization in July, sold participants stock to provide working capital, and set about developing crafts-related industries.[47] He moved his family to Rose Valley soon after acquiring the property and, as George Thomas has put it, set to gathering about him "others committed to William Morris' notion of reintegrating creativity and work, so that the designer and the producer again were united."[48] Even the physical plant, with its red tile roofs, guest house, and small cottages with gardens, reflected the thinking of Morris, who held that "those who are to make beautiful things must live in a beautiful place."[49]

Common ownership and effort were central to the Rose Valley ideal. The eighty-acre central precinct plus some smaller parcels provided a total area of a bit more than a hundred acres, all of which was held in common through the Rose Valley Association. Land and buildings would be rented to those who would live and work in them. Those who insisted on land ownership could buy their own tracts on the periphery of the community proper. In the commonly held core would be created a place where, as Price's biographer Thomas wrote, "the medieval unity of life, art, and work could be renewed."[50]

Meanwhile, in the last years of the nineteenth century a bohemian scene had begun to develop in Philadelphia with the emergence of a group of artists and intellectuals known as the Pepper Pot Club (for one of the favorite dishes at the restaurant where they most often gathered). The spirit of Walt Whitman, who lived just across the Delaware River in Camden, was the chief inspiration of the group; its central figure was the colorful Whitman disciple and cultural radical Horace Traubel, whose prominence was anchored by his editorship of the *Conservator,* a free-ranging Whitmanesque little magazine. Traubel was famed for his unconventional behavior and his enormous appetite as well as for his passion for social justice and beauty.[51] His parents had been friends of Whitman's, and Traubel became, for several years beginning in 1888, Whitman's Boswell, eventually publishing several volumes of intimate records of Whitman's daily life from that period.[52] Traubel was, among many other things, a socialist whose instincts were revolutionary but who seems to have found, as other socialists in America in that era did, brighter prospects for success in small experiments than in converting the whole nation.

Traubel took an early interest in Price's community project and soon became deeply involved in it. After spending the summer of 1903 in Rose Valley, he established the Rose Valley Print Shop in Philadelphia, whence he published the community's magazine, *The Artsman,* beginning that fall. The magazine provided a chronicle of Rose Valley as well as excerpts from the works of Ruskin, Morris, and other guiding lights of the arts and crafts movement. Traubel joined Price and McLanahan as one of the dominant spirits of Rose Valley, a community that would be supported by artistic work and that would stand as a revolutionary vanguard for the coming socialist society. Traubel wrote the manifesto in the first issue of *The Artsman:*

Rose Valley is a cross between economic revolution and the stock exchange. . . . Rose Valley is not altogether a dream or wholly an achievement. It is an experiment. It is also an act of faith. It is not willing to say what it will do. It is only willing to say what it is trying to do. Rose Valley pays its first tribute to labor. In Rose

Valley labor is creed and ritual. Rose Valley reaches life through work. . . . The Rose Valley shops are temples. Here men pray in their work. Here men practice fellowship in their work. The shops have only one creed. That creed is good work. There is only one apostasy at Rose Valley. That apostasy is bad work. Blasphemy is shirk. Blasphemy is neglect. Blasphemy is don't care. . . . Rose Valley has not withdrawn from the world. It is in the world. . . . It is not an ideal. It is a step towards an ideal. It is not standing in the way of any agent of social evolution. It is cooperating with such agents.[53]

As the vision unfolded, Rose Valley attracted increasing numbers of residents who together ran several arts-oriented cottage industries. Students and professors from nearby Swarthmore College also joined the experiment. Price operated his architectural practice at Rose Valley; a furniture shop opened in 1902, and soon there were also a ceramics shop and a book bindery. Ridley Creek, which had powered the old mills, again became a source of waterpower for workshops, as well as the community's water supply. The old bobbin mill was remodeled into a community center known as Artsman's Hall, where theatrical productions were mounted regularly. The residents formally declared themselves the Rose Valley Folk and began to hold monthly meetings called "Folk Motes," patterned after the "motes" held in William Morris's *News from Nowhere*.[54] Social life became lively and elaborate, with lectures, Shakespearean plays, and concerts.[55] Government was democratic, and the community blended individualism and mutual support well. Community members worked side by side on the construction and remodeling projects, fulfilling the arts and crafts vision in which "architect became builder; builder was architect."[56] By the peak years of 1905 and 1906 Rose Valley's predominantly Quaker population probably exceeded fifty.[57] A visitor in that year wrote exuberantly of the colony:

Sometimes we find an oasis. Rose Valley is one of these. We feel that a spirit of artistic freedom pervades; here is a place where the vampire of commercialism cannot find entrance; here is a place where the craftsman may work for the love of his craft, and the artist for the love of art; here is a small but living monument to the lifework of John Ruskin and William Morris.[58]

Despite its convivial social life and idealism, however, Rose Valley was never without problems. At the beginning Price had had trouble finding the craftsman workers he sought; machines had already taken over such arts-oriented industries as furniture manufacture, and traditional craft workers were already in short supply. So rare had such American artisans become that Price had to look abroad for workers, who ended up coming to Rose Valley from France, Norway, and Belgium—and who apparently were never really assimilated into the larger Rose Valley community.[59] Moreover, the community never managed to find a secure financial footing and thus could not provide steady jobs for would-be resident artisans. Its fine furniture was far too expensive to attract any but wealthy customers, especially because much cheaper, if inferior, similar pieces were readily available from a variety of mass-market sources.[60] Thus retaining communally minded artists and workers proved difficult. Many left and few replaced them. By 1907 the shops were moribund, and the Rose Valley Association was finally dissolved in 1908. However, the end of collective work did not mean the end of common social activities; for years afterward Rose Valley enjoyed a rich cultural life, much of it focused on the Folk Mote, the town meeting *cum* social club. The last formal remnant of the cooperative community was erased in 1910 when McLanahan and his father-in-law, Charles T. Schoen, who had already taken over the site of the defunct furniture shop, bought the community shares of the Rose Valley Association and with that transaction took title to all the land and buildings except the Guild Hall. Eventually, the erstwhile community became a prosperous residential neighborhood, many of its residents commuting to jobs in Philadelphia. The Rose Valley Press, operated by Traubel in Philadelphia, continued to operate until his death in 1921, but for the rest of the community the experiment was over. Nevertheless, even though Rose Valley survived for only seven years, Traubel's biographer was downright lyrical in his assessment of the little arts community:

> Traubel and his associates gave to the world something it was not ready to receive. Rose Valley was the premature child of its economic mother. It was not a step backward into industrial competition, but rather a leap forward into the social commune. Rose Valley was the social spirit incorporated into economic fact. It was the harbinger of the co-operative commonwealth heralding its message of freedom in the camp of industrial slavery. It was the expression of "hope that some men, released from the deadening influences of monotonous unthinking toil, may see such possibilities in life as will make them put their shoulders to the wheel and strive to lift society out of the rut of accustomed thought or habit."[61]

New Clairvaux

Another colony that shared Rose Valley's aims and, roughly, its life span was New Clairvaux, founded by Edward Pearson Pressey, a Unitarian minister and Christian socialist, in Montague, Massachusetts, in 1902. Pressey, who deplored the migration to the cities that left behind good but unneeded homes and perennial food crops, saw craft work as a means for reclaiming the countryside and for countering the ravages of urban industrial society.

In 1900 Pressey and his wife moved to the down-and-out village of Montague, where Pressey began preaching in an abandoned church. In 1902 he started publishing a magazine, *Country Time and Tide,* that pushed the entire reform agenda of the day, particularly rural self-sufficiency and salvation through the arts and crafts movement. New Clairvaux, named in honor of the monastery and cultural center led by St. Bernard in twelfth-century France, started in the same year as the magazine and became a fairly freewheeling cooperative of back-to-the-land artists. Components of the community were added one after the other: once the press was running the residents started a farm where they raised produce to eat; then they started a school, the New Clairvaux Plantation and Crafts School, which provided its male students with training in craft work as well as more conventional academic subjects. All the while they were producing a variety of handicrafts for sale. The resident colony population peaked at twenty-nine. Like the other arts and crafts colonies of the same era, however, New Clairvaux was dogged by financial problems; it was finally dissolved in 1908 or 1909. Pressey continued to tackle the problem of repopulating and reinvigorating the countryside as a writer for several years thereafter; in 1918 he moved for the last time, to Schenectady, where he worked on the local newspaper and continued to promote his passion for country living and crafts.[62]

Byrdcliffe

Byrdcliffe was a settlement financially grounded in the patronage of a wealthy friend of art and founded with grand vision. Begun outside Woodstock, New York, in 1902, it was decisive in turning Woodstock into the town of the arts it has been ever since. Byrdcliffe was a multifaceted enclave: a millionaire's personal estate, a summer art school, a handicraft factory, and a rural community.[63]

Ralph Radcliffe Whitehead, the English heir to a fortune created by felt mills in Yorkshire, had been influenced by John Ruskin while a student at Oxford. Whitehead began to formulate his communal theories and plans in the early 1870s as an observer of Ruskin's attempt to establish, in England, a series of utopian colonies collectively known as the Guild of St. George. He seems to have made two or more attempts to start communities based on Ruskin's ideas in Europe, in Austria and Italy, although little is known of them other than that the second colony, near Florence, was a proving ground for the organizational patterns introduced at Byrdcliffe.[64] Back in the United States he became involved in the burgeoning socialist movement and concluded that an arts and crafts colony could help further the social reform agenda as well as promote the arts, of which he was a long-standing patron. According to his original scheme, artists of means as well as wealthy patrons would give 10 percent of their incomes to support their fellow colonists.[65] Like other reformers of his time, he decried the increasing frenzy of life in the new industrial age: "The beauty and the joy of life seems too often to be lost through the haste to get somewhere too quickly . . . nature works slowly . . . and the ties which bind us to her larger soul are torn and weakened by our impotent restlessness and love of novelty."[66] He was also a lifelong advocate of manual labor: "The pleasure of doing good work under healthy conditions, be it with a spade or with a sculptor's chisel,—the joy of a man in the work of his hands,—is not a mere passing satisfaction, but is an element in all sane life."[67]

You have your painting, that is work enough for you, another may have his music; but to others like myself, who have no particular artistic or literary faculty, simpler crafts are still open. We shall want clothes. Why should not the women spin the yarn and the men weave the cloth? Such work, done on hand machines, and not for too many hours in the day, has nothing degrading in it, and would be a delightful occupation to those whose nerves are overstrung by the irrational life they have hitherto been leading.[68]

In the late 1890s Whitehead met Hervey White, an up-and-coming novelist who was working at Hull House in Chicago, and White became Whitehead's agent-in-chief for colony development. About 1899 Whitehead was offered a site for a colony, an idyllic clearing in the ancient forest in western Oregon. He, with White's assistance, set to work on the project, overseeing the building of a large common building and rustic log cottages for the expected artist colonists. Infighting among various individuals involved in the preparations for the opening of the colony, however, ended the venture before it had got under way.

Whitehead, undaunted, undertook to search the mountainous regions of the East for a new site. This time Whitehead and White were joined in the search by the talented painter Bolton Coit Brown, who, like White, would play a major role at Byrdcliffe and later in the larger Woodstock art scene.[69] An anti-Semite, Whitehead at first excluded the Catskills from consideration because the area had a large Jewish summer population, but Brown found what seemed the perfect piece of land near the village of Woodstock, which fortuitously had no resident Jews. The town at the time was an unlikely place for artists and thinkers to gather; one early denizen of Byrdcliffe wrote that the region was "apparently quite without intellectual resources," located in "this most illiterate county of the Empire State."[70] But the topography was stunning, and Brown purchased seven farms totaling more than twelve hundred acres for the colony whose name would combine the middle names of Whitehead and his wife, Jane Byrd McCall Whitehead. Brown began overseeing the construction of some twenty-nine colony buildings in 1902.[71]

Fanciful names adorned the rude but durable structures: Lark's Nest, Yagdrisil, Camelot, Morning Glory, Fleur-de-lys, Carniola.[72] It was locally rumored that Whitehead had spent $500,000 on the building of the physical plant.[73] By mid-1903 he had issued a call for "any true craftsmen who are in sympathy with our ideas and who will help us to realize them" to come to his new haven for the creative; while denying that Byrdcliffe would be a "community," Whitehead projected that

there are many ways in which coöperation is possible, and we shall use any of them which are convenient. To make and sell our products, to supply ourselves with some necessaries of life, we shall organize means in common. By combining in groups we can have many things which would be impossible as individuals. We can in time have a good library; we can have music played by first-rate musicians. . . . We can arrange for the education of our children on some more rational lines than those of the public schools.[74]

A number of craftsworkers moved in in 1903, along with a salon of free-spirited writers recruited by White. With the advent of summer came new arrivals, students at the Byrdcliffe Summer School of Art, an important part of Whitehead's concept (indeed, summer schools of art, which attracted a seemingly limitless clientele, became financial lifelines for any number of artists' colonies). In accordance with the benefactor's wishes, Byrdcliffe was a happy-go-lucky Bohemia, a benevolent dictatorship, and artists worked on the premises for many years.[75] As historian Alf Evers later wrote, "The young students of painting, drawing and of woodworking, carving, weaving and metalwork felt the Byrdcliffe experiment as a fore-runner of a future similar to the one they had read of in William Morris' *News From Nowhere*, in which pollution of air and water had ended, money had become a mere curiosity, and all shared in a life of creative fulfill-ment."[76] Such optimism was easy in the pleasant life at the colony. One early resident recalled years later, "The birds sang as if the earth had just then been newly created. And the Byrdcliffers sang too, and danced and made love to each other, just like the birds. Later the summer came on—with wonderful warm summer nights, when fireflies danced over dew-laden meadows, and when we gathered in bands and climbed the Over-look, in search of adventure and romance."[77] Certainly the gathering of great minds infused Byrdcliffe with vitality. Among those reported to have stayed there are Clarence Darrow, Charlotte Perkins Gilman, John Bur-roughs, John Dewey, Harry Hopkins, George Bellows, Will Durant, and Heywood Broun. One report has it that folksingers Pete Seeger and Bob Dylan lived there for a time, although long after the glory days had passed.[78]

The community's main industry did not fare well, however. The William Morris–style furniture that the colony shops turned out was go-ing out of style in favor of art nouveau designs, and the handcrafted works could not be delivered at prices within reach of any but the wealthy. Leslie Greene Bowman reports that the community ultimately produced fewer than fifty pieces of furniture.[79] Many were huge items made of oak, so heavy that they could scarcely be transported to the local freight depot for shipment by rail to market. Thus they were consigned to White Pines, the Whitehead home at Byrdcliffe. The Byrdcliffe Pottery did somewhat bet-ter with its wares, but it was hardly extensive enough to support a whole community of artists.

There were also the inevitable personality clashes, early on one between Whitehead and his lieutenant, Bolton Brown, which resulted in Brown's departure from the premises in 1903, and later with various others. Brown, White, and other artists were disgusted with the rather British, class-con-scious atmosphere of the place, one in which friends of the Whiteheads visited frequently and dominated the colony, to the detriment of the work-ing artists. Although artists were given wide creative latitude, in nonartis-tic ways the founder's rule was heavy-handed; as one reporter put it, "Whitehead operated his commune almost as a czar."[80] Another contem-porary observer described Byrdcliffe's government as "feudal."[81] One particularly nettlesome matter was Whitehead's demanding that the residents of his fiefdom perform Morris dances three times a week. Even benevolent regimentation did not sit well with many free artistic spirits, and they sought less structured settings in which to pursue their work.

Within a few years many of the resident artists had left the mountain-top community and headed for the burgeoning art community in town. As Karal Ann Marling wrote in 1977, "The intentional colonies, founded in a wave of social reform, articulated an elaborate program of goals to justify the existence of their retreat communities; by regulating the lives of their members to further those goals, they left little room for individual initiative and, consequently, for the chaotic results of organic communal growth."[82] It may be a testimony to some kind of spirit of Byrdcliffe, however, that most of those who left settled nearby, stimulating the center of the arts that Woodstock has been ever since—even though by about 1912 the town artists were condescendingly calling the pioneer colony "Bored-stiff."[83] And in any event not all the creative spirits departed; artists and writers were active there until the 1930s, and in some cases longer. Anita M. Smith reported in 1959 that one jewelry maker and silversmith apparently still living and active at that time "remained through all the years in Byrdcliffe."[84] The Whiteheads themselves continued to do craft work, especially pottery, at least as late as 1926.[85]

After Whitehead's death in 1929, his widow, Jane, lived on at Byrdcliffe[86]; as she grew older, management fell to her son Peter, who stalwartly maintained the core of the property as an arts and crafts center, although he had to sell much of the peripheral acreage to pay taxes and maintenance. When Peter Whitehead died in 1976, title to most of the remaining property passed to the Woodstock Guild of Craftsmen. Most of Byrdcliffe's buildings still stand and some have been used intermittently for the creation of art in recent years. The Guild, trying to preserve the deteriorating buildings, was reportedly renting studios out at $500 per season after Peter Whitehead's death.[87] Perhaps a communal settlement of artists will eventually emerge again there.

The Maverick

The personality clashes between Whitehead and his lieutenants at Byrdcliffe led to the creation nearby of another, more egalitarian, colony known as the Maverick. Hervey White resigned his Byrdcliffe position in

1904 after an altercation with Whitehead and, with help from a friend, purchased a 102-acre farm three miles away.[88] The Maverick, with no wealthy patron, was an artists' colony, active mainly in the summer, in which the poverty was shared; White, the lord of the manor, lived in a tiny six-by-eight-foot cabin. From 1908 onward White began to build other simple cabins for use as studios and residences, and gradually a community of the arts took shape. Although those who could afford it paid rent to live there, White, a lifelong socialist, provided free lodging to indigent young residents at what he sometimes called his "rural Hull House" and even bought groceries for them.[89] The Maverick only later appealed to visual artists, but it quickly became popular among writers, musicians, and bohemian intellectuals. Among its residents and visitors were Clarence Darrow, Charlotte Perkins Gilman, and Thorstein Veblen. White established the Maverick Press by printing three of his own books in 1910; he had had trouble interesting commercial publishers in his work, which was well received critically but never had good sales. The following year he founded a new monthly literary magazine, *The Wild Hawk*. That periodical gave way after five years to a magazine with broader focus, *The Plowshare*, which featured reviews and art as well as literature and in time received a fair amount of acclaim in independent literary circles.[90] Other publications emerged from the press at the Maverick as well, providing the foundation for the literary tenor of the community.[91]

A growing new wave of bohemianism in America early in the century helped feed and support the Maverick. White kept building more of his simple little cabins to house arriving artists, and overhead mounted. In 1915 the proprietor, needing to pay some colony debts, especially a huge one occasioned by the drilling of a deep-water well, concocted the idea of holding an annual chamber music festival. Many locals, farmers and townspeople as well as resident artists, pitched in to construct an outdoor theater in an abandoned bluestone quarry, and the Maverick Festival was born. The next year a concert hall was constructed, and the Maverick Concerts, an important part of the Woodstock cultural scene ever since, were initiated.[92]

The most fully communal phase of the life of the Maverick occurred late in White's life. In 1938 the aging proprietor of the colony turned his Maverick Press over to a younger crowd who published a literary and political sheet called *The Phoenix*. The editor and head of the group, James P. Cooney, believed that the world was falling apart and that the only hope of salvation lay in putting into practice the social theories of the late D. H. Lawrence, who had urged the development of a new culture based on American Indian traditions. A sense of the direction of this communal group can be grasped from Cooney's announcement in 1939 of their "complete renunciation of machines and mechanized modes of life; the unequivocal condemnation of Industrial forms of society" and their intent "to break away in small communities" and "return to the dignity and purity and religiousness of a mode of life rooted in agriculture and the handicrafts."[93] Tales of bizarre behavior circulated in the town; Anita Smith has recounted two of them, "of one man who quite openly had two wives on an equal status; of another man who believed he could acquire a mate by bellowing like a bull in the night, and it was said he was successful!"[94] The *Phoenix*, in any event, was much admired for its editorial quality until it suspended publication in 1940 when the Cooneyites moved to Georgia to pursue the simple life in a more isolated location.[95] The Maverick kept to its original course, and at last report was still functioning in more or less the spirit in which it was founded.

Beaux Arts Village

One of the last of the arts and crafts colonies to be founded was Beaux Arts Village, located across Lake Washington from Seattle. It arose somewhat spontaneously from a group of artists who worked commonly in a former University of Washington building and, in the spirit of the arts and crafts movement, decided to found a colony. Frank Calvert and Alfred T. Renfro, among others, played leading roles in the group, which came to be called the Beaux Arts Society. With $16,500 of borrowed money, they purchased an attractive fifty-acre site with a nice beach and heavy timber. They held as common land the beach and a central ten-acre enclave called "Atelier Square," which was designated as a site for studios for all kinds of arts; the square was laid out in the shape of the outline of the society's emblem, an arts and crafts bungalow. The rest of the land was divided into 114 lots.

Renfro was the first builder and first resident, moving in in October 1909. By 1916 there were fifteen houses, and the Beaux Arts Society had seventy-eight members, each of whom owned village property. Although there was some common life (an annual picnic on the beach was held for years, for example), the studios were never built at Atelier Square, and

that land was eventually subdivided into homesites. Many charming houses were built in a variety of architectural styles, and before long the village
became entirely too expensive and too middle-class to provide a haven for
starving artists. The bourgeois normalcy of the place is attested to by the
scandal that erupted when a couple living in a rented house were discovered to be not only practitioners of yoga but unmarried; they were ousted. In relatively short order Beaux Arts Village became a pleasant suburb
of Seattle, although it remains a neighborhood with interesting houses,
large trees, and a communal beach.[96]

Macdowell and Yaddo

Other arts-oriented communities of the era were farther removed
from the arts and crafts movement, and often had only limited cooperative features. Nevertheless, they too embodied a bit of the collective spirit
of the age.

THE MACDOWELL COLONY

A few years after the early glory days of Byrdcliffe, another subsidized
enclave of artists, the MacDowell colony, began to take shape at Peterborough, New Hampshire. Edward MacDowell, a prominent composer and
music professor at Columbia University, had proposed to establish an art
colony, although mental illness kept him from realizing that goal. His
wife, Marian, believing that he had been driven mad by the pace of city
life, tried to help him by moving him from New York to Peterborough
and building him a log cabin where he could compose without inter-
ruption. By 1907 some other artists had begun to arrive to join the
MacDowells.

After Edward's death in 1908, Marian promoted the artists' community more earnestly. Old farm sheds became men's and women's dormitories
(dubbed "M'Annex" and the "Eaves"); the barn was turned into a dining
room and clubhouse. By the mid-1920s there were several hundred acres
of land and many studios and homes.[97] Artists were allowed to disperse to
scattered studios—eventually more than twenty-five of them, each out of
sight and sound of the others—each morning; lunches were delivered by
silent couriers, and interruptions were discouraged. (Indeed, the no-inter-
ruptions, no-visitors policy was so firm that it took thirty years for the
colony to decide to hold its first open house.[98]) At the end of the day came

lively suppers and sometimes roisterous evenings. Artists—composers and writers were the most frequent residents—thrived on the regular cycle of solitude and stimulus. Those who lived at the colony were charged a small fee for room and board, but it could be waived when need required. Although it was begun as a summer colony, it eventually had some population all year.[99]

The MacDowell colony was popular among artists from the first. By 1911, when the colony was just three years old, a visitor reported that fifty artists had lived and worked there and that a number of significant literary and artistic achievements had been created on the premises.[100] When the "place of dreams untold" celebrated its fiftieth anniversary in 1957, it had reached six hundred acres in size, had about a thousand applicants for the approximately ninety-five spaces available, and had seen its denizens pick up no fewer than eighteen Pulitzer Prizes (a number that continued to grow in subsequent years). The most enduring presence was Edward Arlington Robinson, who, after at first regarding with grave misgiving the concept of writing in a colony setting,[101] spent his summers there for two or three decades.[102] Other prominent sometime residents included Willa Cather, Aaron Copland, Sara Teasdale, Thornton Wilder, William Rose Benét, and Stephen Vincent Benét. Nearly a century later MacDowell continues to carry on the tradition of the creation of art in a community setting.

YADDO

Yaddo is similar to the MacDowell colony in many ways. Formally opened in 1926 near the spa of Saratoga Springs, New York, Yaddo is located on land that encompasses five hundred acres of pine groves, vast lawns, lakes with ducks, rose gardens, and marble fountains, along with a fabulous fifty-five-room Victorian mansion built by patrons of the arts Spencer Trask and his wife, Katrina Nichols. Yaddo—its name came from the Trask children's mispronunciation of its original name, The Shadows—started out as what Marling has called "an interminable summer house party where writers and artists hobnobbed with statesmen and celebrities."[103] The death of Spencer Trask in 1909 delayed their plans to turn Yaddo into a more focused artists' colony, but Katrina's second husband revived the project and finally oversaw its completion. Yaddo was (and is) like its predecessor at Peterborough in its provision of early breakfasts, far-flung studios, and delivered lunches. Most guests stayed in private rooms in the mansion. As was the case at the MacDowell colony, nonartistic spouses were usually not invited to accompany their mates.[104] In 1946 it was reported to be averaging twenty resident artists each summer. Among those who had worked there by that time were James T. Farrell, Katherine Anne Porter, Malcolm Cowley, Aaron Copland, and Truman Capote.[105] Like MacDowell it continues to be a center of creative activity today.

WHEREVER TWO OR THREE ARTISTS
ARE GATHERED TOGETHER . . .

There were other communities as well, generally small and short-lived but testifying to the power of the communitarian impulse in the arts and crafts movement. In most cases little is known of them. The Elverhöj colony, for example, was founded in 1913 by A. H. Anderson and Johannes Morton, both painters and silversmiths, at Milton-on-the-Hudson, New York, and took for its motto "Live close to nature for inspiration." Housed in an old colonial mansion on 150 acres, in 1916 the colony was reported to have eight permanent members, male and female, and a good crop of summer students for its painting, etching, gold and silversmithing, other metalwork, weaving, and bookbinding courses.[106] Another New York colony called Briarcliff made furniture, but it is difficult to determine whether or not it had substantial communal features.[107] It did, however, market its furniture as being made by "The Craft Settlement Shop" in Ossining.[108] Gustav Stickley, a leader in popularizing arts and crafts furniture among the American public, purchased land near Morris Plains, New Jersey, and spent several years trying to develop a cooperative community called Craftsman Farms there, although at times he seemed to envision his enterprise more as a private country school for boys than a typical intentional community, and his energies were in any event more than absorbed by his many other projects.[109]

In later years, past the heyday of Morris and the arts and crafts movement, colonies of artistic bent popped up again here and there. In 1933 John A. Rice, who had been fired from his faculty position at Rollins College in Florida for his unconventional behavior, led a group of bohemian artists to establish Black Mountain College in North Carolina. The experiment, as much a colony of the arts as a college, attracted such creative minds as John Cage, Anaïs Nin, Buckminster Fuller, Charles Olson, and Robert Rauschenberg to its campus where students and faculty lived in communal poverty. Although the wolf was never far from Black Mountain's door, the colony survived until 1956. Its story is recounted in another chapter of this volume.[110]

Any number of small and informal communities of artists have undoubtedly been in existence at any given moment, even if they have been little documented. In 1940, for example, George Davis, a New York magazine editor, with the young novelist Carson McCullers rented a large brownstone in Brooklyn Heights and started a memorable residential colony of the arts, generally known after its location as Seven Middagh Street, that lasted five years. Of the company that settled there McCullers's biographer, Oliver Evans, gushed, "Not since the Brook Farm venture in Massachusetts a hundred years earlier had so many American intellectuals attempted the hazardous experiment of living together under one roof."[111] Black Mountain College might challenge that claim, but the congregation was notable: among the many residents at one point or another were Benjamin Britten, Paul and Jane Bowles, Christopher Isherwood, Richard Wright, and Gypsy Rose Lee, and among a torrent of visitors were Anaïs Nin, Salvador Dali, Virgil Thomson, Aaron Copland, and Leonard Bernstein. W. H. Auden was the self-appointed housefather in the early years, preserving some decorum and collecting the rent from residents. Auden's sense of order contrasted sharply with the freewheeling camaraderie of the other residents, however; one observer recalled seeing "George [Davis] naked at the piano with a cigarette in his mouth, Carson on the ground with half a gallon of sherry, and then Wystan bursting in like a headmaster, announcing: 'Now then, dinner!'"[112] The lively scene persisted throughout the war years, the latter members departing in 1945.[113]

And more recent, longer-lived art colonies have appeared since the turn-of-the-century heyday as well. One, Quarry Hill, was founded near Rochester, Vermont, in 1946 and has been a "haven for creative and open-minded people" for half a century.[114] At this writing it is apparently the largest intentional community in Vermont, with about a hundred members, a private school, a community building, and a clutch of wonderfully varied owner-built homes. Still later, Drop City was founded as an art colony in Trinidad, Colorado, in 1965, and with its beyond-bohemian flair became a prime founding location of hippie communalism.[115] Drop City spawned several offspring communes, among them Libre, near Gardner, Colorado, which remains a vital center of the visual arts. There were, moreover, undoubtedly many dreams of community for every one established. The arts and crafts movement espoused and produced art with a mission, and communitarian values had much to do with it.

3

New Communes, 1900–1920

Throughout the early decades of the twentieth century, dozens of new intentional communities were founded and augmented the ranks of the many already in place as the century opened. The communal world has always been one of ebb and flow; some of the established communities would not survive long into the new century, and for that matter some of the newcomers would themselves be short-lived. In sum, however, this largely optimistic period was a fruitful one for communitarianism.

The Communities of Evangelical and Pentecostal Christians

Early in the twentieth century, Pentecostalism swept like a firestorm through certain segments of American Christianity. Because the enthusiastic new practices of the Pentecostalists (and the marginal social status of many persons involved in the movement) offended many members of the more staid churches, believers in such things as speaking in tongues and faith healing often were forced to build new institutions. Thus they founded many churches, missions, and other organizations, including, occasionally, intentional communities. Nonpentecostal conservative Protestants were also often marginalized, and they too in several instances built intentional communities that helped them define and affirm their distinctiveness.

BETHEL COLLEGE

The Pentecostal movement was founded in a communal setting, and the seminal community deserves a mention here, even though it was neither large nor long-lived. Charles Fox Parham, a holiness preacher who at the end of the nineteenth century had been involved in faith healing, opened the College of Bethel in October 1900 in an ornate Victorian mansion on the outskirts of Topeka, Kansas. In late December he and his students became convinced that the outward proof that a believer had been baptized in the Holy Spirit was speaking in tongues, and at a new year's eve watch service on the last evening of 1900 they began to pray that the gift of tongues might come to them. At one point just into the new year—and new century—Agnes Ozman, a student at the school, felt a surge of spirit and began speaking in what the others took to be Chinese. Soon many others began to make strange utterances as well, and within a few years Pentecostalism would establish itself as the preeminent new religious movement of the twentieth century.

Bethel College had about forty students; Parham was the sole teacher, and the Bible was the sole textbook. They all dwelt together in communal poverty, living "on faith"—subsisting entirely on donations. Once they had achieved the remarkable feat of speaking in tongues, however, they felt impelled to travel to spread their new version of the Gospel, although their efforts were little noticed until 1906, when, under the leadership of William Seymour, a later student of Parham's, the first widely noticed Pentecostal revival took place in Los Angeles and became the fountainhead from which the worldwide spread of the apostolic faith issued. In any event, the school and commune in Topeka evaporated. A few months into 1901 the house they had been using was sold to a bootlegger, who operated the premises as a roadhouse until it burned just a year after Agnes Ozman had ushered in Pentecostalism within its walls.[1]

ZION CITY

After the catalytic experiences at Bethel, the first commune within the Pentecostal movement, broadly defined, was Zion City, the communal center of the work of John Alexander Dowie, whose first settlers arrived in 1901. Dowie's work predated the definitive founding of Pentecostalism by Parham and his students at the beginning of 1901, but his emphasis on faith healing and holy living meshed well with the Pentecostal surge that spread worldwide early in the twentieth century (indeed, Parham himself visited and was quite taken with Zion City), and historians have come to characterize Dowie's Christian Catholic Apostolic Church as fitting within the larger Pentecostal movement despite its separate origins. Dowie, Scottish by birth and Australian by upbringing, moved his revival and faith-healing work to the United States in 1888. He first achieved some measure of publicity when he opened a revival tabernacle at the Chicago World's Fair in 1893; his vitriolic attacks on medical doctors as well as Roman Catholics, Masons, and others drew notice in the Chicago press, and reports of many miraculous healings at his services aroused even more attention. Dowie's following grew rapidly, and by the middle of the decade he was laying plans for a community of believers.

In 1899 Dowie's agents purchased sixty-six hundred acres of land about forty miles north of Chicago on Lake Michigan, and work on the necessary infrastructure began the following year.[2] In 1901 the first of what were eventually thousands of families—estimates of Zion's population under Dowie range up to ten thousand—began to settle at Zion City. The community was designed as a theocracy from the first, firmly under the control of Dowie, the owner of all of the businesses and real estate. Perhaps the most notable feature of the community was its high moral tone; Dowie condemned not only conventional medicine but also a host of modern vices, including smoking, drinking, and lowbrow behavior generally. The most important of the diverse industries was a lace factory, which for a time was a solid financial success; also important was a candy factory that developed a reputation for producing high-quality products. Financial mismanagement, however, dogged the industries and ultimately was important in Zion City's demise as an intentional community.

Although Dowie's rise to prominence had been rapid and spectacular, he proved incapable of providing consistently strong leadership. His claims about his personal powers and role became increasingly extravagant; among other things, he began to call himself Elijah III, the third manifestation of the ancient prophet (the second, he said, had been John the Baptist). He and his wife lived increasingly luxuriously, and despite his strict moral teachings, rumors of lapses in his personal behavior began to circulate. In 1903 he spent an enormous amount taking a large contingent of Zionists to New York for an evangelistic crusade that by all accounts was an abject failure, and Dowie and Zion City never quite recovered from the bad press that fiasco received.[3] In 1904 he undertook a world tour during which his vitriolic denunciations of those with whom he disagreed raised considerable ire among local citizens in several countries, further tarnishing his movement. In 1905 he sought to start a new Zion in Mexico at a time when the empire in Illinois was beginning to crumble. In September 1905 he suffered a stroke while presiding at a worship service at Zion City, and divine healing did not avail him. He left for Jamaica to heal himself in a warmer climate, and while he was gone several of his deputies deposed him as general overseer. Wilbur Glenn Voliva emerged from the coup as the leader of Zion City. Dowie died in 1907, but Voliva restored a measure of stability to the city whose fortunes he directed for many years thereafter. Voliva, though not in Dowie's class as a showman, nevertheless had one eccentric doctrine that was widely publicized: he taught that the earth was flat.[4] Zion City through most of the twentieth century has drifted away from its distinctive roots, although the Christian Catholic Church remains a strong force in the town.[5]

LOPEZ ISLAND

As the Dowieites were turning from their years of exuberant growth under their founder to consolidation under Voliva, another Pentecostal preacher founded a colony separated from "the world," this time in a remote part of Washington state. Thomas Gourley in his earlier life had done police work and carpentry in Kansas City, but by 1908 he had opened a Pentecostal mission in Seattle and was dreaming of a community of the faithful. The initial enclave emerged in Seattle, where in a fairly remote part of the waterfront area, Gourley oversaw the building of a settlement of forty-two houses, a common dining hall, private school, and, as with most intentional communities of that era, a print shop for the production of the colony publications. However, as a "come-outer," one who believed that the saved had to remove themselves from the corruptions of the secular world, Gourley was driven to remove his colony as far as possible from "civilization," and in 1911 he and more than 150 of his followers boarded a variety of boats and sailed to Lopez Island in the San Juans. There, after a false start on a piece of land that proved unworkable, Gourley obtained permission from an absentee landlord family to settle on a few acres on Hunter Bay.

The colonists immediately began constructing homes and other structures, including a communal dining room, a school, a laundry, and bathrooms. Life was never luxurious; the food was characterized as plain and monotonous, and Gourley's teaching against killing meant that even the harvesting of the abundant seafood was impermissible. Repeated epidemics—typhoid, tuberculosis—took a substantial toll in lives. Some members left, unable to abide the austerity of it all, but most stayed on. Although the colony did not seek new members, some did join, attracted by Gourley's powerful preaching and the colony's willingness to take in the destitute. Faith was dominant in colony life; two worship services were held each Sunday, and the daily schedule always included a good dose of Bible study and prayer.

World War I helped end the colony. Gourley counseled his followers to refuse military service, a position not welcomed by the colony's neighbors in the islands. In September 1918 he was charged with violating the Espionage Act. Although the charge was eventually dismissed, dissatisfaction arose within the colony, abetted by the ongoing hardships of daily life and rumors of Gourley's mishandling of colony funds and business affairs. Gourley finally apparently left the disorderly situation for good at the end of 1920. He would go on to further preaching and an untimely death in a train wreck in 1923. Most of the remaining colonists divided the scant resources left to them and reentered "the world." A few may have lingered on Lopez Island,[6] but the colony was finished.[7]

BURNING BUSH

The movement that led to the creation of the Burning Bush community emerged in Chicago about the turn of the century, fueled by the dissatisfaction of a group of Free Methodists with what they saw as the growth of formalism in their denomination. In due course they organized their own movement called the Metropolitan Church Association, which eventually opened a headquarters at Waukesha, Wisconsin. According to the one substantial historical account of the Burning Bush colony, several intentional communities called "Christian commonwealths" were formed within the larger organization, but the author provides no information on any of the others.[8]

Two wealthy leaders underwrote much of the work of the Metropolitan Church Association, and one of them, Duke M. Farson, a Chicago bond broker, became the angel of the colony. Farson purchased 1,520 acres with a large plantation-style house in east Texas, and in 1913 375 church members arrived on a chartered train. They built a large tabernacle and many small houses and dormitories. Members donated all their worldly possessions to the movement, thus getting the colony rolling, but most of the members were not prosperous, and the small amounts donated soon ran out, meaning that the colony remained dependent on Farson's benevolence. Nevertheless, the colonists struggled for self-sufficiency, with a large agricultural operation (extensive fruit orchards were on the property when the colony acquired it), a sawmill, and a cannery.

Theologically, the Burning Bush colony was Arminian and Pentecostal. Daily life was dour; worldly amusements were disdained, and members were expected to spend their spare time in Bible study. The worship services, however, were freewheeling affairs, and the Saturday night meetings came to attract a goodly crowd of locals who attended just to see the show. Speaking in tongues and other dramatic spiritual outpourings, it seems, had not otherwise yet penetrated that part of Texas.

The Burning Bush broke up in 1919. Farson's bond business ran into hard times, and when he became unable to pay the bills, the colony's debts mounted. A local creditor went to court and received a substantial judgment and in April 1919 he acquired the colony's land. But the colonists had dispersed by then and the Burning Bush was history.[9]

PISGAH GRANDE

Yet another community to emerge from Pentecostalism in the early twentieth century was Pisgah Grande, founded in 1914 in southern California. Finis Yoakum, a physician, had been critically injured when run over by a horse and buggy in 1894, and attributed his cure to prayer. He thereafter dedicated himself to work among the down and out of Los Angeles; his Pisgah Home, whose motto was "All Things in Common," became a refuge for the homeless and a center of faith healing. It also featured a free store, providing necessities of life to the needy without charge. In 1914 Yoakum bought a thirty-two hundred-acre cattle ranch in the Santa Susana Mountains north of Los Angeles and began to build what eventually became a substantial, if not prosperous, settlement for his followers. Yoakum's openhanded generosity attracted more than a fair share of misfits and derelicts, and one critic who lived there for six months in his youth wrote of the undercapitalized colony that "most of the dwellings were mere shacks" and that Pisgah's ambience was that of a "fair refugee camp" run by a leader with an "enormous display of ignorance of the fundamental laws governing human behavior."[10] Whatever its shortcomings, the colony survived for years, but decline set in after Yoakum's death in 1920, leading to the closing of Pisgah Grande; James Cheek,

Yoakum's successor as leader, eventually moved the movement's head-quarters to Pikeville, Tennessee. In the meantime, the old Pisgah Home property in Los Angeles was rehabilitated and at last report was still reaching out to the needy with a Gospel message. The abandoned buildings at the colony site in the mountains were reported to be largely still standing in the 1970s.[11]

BETHEL HOME

The early Pentecostals were not the only conservative Protestants founding intentional communities in the early years of the twentieth century. Several other organizations kept alive an American Christian communal tradition by now more than two centuries old, and one new nonpentecostal conservative movement launched, early in the new century, one of the largest American communal ventures ever. Bethel Home (commonly called simply "Bethel"), the communal headquarters of what is now known as the Watchtower Bible and Tract Society, or more popularly the Jehovah's Witnesses[12]; Watchtower Farm, the source of agricultural products for Bethel Home and for its communal workers[13]; and a few other smaller facilities embrace residential communities of probably more than two thousand workers whose common goal is the propagation of the Gospel as understood by the Witnesses.

Jehovah's Witnesses emerged from the Adventist movement of the nineteenth century, which peaked in public renown and controversy when thousands of believers prepared for the visible Second Coming of Christ on October 22, 1844, a date predicted by Adventist prophet William Miller. Although among the Adventist faithful the failure of the spectacular predicted events to happen occasioned a "Great Disappointment," various groups kept alive the belief that the end of the world as we have known it was still literally close at hand.[14] Out of this milieu emerged Charles Taze Russell, who by the 1870s was coming into prominence as a leading preacher and publisher of Adventist ideas—his own version of such ideas, to be sure, ideas that stressed the eschatological significance of certain specific dates, the most important of which was 1914, Russell's key date for the end of the world.

In the early years of the twentieth century, Russell moved his head-quarters from Pittsburgh to Brooklyn, just across the East River from lower Manhattan, where members of the movement's central staff began living communally. By 1909 the community became formalized in structure with the incorporation of what was then called the People's Pulpit Association. Bethel has grown steadily since then as the organization has purchased additional land and buildings. Barbara Grizzuti Harrison, who lived and worked at Bethel for three years as a young woman, reported the population of Bethel as 1,449 as of 1970; 500 more lived at Watchtower Farm.[15] With the worldwide growth of the Witnesses movement since then, the numbers of worker-residents are likely higher today.

Life at the Witness communities is thoroughly regulated. At Bethel all rise at the 6:30 A.M. bell, take their meals communally, live in adequate but simple living quarters, and have prayer and Bible study together regularly. Rules about dress, grooming, use of tobacco (forbidden), and other such things govern all residents. The employees perform a variety of chores to keep the facilities running, and fan out into the New York area to participate in local congregations as exemplary Witnesses. Although some critics of the Witnesses see the regimentation as stifling, even repressive of proper human expressions and freedoms, the system seems to work at least in doing the tasks on which the organization depends, for out of Bethel pour the hundreds of millions of books, magazines, and tracts that the rank and file of the movement annually use "in service," in their ongoing program of door-to-door canvassing for which they are so well known.[16]

Jewish Farm Colonies

The heyday of the Jewish farm colonies was the late nineteenth century, when dozens of them were formed, largely populated by members of the wave of Ashkenazic immigrants who fled persecution in eastern Europe after 1880. Several New Jersey colonies, the Palestine colony in Michigan, and possibly others still existed in 1900. However, the story of Jewish communitarianism does not stop with those earlier colonies. Other settlements have been founded from time to time, typically as Jews settled in places far from their traditional population centers in the eastern cities.[17]

ELLICOTT CITY

The first Jewish communal settlement begun after 1900 seems to have been located at Ellicott City, Maryland, but little is known about it. The record indicates that about twenty-five Baltimore Jews pooled their resources to purchase 351 acres ten miles from Baltimore and moved there in 1902. It seems that the group soon ran into financial problems, and apparently some left, but others remained, and by the time another report was written in 1908, eight to ten families were at the site and had overcome their early obstacles. Just how long the group ultimately survived, however, is a mystery. The best guess is probably that the Ellicott City colony, like some of the New Jersey enclaves, gradually shed its communal features and became an ongoing neighborhood in suburban Baltimore.[18]

TYLER

The year 1904 saw the founding of two more Jewish communities, one in Texas and one in Wisconsin. The Texas one was the more ephemeral lasting only a year or so. The land involved, 220 acres near Tyler in east Texas, was purchased by the Jewish Agricultural and Industrial Aid Society and made available to communal settlers. Five families constituted the vanguard at Tyler, and for a time the small colony reportedly flourished. In 1905, however, disaster struck in the form of a malaria epidemic. The devastated colonists abandoned their community and, believing the location inherently unhealthy, campaigned to keep other Jews from settling there. They were apparently successful, because the Tyler colony quickly disappeared from the record.[19]

ARPIN

The year 1904 also saw the founding of a much longer-lived colony in Wisconsin. A decade earlier the Arpin Brothers Lumber Company had built a company town in Wood County, about 150 miles northwest of Milwaukee. After ten years the company had exhausted the local timber and moved the sawmill to another site, but a few workers chose to stay behind and farm rather than move to the new location. Thus it was that a town of two hundred had housing for many more persons than were resident in 1904.

In the meantime, a major exodus of Jews from Romania had taken place in 1901 in response to severe persecutions there, and the Jewish community of Milwaukee volunteered to help settle some of the newcomers. Adolph W. Rich organized the Milwaukee Agricultural Society and purchased 720 acres at Arpin as a colony site. The first families arrived in December 1904, living in vacant lumber company houses until they could build more substantial homes the following summer. The seven initial families and others who joined later mainly farmed and cut firewood for sale. Although bad economic times occasionally burdened the settlers, the small community largely prospered and grew. In 1913 the members started a Jewish school, and in 1915 they dedicated a synagogue, complete with *Se-fer Torah* (Torah scroll). The seventy to eighty persons typically resident had an active social life, and farming supplemented by an occasional bit of peddling gave them adequate, if not luxurious, livelihoods.

The community finally declined with the passage of time. Children grew up and moved away. Families occasionally moved back to Milwaukee, tired of the hard farming life, the cold rural winters, the lack of a large Jewish community—and, in several cases, fearful that their children in this isolated location might commit the dreaded act of intermarriage. After 1922 only five families remained; in 1940 only two were left. By 1958 the last colony member had departed.[20]

One little-known Jewish colony came about because of a rural region's push for economic development. South Carolina's economy was stagnant for decades after the Civil War, and boosters by about the turn of the century increasingly sought to put unused farmland into production and to build the state's small industrial base. Recognizing that they would have to lure newcomers to the state to bring their scenario about, the economic and governmental leaders pushing revitalization started a state immigration bureau to induce the sought-after entrepreneurs to move to the state, even opening a New York office on Wall Street to help beat the bushes. The many relatively recent Russian Jewish immigrants provided a likely pool from which new South Carolinians could be recruited.

Charles Weintraub was the first of the Russian Jews in New York to become interested in the Carolina plan and in the summer of 1905 began looking at property for a possible colony. At the same time, he and his associate, Morris Latterman, organized the Incorporative Farming Association, a collective of twenty-five families of socialist Russian Jews interested in colonization. In October they purchased a twenty-two hundred-acre plantation near Aiken and within three months over a dozen families had moved into the new colony of Happyville. They began farming the land and building houses at once.

By the spring of 1906, when the colony's prospects looked good, the weather took a turn for the worse, with frost and rain wreaking havoc. The colonists persevered, and the summer of 1907 provided much more beneficial weather. But nothing like real prosperity ensued, and financial problems that had been there from the beginning refused to disappear. The colonists, looking ahead, could see nothing but hard work and deepening debt, and in July 1908 the land was sold. Most of the colonists had already left by then, mainly for New York and New Jersey. Weintraub at first had some hope of attracting new settlers and extending the experiment, but his efforts came to naught and eventually he sold his interest to several members of the Surasky family, prominent Jewish merchants in Aiken. Weintraub disappears from the record at this point; he may have moved to Atlanta. Happyville soon thereafter was sold to Gentiles, and one of the last experiments in Jewish colonization in the Deep South was reduced to memory.[21]

LARAMIE

Wyoming has never been very hospitable to agricultural settlers; its cold and dry climate and rugged terrain have always kept its population low, and the Jews who tried to settle there were no more fortunate than anyone else. Richard Singer reports that a colonization project was begun in 1907 in Laramie County by urban Jews who had tired of city life, but that these pioneers were not prepared for Wyoming. The plan had it that the colonists would support themselves by farming, but irrigation would have been required for that, and it turned out to be unavailable. Just how long the communitarians stayed in Laramie County is unknown, but the sojourn was undoubtedly brief. A second colonization project fell even further from fruition; Singer describes a grand plan to settle hundreds of Jewish families from Chicago in Platte County, but that one apparently never got off the ground.[22]

MONTEVILLE

A colony founded in Massachusetts in 1908 is another about which little has been written. Monteville was begun at Sandisfield in 1908, and virtually nothing beyond that seems to be known of its founding or early development.[23] Its member families seem to have done well, however; nearly three decades later the Federal Writers' Project found it a going concern and provided directions for finding it. However, no further historical information on the colony seems to have been preserved.[24]

PLACER COUNTY

The record is especially thin for the colony reported to have been founded in Placer County, California. Richard Singer, in his exhaustive work on all the Jewish agricultural colonies, mentions it only briefly. One other account exists of Jewish colonies in California, Orangevale and Porterville, both reportedly founded in 1891.[25] Because Orangevale seems to have survived in some form well into the twentieth century,[26] and it was near Lincoln, California, it could be the colony Singer mentions as having been founded in 1909. In any event, Singer places Placer six miles from Lincoln and says that the land was divided into tracts of six to eighteen acres and cooperatively farmed. It consisted mainly of orange groves.[27]

CLARION

One of the last Jewish colonies to be founded, and one of the longer-lived ones, was established in a remote part of central Utah in 1911. The Clarion colony grew out of the work of Benjamin Brown, a Russian immigrant who arrived in the United States about 1900 and soon thereafter became a farm laborer near Philadelphia. His stint in the American countryside convinced him that colonies would better the lot of American Jews, and in 1909 he began making speeches outlining his plans. In brief, he sought a rural colony that would at first be economically communal but that would, as it became prosperous, evolve into a moshav, or group settlement with private property holdings. His colony would be in the West both because land was cheap there and because the location would make it difficult for members who might become dissatisfied with the colony to return to the city. Eventually, be believed, it would house as many as a thousand families.

In 1911 the first dozen of the heterogeneous band of adventurers who had joined Brown's cause made their way to the location chosen earlier that year, 6,085 acres along the Sevier River in Sanpete County near the small town of Gunnison. These first settlers, all men, quickly erected temporary living and dining structures with help from friendly neighboring Mormon farmers. Although serious agricultural problems—lack of water, a disastrous initial harvest—had been encountered from the beginning, at the end of the first season the colonists were optimistic about their future. Contemporary accounts of the colony paint a picture of glorious success.[28] As Robert A. Goldberg has recounted the story,

When winter's cold made farm work impossible, the colonists retired to their tents and hammered out the principles and purposes of their experiment. They anticipated that their colony would be the first of a multitude of similar Jewish settlements throughout the United States. Initially, the colony would engage solely in the cultivation and marketing of agricultural produce. Later, the settlers would diversify and establish a canning factory to process their crops. From these beginnings, a town would grow where every branch of agriculture, commerce, manufacturing, and mining could be undertaken. A new society rooted in all of these economic endeavors would revitalize the Jew in his as well as others' eyes. Perceiving themselves as the harbingers of the economic and social future of Jewish America, they appropriately named their colony Clarion.[29]

But things did not long go well. Start-up expenses for tools and livestock had been high, and the mortgage payment on the land the colony was buying from the State of Utah would soon be due. Brown succeeded in staving off disaster with a fruitful money-raising trip back East, and the working of the land for the second season commenced. New families continued to arrive. But the lifeline of the colony, a new state canal that had been pivotal to the selection of the site, failed to deliver nearly enough water—when it was running at all. The year's crops were poor, and internal squabbling among the diverse group of settlers increased. In the fall of 1912 the colony decided to break up some of its land, giving each family forty acres, which proved not to be enough in that arid climate to support a family. Ironically, the building of a colony school added to the dissension as colonists utterly failed to agree on subjects to be taught, or for that matter even what languages (Yiddish? Hebrew?) would be studied and used. But still the colony survived, by the spring of 1913 finding itself with 156 residents and nearly twenty-four hundred acres under cultivation. Indeed, despite all the problems, new colonists continued to arrive as late as January 1915.

Eventually, the problems swamped the colony. Brown, by now distinctly unpopular, resigned in 1915. Creditors demanded payment, and the colony was not nearly ready to pay its own way. Finally, in November 1915 the state foreclosed its land mortgage, and the following January it auctioned the colony's real estate. The colonists scattered; a few remained to farm in the area on their own, but during the 1920s even this remnant departed, largely over fears that their children, far from significant Jewish populations, would become assimilated.[30]

Other Religious Communities

A SERVICE COMMUNITY: GOULD FARM

What could be called the last of the social gospel colonies was Gould Farm, founded near Great Barrington, Massachusetts, in 1913. William Gould, an energetic Congregational layman, was infused with the characteristic social gospel drive to alleviate the problems of the world—to build the "Kingdom of God Here and Now," as he often put it.[31] After starting a variety of relief programs, such as summer camps for boys, he and his wife, Agnes Gould, bought the Great Barrington property and, with the help of a staff that grew steadily, brought in persons in need of care or therapy—principally alcoholics and sex offenders, but also those undergoing lengthy convalescences after hospital stays, the mentally ill, the physically handicapped, and others in similar straits.[32]

The staff members from the beginning were determined to live as a family, and at least in the early years Gould Farm was economically as well as physically communal, the staff living in dedicated, voluntary poverty. To Gould, the entire project was a ministry; he imbued the farm with a heavy spiritual emphasis and held frequent worship services. After his death at fifty-seven in 1925, Agnes Gould assumed the leadership and expanded the work still further over the next several decades. Although the total commonality was eventually relaxed—staff members began to be paid small stipends—the communal, family atmosphere has persisted.[33] In 1989 Gould Farm reported forty "guests," a staff of more than thirty-five, and a therapeutic program that included the working of a hundred-acre farm. Will Gould's charitable purpose continues; Gould Farm still refuses to turn guests away for lack of money, and reports that "basic to our program is providing a warm and caring atmosphere in which the healing process can take place."[34]

THE COMMUNES OF INDEPENDENT RELIGIOUS VISIONARIES

Some of the more memorable communal experiments in the early twentieth century were founded by religious visionaries, persons convinced that they were prophets or even deities and that they, exclusively, therefore understood the truth of the ages. From such convictions came a steady stream of communal villages in the World War I era. Pisgah Grande, previously discussed, bordered on this model, but three communities above all others embodied it flamboyantly: the House of David, Holy City, and Father Divine's Peace Mission Movement. The first two will be characterized here; Father Divine's movement, categorized differently because it may also be seen as an African American liberation movement, will follow immediately in the next section.

The House of David. One of the most fascinating communal groups to emerge in the twentieth century was the House of David, which settled in

Benton Harbor, Michigan, in 1903, where, in two factions, it remains to-day, although with much less public attention than it received during its early years under founder Benjamin Franklin Purnell. Although the House of David was definitively shaped by Purnell himself, it did stand in a fairly well-established nonmainstream Christian tradition. A century before Purnell's heyday Joanna Southcott had established herself as a religious visionary with a considerable following in England. Her many predictions and warnings brought her thousands of adherents, many of whom she designated among the elect 144,000 who would inherit eternal life. Southcott thoroughly repelled the officials of the dominant churches, who denounced her as a blasphemer, if not worse. The climax—and de-nouement—of her career began in 1814 when, at age sixty-five, she announced that she was pregnant and would deliver the Shiloh, a messianic figure, in a virgin birth. At the end of the year, however, she announced that her pregnancy had been a delusion, and shortly thereafter she died.[35]

Southcott's followers were left without leader or movement, and various would-be successors rushed in to claim her mantle. Several of them developed movements of their own, and the story over the next few years has many personalities and twists and turns too complex to recount here, but some of her successors developed followings in the United States. One of them was a onetime British soldier in India who migrated to the United States and changed his name from James White to James Jezreel, pursuing his own version of the Southcott work by trying to gather a lat-ter-day House of Israel that would consist of 144,000 believers, 12,000 from each of the Hebrew tribes of antiquity. Jezreel, like his predecessors, amassed a goodly band of disciples, and a few years after his death in 1885 one of his would-be successors, Michael Mills, organized the important body of Jezreelites in Detroit into a short-lived intentional community.[36] One member of that colony was Benjamin Purnell, who at some point had become a Jezreelite minister. Purnell saw himself as the seventh "mes-senger" in the Southcott line, the seventh son who would oversee the in-gathering of Israel.[37]

Purnell began acquiring a body of followers in the 1890s, and in 1903 they first began to settle communally at Benton Harbor. They stayed for a time with a Jezreelite family there, but soon acquired land east of town and began constructing what would become an elaborate campus of communal buildings. The first of them, the Ark, would be a residence, a print shop, and a school building. Soon a second building, Bethlehem, was under way. Meanwhile, Purnell was working busily on the ingathering. Journeying to Australia late in 1904, he and his family worked among the many Australian Southcottians and the following spring led some eighty-five of them back to Benton Harbor. More buildings were needed to house the rapidly growing flock, and accommodating the in-gathering dominated House of David life for the next few years. By 1907 the population had grown to 385, and more were kept on a waiting list. More land had been purchased, more buildings built, and new enterprises undertaken.[38]

Hordes of curious onlookers came to marvel at the strange colony as it took on large proportions in the small Michigan town, and to entertain them as well as to divert them from the colony proper (not to mention provide the burgeoning colony with a profitable business), Purnell late in 1907 began to build the Eden Springs Amusement Park. By the summer of 1908 it was functioning successfully, with rides, a zoo, stage shows, games, and renowned ice cream cones. A hugely successful commercial venture, the park became the first in a series of amusement enterprises.

Outside the local area the House of David was probably best known for its baseball teams, in part because the players, like all House of David members, did not cut their hair. The community had some good athletes among its members, and quietly hired a few outside professionals to shore things up; a House of David nine barnstormed North America and Europe for years, getting munificent gate receipts and flying the House of David flag for the world to see. A separate home team played in a stadium next to the amusement park, and attracted large crowds there as well. Eventually, a similar exhibition basketball team was developed, one that played a number of African American teams and, as an entertainment enterprise, put a lot of razzle-dazzle into its fast-paced games. According to House of David historians, the basketball team was the inspiration for the founding of the Harlem Globetrotters.[39]

Yet another entertainment-oriented enterprise was the colony band, which like the baseball team had home and traveling units and became well known for its musicianship as well as its smart marching formations. The band featured several musicians who became popular favorites, and the musical resources of the colony also served it well in worship.

Meanwhile, other less flamboyant but if anything more essential businesses were developed. A lumbering and sawmill operation on an island in Lake Michigan supplied needed building supplies for the colony and for the Benton Harbor area. Eventually, the colony bought and operated the local streetcar company. With its own power plant, water wells, tailor shops, and extensive farms as well as building supplies and construction crews, the House of David came remarkably close to self-sufficiency. In sum, the colony prospered, and its prosperity spilled over on the surrounding area, with whose residents the colony had predominantly cordial relations.

Purnell, steadily assisted by his wife, Mary Purnell, was the unquestioned charismatic leader of the colony. His ability as a speaker was legendary. His teaching emphasized the integrity of the body, and as a result the House of David practiced vegetarianism and abstinence from alcohol as well as the avoidance of cutting one's hair or beard. He valued the contributions of the women of the community and made sure they were well represented on the colony's governing bodies—more so than in most religious or secular organizations at that time. Most important, perhaps, Purnell required celibacy of all his members. Members could and did marry, but marriage partners were to live as brother and sister, retaining their virginal purity for the Second Coming, which was believed to be at hand.

Despite its size and seeming success, the House of David inevitably had detractors. Apostates occasionally published sharp criticisms of colony life, alleging, among other things, that members lived in undue austerity even though Ben and Mary lived quite well.[40] In 1914 sensational allegations were published that Purnell, supposedly celibate like his followers, had had sexual relations with most of the young women of the colony, but Purnell managed to deflect the charges, and colony life went on much as before. A more serious challenge came when apostate John Hansel and his family sued for recovery of money and work they had contributed and won a substantial judgment.

Legal problems intensified with the passage of time and the emergence of more charges of sexual impropriety on Purnell's part. In 1923 two sisters, both minors, filed a civil suit claiming that Brother Benjamin had raped them. Purnell was subpoenaed, but he could not be found. Perhaps he had fled. Perhaps he was dead. Perhaps he was living incognito in the area. Finally, after a long period of intense public speculation about his fate, in late 1926 the police raided Diamond House at the House of David, where in fact Purnell had been living throughout the search, as many of his faithful well knew. He was quickly found and arrested for statutory rape. His trial, which spanned the summer of 1927 and was a media sensation, ended up turning more on the demand that the House of David be dissolved as a public nuisance than on the activities of its leader. Purnell was eventually found guilty—of perjury. In November the judge ordered the House of David into receivership. Ben and Mary were ordered to leave the colony, but within about a month of the judge's order Purnell was dead of tuberculosis.

The colony had been allowed to continue, under the direction of an outside receiver, and might have survived comfortably for some time. Disunity, however, soon set in. Thomas Dewhirst and Mary Purnell ended up as leaders of warring factions and more legal action ensued. A settlement in 1930 gave the Dewhirst faction the main colony property; Mary Purnell took other nearby buildings and $60,000. The more than four hundred members still in the community split nearly equally between the two.[41] And so things have been since; the two movements have declined slowly over the years but at this writing still endure, each with fewer than two dozen members.

Holy City. In 1918 William E. Riker founded Holy City as a complement to the Perfect Christian Divine Way (PCDW), an organization he had established to promulgate his theories nine years earlier. Although Riker preached a somewhat convoluted version of Christianity, what earned him the greatest notice was his espousal of outright racism. Riker was the peer of the Ku Klux Klan in his preaching of white supremacy. On that basis he and a band of about thirty followers built their colony in the Santa Cruz mountains near the California coast in a location that provided a convenient rest stop for motorists traveling between San Jose and Santa Cruz; residents eventually numbered in the hundreds. The "Headquarters for the World's Perfect Government" featured gaudy, ornate architecture, a raft of tourist attractions ranging from a soda pop factory to a zoo, and innumerable large signs advertising Riker's theories, which included strange depression-era economic schemes as well as the familiar white superiority line. Major trouble came in 1942, when Riker, an admirer of Hitler, was arrested for sedition; although he was eventually acquitted, Holy City was already by then in decline. A few unsuccessful attempts to revive it were made until the late 1960s; Riker, rather surprisingly, converted to Catholicism at the age of ninety-four in 1966, three years before his death.[42]

COMMUNITARIAN AFRICAN AMERICAN LIBERATION MOVEMENTS

Father Divine's Peace Mission Movement. Close on the heels of Holy City came one of America's most remarkable communitarian religious movements, the Peace Mission Movement of Father Divine. Divine, who deliberately obscured his personal history,[43] turned up preaching in New York City about 1915. By the end of the decade, he had purchased a house in the prosperous suburb of Sayville, Long Island, where the nascent movement provided a communal residence for some of its members, who increasingly came to consider their leader God in human form. In the early 1930s, when the largely black movement was pressured to leave overwhelmingly white Sayville, Divine moved his headquarters to Harlem, where the group boomed.

Divine ministered to bodily as well as spiritual needs, providing his followers with food, clothing, and jobs as well as spiritual manna even in the depths of the depression. As the movement swelled and became more thoroughly communal, Divine purchased hotels and apartment buildings as communal homes, known as "heavens," for followers. The heavens were hardly luxurious, providing cramped quarters for the legions of celibate believers who streamed into the movement, but they were austerely adequate and, given Divine's emphasis on cleanliness, always neat and attractive. Food, too, was provided for followers and visitors. At its peak the movement was best known for its lavish banquets, at which Father Divine personally presided over the distribution of endless platters of dozens of kinds of food to thousands gathered to eat it. The low cost of high-density communal living plus the industry of followers, many of whom operated retail businesses whose proceeds supported the movement, meant that for several years the Peace Mission was a resounding economic and spiritual success.

With the return of national prosperity in the 1940s, however, a slow decline set in. The movement was losing its millennial fervor and becoming increasingly bureaucratized. Since Divine's death in 1965, his widow, Mother Divine, has presided over an aging remnant group that still lives communally and is supported by small businesses.[44] At this writing one can still stay in one of the Father Divine hotels, if one is willing to stay without company of the opposite sex, and eat at a Divine restaurant—all at a bargain price. The Divine spirit lives on, at least for now.[45]

BLACK JEWS

A special set of cases in the history of African Americans consists of the black Jews—African Americans who have created new religions that have some degree of Jewish content but that are generally not acknowledged as truly Jewish by those more universally recognized as Jews. Much of the momentum for black Judaism, as well as for the more prominent black Islam, came from the wave of black nationalism that surged through urban black America in the early twentieth century. Several black Jewish groups arose after 1890, and two of them operated communally early in the new century.

The Church of God and Saints of Christ. The pioneer black Jewish movement, and one that had an important communal phase in its development, was the Church of God and Saints of Christ, founded before the beginning of the twentieth century but not communal until several years after its founder's death in 1908. Despite its Christian-sounding name, the CGSC was the first known movement of black Jews. William Saunders Crowdy (1847–1908) began to have visionary experiences while living in Guthrie, Oklahoma, in 1893, and soon was preaching his message of a return to Jewish traditions to street audiences in various places. In 1896 he picked Lawrence, Kansas, which had a large black population, to found his new religious organization. From Lawrence the movement spread quickly; by 1899 Crowdy had followers in at least a dozen states and Canada and had divided his far-flung church into administrative districts. Today the denomination's American congregations are mainly on the East Coast, but it has had good worldwide growth and now has a presence in several other countries, notably Jamaica and South Africa.

The communal course of the CGSC was set in 1901 when Crowdy purchased a forty-acre plot of land in Belleville, Virginia (near Portsmouth). In 1917 his successor as head of the church, William Henry Plummer, moved the headquarters of the denomination to the site, which over the years has been expanded to more than a thousand acres. Plummer soon established a private school and a home for widows and orphans. Buildings were added over the next few years for worship space and other needs of the church. Eventually, the Belleville property included various communal residences, dining halls, a print shop, offices, a music hall, and a commissary. Thus it was that the core members of the church lived communally; most of the members, in outlying congregations, did not. The communal structure of the headquarters church was abandoned in the 1940s, but the church plans to resurrect it, in a sense; in a relatively recent report, denominational leaders were preparing to build group homes for the elderly on the property.[46]

Titular nomenclature notwithstanding, the CGSC has had substantial Jewish content from the first, although, as with most other movements of black Jews, the members have never been converted to "official" Judaism and thus are not recognized as authentic by the main body of world Jewry. Crowdy preached that African Americans had strong affective ties to ancient Israel, and in fact were descended from the ten lost tribes of Israel—a claim echoed by most of the other groups of black Jews—so they were now the true Jews. The group observes a Saturday Sabbath and uses much Jewish terminology. The high point of the ceremonial year is Passover, the celebration of which features a Seder meal. Jesus is regarded as an advocate of racial equality, but not as divine Lord and Savior; the Christ in the church's name refers to the Messiah that CGSC members still await. Today the church continues to thrive, albeit essentially noncommunally, preaching its distinctive mixture of Judaism, Christianity, and black nationalism.[47] Another branch of the church, headquartered in Cleveland, considers itself Christian, although it too retains some Jewish features, such as a Saturday sabbath.

The Temple of the Gospel of the Kingdom. Within a few years of Crowdy's founding of the Church of God and Saints of Christ, other groups of black Jews appeared on the American scene. Most of them were related to the rise of black nationalism among urban African American populations, and most did not involve communal living. One more of them, however, did adopt a communal model. About 1900 one Warien Roberson founded his Temple of the Gospel of the Kingdom in Virginia, teaching a version of Jewish orthodoxy that included learning Yiddish and emulating various Jewish cultural patterns. He also established lifestyle standards, including communal living and celibacy, that resembled ones that Father Divine, among other African American religious movement leaders, would adopt before long. By 1917 Roberson had moved his core group of followers to Harlem, where snide reporters dubbed it the "Live Ever, Die Never" society, after Roberson's teaching that followers would have eternal earthly life. Profiting from the surge of racial pride then current among African Americans, Roberson's movement grew swiftly in Harlem and in outlying locations, establishing as many as 150 "kingdoms" (communal households).[48] But the movement came crashing down when news reports charged that one kingdom, near Atlantic City, was a "baby farm" where various women bore the leader's children. Apparently, the strict rule of celibacy was not binding on Roberson himself. He was charged with transporting women across a state line for "immoral purposes" in 1926,[49] and, pleading guilty, was sentenced to a prison term.[50] The Temple movement collapsed and subsequently was regarded as an embarrassment by leaders of the black Jewish movements that emerged in its wake. It had, nevertheless, provided the necessities of life for its members and supplied a model of racially based community for other African American leaders for years to come.

LATTER DAY SAINTS COMMUNITARIANISM

The Church of Jesus Christ of Latter-day Saints and its various off-shoots have long had a tradition of communitarianism. Virtually the entire church was in a single locality (albeit a moving one, from upstate New York to Kirtland, Ohio, to Independence, Missouri, to Nauvoo, Illinois) in the movement's early years, and early on founder Joseph Smith Jr. proclaimed it the will of God that members hold their goods in common. The Law of Consecration and Stewardship, first disclosed in 1831, less than a year after the founding of the church, was implemented to some degree in the Ohio settlement, and again in Missouri.[51] But these early efforts to establish the United Order of Enoch, as the Latter-day Saints called their theocratic communitarianism, amounted to little more than directing the better-off Mormons to provide assistance to the poorer ones within the flock.[52]

Not until well after they had moved to Utah in the late 1840s did the Mormons adopt a more comprehensive communitarianism, and then only a few members participated in the venture. The early years in Utah were marked by cooperation in agriculture, notably in essential irrigation projects, and in retail trade. Then in the early 1870s church leaders, including the president, Brigham Young, began to talk about implementing the United Order more fully than had been done in the past. Early in 1874 the first local United Order was developed at St. George in southern Utah, and other local units emerged not long thereafter. The various experiments differed in their details, because the church never set forth an explicit operational scheme, but in several cases living the United Order, especially in rural and small-town areas, meant communal living including pooling of resources. The order was less completely developed in the cities, where it resembled the modern Mormon welfare system that provides assistance to church members in need.

The textbook case of a fully developed United Order community with a highly communal lifestyle, and the longest-lived of them, was that at the appropriately named Orderville in southern Utah. Settlement at the chosen site began in March 1875, and the roughly one hundred members immediately set to work growing crops and building a communal village. They agreed that no private property would be held by anyone, although a person was given a "stewardship" over his or her clothing and other purely personal items. Through hard work the group, though never becoming rich, achieved high self-sufficiency and was regarded as a model of what the United Order could be. It fine-tuned its system from time to time and developed a healthy society that might have continued for some time had not outside events intervened. As it happened, in the 1880s the federal government launched an all-out attack on Mormon polygamy, and devout polygamists in many cases had to go into hiding. Because most of the Orderville leadership was polygamous, the community lost its helmsmen, and soon the order was dissolved. Orderville became just another rural farming community and remains that today.[53]

In the meantime several churches of the LDS diaspora that came in the wake of Smith's death in 1844 had conducted their own nineteenth-century experiments in communal living. One of the earliest splinter groups gathered in Voree (now Burlington), Wisconsin, under the leadership of James J. Strang. The Strangite church grew quickly, perhaps counting as many as two thousand members at its peak. In 1847 Strang, seeking greater isolation, moved his group to Beaver Island in northern Lake Michigan. There a fairly prosperous commune flourished until Strang's assassination in 1856, after which the group dissipated. The few remaining Strangites do not live communally.[54]

Other Mormon splinters, however, continued to keep the communal tradition of the Latter-day Saints alive much longer than the Strangites did. Alpheus Cutler led a group into community at Manti, Iowa, in 1853; after Cutler's death in 1864 the group moved to Clitherall, Minnesota, where an inwardly focused commune operated for many years. Later some of the Cutlerites moved to the LDS Mecca of Independence, Missouri (where, all factions agree, the saints will ultimately gather for the Second Coming of Christ), and there the very few members of the church continue their work, although communal living was abandoned some years ago.[55]

Several other communal LDS groups, all of them short-lived, were active as well in the middle and latter parts of the nineteenth century, but many, perhaps most, did not survive into the twentieth. One successful early faction, under the leadership of Lyman Wight, operated a colony near Fredericksburg, Texas, in the 1840s and 1850s whose financial under-pinning was a gristmill. In the early 1850s another colony, known as Preparation, was opened in Monona County, Iowa, under the leadership of Charles B. Thompson, but it collapsed in 1858 primarily because of Thompson's venality. Joseph Morris organized a communal settlement of schismatic Mormons on the bank of the Weber River thirty miles from Salt Lake City in 1861; it was crushed by a Mormon posse after an armed battle in June 1862. Other nineteenth-century schismatic Mormon com-munal experiments included various ones under the leadership of Sidney Rigdon, who ended up in New York State, and Colonia, headed by James C. Brewster, in Texas.[56] Some, but not all, of the breakaway groups prac-ticed polygamy.

Such was the nineteenth-century prelude to further United Order ac-tivity in the twentieth century, all of which occurred outside the formal borders of the main Mormon church. The LDS church never repudiated the United Order, but after the 1880s no longer promoted it, focusing in-stead on developing the church welfare system. For all that activity in the nineteenth century, no LDS communal experiments seem to have been operating as the new century dawned.

The eclipse of LDS communalism proved transitory, however, as the main church began to get serious about forcing its members to abandon polygamy in the early years of the twentieth century. Dissident "fun-damentalists" noted that church leaders never claimed that any divine rev-elation had caused them to repeal the law of polygamy, which had been instituted in the first place because of a purported revelation to church founder and prophet Joseph Smith Jr. and they became resolute in their own view that they were simply remaining faithful to the will of God in maintaining plurality of wives. In that spirit several polygamous United Order communes were founded outside the confines of the now-monoga-mous main church, typically by charismatic leaders who, in classic LDS fashion, claimed special revelation directing them to found intentional communities as well as to practice polygamy. As the twentieth century has progressed, dissident LDS communitarianism, both polygamous and monogamous, has thrived. The groups founded in the first two decades of the century are here presented, following LDS historiographic conven-tion, by the names of their founders.

Peterson: The United Order of Equality. The first communal LDS splin-ter group to emerge in the twentieth century, and one of the few that did not embrace polygamy, developed in the first years of the new century in Independence, Missouri, the traditional LDS bastion. Ephraim Peterson and associates, wanting to get on with building Zion at Independence, published a plan for an ideal city and over several years, from perhaps 1905 until 1912 or so, urged others to join in their effort.[57] But the movement seems to have attracted few adherents, and except for a bit of surviving literature it long ago vanished.[58]

Bickerton: The Church of Jesus Christ. At about the same time Peterson was establishing his small group in Independence, another venerable LDS faction instituted a colony in nearby Kansas. In 1845 William Bickerton had joined one of the many LDS groups existing in the turmoil in which the Mormon movement found itself after the assassination of its president in 1844. Eventually, he concluded that the factions with which he was familiar, including the largest, by now headquartered in Utah, were all in error and felt called to establish his own branch denomination.

Formally organized in 1862, the Bickertonite church, officially called the Church of Jesus Christ, survives today. At some point in its early history the church established a colony at St. John, Kansas, where Bickerton himself lived for a time. Just how long that colony endured is unclear. In any event, another colony using the name of the Church of Jesus Christ was established in Comanche County, perhaps seventy-five miles south of St. John, in 1909. Whether the colony was an official outpost of the Bickertonite church or a separate splinter group is unclear, but it is known that under the leadership of Charles Tickhill and later A. B. Cadman, the church purchased 1,920 acres of ranch land near the Kansas-Oklahoma border in the hope of providing missions to American Indians in the Oklahoma territory. Erecting at least two buildings, the settlers grew grain and raised livestock to support their missionary work. More than eighty persons are said to have participated in the colony at one time or another. Details of colony life are largely missing, but it apparently endured for nearly two decades, closing amid disagreements and misfortunes in 1928.[59]

Zahnd: The Church of Christ, the Order of Zion. The family of Joseph Smith Jr. did not join the dominant Utah faction but stayed in the Midwest, eventually settling in Independence, Missouri, and assuming the leadership of the Reorganized Church of Jesus Christ of Latter Day Saints. Like the other branches of the larger LDS movement, the Reorganized Church has experienced schism and division, and one of them came with the withdrawal of one John Zahnd, who among other things objected to certain features of the organizational structure of the RLDS church and also believed the LDS movement should return to its tradition of communitarianism. In 1918 Zahnd organized the movement that he called the Church of Christ, the Order of Zion, in Kansas City. What happened thenceforth, however, is mysterious. The fragmentary surviving publications of the group indicate a sufficient membership to carry on a small communal experiment, but do not tell what happened after 1918. One surviving article written by Zahnd in 1928 suggests that the group was by then no longer active.[60]

Gudmundsen. About the time John Zahnd was forming his new church in Missouri, Moses Gudmundsen started a United Order community that at first was a part of the main Utah church but eventually became a separate organization. Gudmundsen, who taught music at Brigham Young University, began to develop his movement in 1918, when he and his brother, Octavius, took out homestead claims at West Tintic, Utah. Because more homestead land was available, Gudmundsen encouraged others to join them and take more claims; before long some sixty residents were living and farming communally. Over time, however, the teachings of Gudmundsen, who headed the local Mormon congregation, began to deviate from the official stance of the LDS church, and Gudmundsen, failing to heed requests that he resign from his leadership position, began, in the familiar LDS manner, to claim that he had special revelations of his own. In the fall of 1920 he introduced his most controversial teaching, that of "wife sacrifice," in which a man could abandon his wife for a new, "true," spouse. Soon thereafter, in 1921, the colony was disbanded and Gudmundsen left Utah.[61]

More Latter Day Saints communes would arise in later years and will be discussed in later chapters.

VEDANTA COMMUNALISM

One of the earlier Asian religions to make an impact in the United States was the Ramakrishna movement, which became organized in the 1890s as the Vedanta Society after the spectacular appearance of the charismatic Swami Vivekananda at the World's Parliament of Religions in Chicago in 1893. The path elucidated by Vivekananda encompassed toleration of all religions, social reform activities and works of charity, the recognition of a higher reality than the material, and inner peace—themes that many Americans found attractive. Vivekananda pointed the way toward Vedanta communities as early as 1895, when he gathered a small group of his new female converts at the Thousand Islands in the St. Lawrence River for intense spiritual instruction, where the women came to the conclusion "that they should live as a community, without servants, each doing a share of the work."[62] The master himself soon returned to India, but his successors built more substantial institutions, including some that responded to Vivekananda's call for community.

A 160-acre retreat called Shanti Ashrama was opened near San Jose, California, under the leadership of Swami Turiyananda in 1900; a community of devotees there lived in tents under harsh conditions until the community faded away in the 1910s. Another of the swamis, Trigunatita, in the summer of 1906 responded to requests from disciples for a more intense spiritual experience by opening a monastery on the top floor of the Vedanta temple in San Francisco, an eclectic structure that had been completed and dedicated earlier that year and had miraculously survived the earthquake that devastated the city in April. With a strict ascetic regimen, the monastery functioned well until it was closed after Trigunatita's death by assassination (at the hands of a mentally unstable former student) in 1915. Even though the male Ramakrishna leaders had rather traditional Indian ideas about the place and role of women (but reflecting the fact that a solid majority of American Vedantists were always female), they established a convent for nuns in a nearby rented house as well.

The monastic institutions were sufficiently popular with the faithful that Trigunatita soon decided to expand the program with a rural colony, in part because he thought that such a colony would help make the movement more permanent and self-sufficient. He thus purchased some two hundred acres of land on the outskirts of Concord, across San Francisco Bay, of which twenty-five acres were retained by the Vedanta Society and the balance sold to members for homesteads who created what one historian has called "a sort of Brook Farm."[63] The swami's plan called for a temple, a library, an orphanage, a retirement home, and a hospital. A number of members participated, erecting houses and planting orchards and crops, but the community never achieved financial stability. In any event, as with the urban center, Trigunatita's death effectively ended the project. Although his assistant, Prakashananda, took the reins of the society in San Francisco, the work was hobbled by the loss of the dynamic Trigunatita.[64]

A Vedanta community on the East Coast was opened in 1907, a year after the establishment of the San Francisco monastery. The Vedanta Ashrama, on 375 mountainous acres at West Cornwall, Connecticut, was originally a summer retreat center, but it soon turned into a year-round colony under Swami Abhedananda. Residents lived in two former farmhouses called Lotus and Peace, doing hard farm and gardening work as well as pursuing the spiritual life.[65]

A few years later the communal vision was rekindled among the Vedantists, this time under Paramananda, the most influential of the Vedanta swamis working in America in the early twentieth century, who, after arriving in America in 1906, had established a successful Vedanta center in Boston, and shortly after Trigunatita's death had begun working in Los Angeles as well. In 1923 he established the Ananda Ashrama on 135 hilly acres at La Crescenta, near Pasadena. Designed as a center for meditation and retreat, it was soon the site of lectures and public programs as well, and became the base from which work branched out through the Los Angeles area. The community contained homes and other buildings, including a "Temple of the Universal Spirit" open for worship to persons of all religious persuasions. In a beautiful location and stabilized by cottage industries, the center attracted visitors from east and west, among them such celebrities as Jiddu Krishnamurti and Greta Garbo. Branch centers in Massachusetts—a beautiful wooded site at Cohasset, twenty miles from Boston—and India followed the Ashrama's success, and Paramananda's partly communal work continued to develop until his sudden death of a heart attack in 1940. Even the loss of such a charismatic leader did not lead to immediate extinction for the communities; they survived for many years afterward and constituted, according to the judgment of historian Laurence Veysey, the "most long-lived communitarian venture founded during the twentieth century in the United States."[66]

Other monasteries and experimental Vedanta communities were established in later years. Sister Shivani, born Mary Hebard, and her husband, Haridas (Thomas LePage), established Abhedananda Acres, named for their swami, after homesteading in California's Antelope Valley (near the site of the former Llano colony) in 1923.[67] Followers of Swami Prabhavananda developed several more monasteries and convents in southern California in later years; one of them, Trabuco College, was populated by a remarkable literary crowd and will receive more attention in a later chapter.[68] In the 1930s and 1940s new communities of women were established (the earlier first one, in San Francisco, having lasted only about four years); eventually, four of them took shape, two each in northern and southern California.[69]

A tracking of all the Indian ashrams and monasteries in America after the founding era could occupy a large volume in itself. From Vivekananda's time on, Indian religious communities have been a fixture on the American scene, and some of the longest-lived of them all were the Vedantist originals.

Ethnic Communities

Much of American communal history is steeped in ethnic distinctiveness. North America's largest communitarian movement (apart from the Catholic communities), that of the Hutterites, constitutes a prime example of an ethnic group that has chosen to live communally. The Hutterites, however, have been unusual in their persistent dedication to the communal ideal. More typically, groups of immigrants seeking to preserve their ethnic distinctiveness have banded together soon after (or even before) their arrival on American shores, hoping that the mechanism of intentional community will help keep their traditions from being dissolved in the cultural melting pot of the larger society. Such communities, which might be branded defensive ones, have tended to last less than a generation. The immigrants (and especially their progeny) have almost always adjusted to the new land and culture relatively quickly, and the dynamic that made community seem compelling has disappeared.

The banding together of immigrants for cultural self-defense has gone on since European immigration began; here we will sample four notable examples of ethnic enclaves that adopted communal features when their participants were newly landed in the United States but reverted to private economic life once the new Americans had become more secure in their grip on their new environment.

DRUMMOND ISLAND

The determined efforts of Maggie Walz, temperance crusader and social activist, led to the creation of a cooperative colony of Finns on Drummond Island in Lake Huron early in the century. Walz arrived in the United States from her native Finland in 1881 and soon established herself as a leader in the Finnish immigrant community in Michigan, becoming, among other things, manager of the *Suometar*, the first Finnish newspaper in America. In 1903 she formulated a plan for a colony that would embody cooperative economics and also, importantly, be a temperance haven. "I found I could not take the saloon from the man, so I took the man from the saloon," she later commented.[70] To carry out her plan she became the government land agent for Drummond Island, and in 1905 began parceling out land to those who joined her cause. Soon there were four settlements (including one called "Kreeta," Walz's nickname) and nine hundred residents who worked at lumber camps, sawmills, and sugar beet farms. Some accounts depict an idyllic scene, with good houses, a sauna for every home, churches, and farms and other industries all producing general prosperity.[71] After several years, however, the utopian vision faltered; life was hard in the remote North, and some of those attracted to the colony found it insufficiently socialistic and rebelled against Walz's rather loose cooperative scheme. In 1914 the socialists took control. Ironically, the common features of life on Drummond Island soon vanished.[72]

THE MOLOKAN COMMUNITIES

The Molokans, or Russian Spiritual Christians, split from the Doukhobors in the eighteenth century chiefly over disagreements about the relative status of scripture and human leadership. The Doukhobors tended to emphasize the teachings of their leader as the ultimate spiritual authority; the dissenting faction believed that the Bible should be final. As with other Russian sectarians, the issue that led to emigration was military conscription; the pacifist Molokans wanted exemption from the draft, and after much recrimination the Russian government finally let them go in 1904. They considered settling near the Doukhobors, with whom they had retained close ties despite the groups' theological differences and who had themselves recently migrated to Canada, but found the Canadian climate too chilly and chose southern California instead, finding the climate and topography like that they had known in their homeland, the Transcaucasus.[73]

Communitarianism was part of the Molokan lifestyle in America from the beginning. The first settlement was in East Los Angeles, where several families lived communally in each of many houses and together opened a cooperative grocery store. Soon afterward a Molokan presence was established in San Francisco, around Potrero Hill, and about the same time the first of several agricultural communal enclaves was established in the

Guadalupe Valley, near Ensenada, Baja California. There in 1906 the Molokans bought thirteen thousand acres of land and attempted to reestablish
their traditional social structure—a village surrounded by communally
tended fields.[74] Fifty families moved to the colony, which endured for
about half a century, until conflicts with Mexican squatters in the 1950s
caused most of the remaining families to return to the United States.[75]

Other cooperative experiments followed, the rest of them in the United States. One group of ten to twenty families established a colony near
Potter Valley, east of Ukiah, California, about 1910, staying until their
sense of isolation impelled them to return to the larger Molokan community in San Francisco in 1918. Another group of families moved to land
near Kerman, California, in 1915, holding land individually but establishing a distinctive religious community that endures today.[76]

Meanwhile, a more thoroughly communal settlement was founded in
1911 by a group of families from Los Angeles (joined over the next few
years by families from other Molokan enclaves, until the settlement embraced more than a hundred families) near Glendale, Arizona. Four separate village settlements were created, one calling itself the *Obshchaia
kommuna,* or commune. A new irrigation district had just been established
in the area, and soon a wartime cotton boom brought much prosperity to
the hardworking immigrants. Things went well until 1921, when the postwar economic recession saw the bottom drop out of the price of cotton
and of Molokan prosperity. Once again most returned to the city, in this
case Los Angeles, leaving only a few families to continue as farmers in the
Glendale area.[77] Today ethnic enclaves of Molokans remain in several locations, but the rural communal ventures have disappeared.

VAN EEDEN COLONY

Dutch immigrants constituted one of the groups of ethnic colonizers,
although their community rates low in cooperation achieved. Frederik van
Eeden, a Dutch cultural dissenter of the late nineteenth century, founded
an ambitious intentional community called Walden in the Netherlands in
1898, although a few years later it collapsed amid financial mismanagement and ideological strife. Van Eeden thereupon made three speaking
tours to the United States and met associates with whom he proposed
founding the Cooperative Company of America, the parent body for a
proposed American colony. After some years of planning, a colony site
was located and purchased in North Carolina in 1909.

Van Eeden never implemented his socialist ideas personally; oddly, he declined to visit the colony, instead staying in the Netherlands and funneling Dutch settlers to the American premises. In any event, the grand socialist economy Van Eeden had promised the twenty or so families who ended up at his colony never materialized; the land was low in quality, so much so as to make agriculture impractical. The settlers drifted away, the last ones departing in 1939.[78]

THE BOHEMIAN COOPERATIVE FARMING COMPANY

One other notable ethnic group arrived and founded a settlement with important communal features in the second decade of the twentieth century. The Bohemian Cooperative Farming Company purchased fifty-three hundred acres a mile west of Mayland, Tennessee, and began settling the land in the spring of 1913. The colonists had a model to inspire them; earlier, in 1897, another group of Bohemians had established a colony named Rys in Virginia, one that featured a totally communal economy but that had broken up owing to internal dissension within its first year. Not deterred by the problems their forebears had encountered, at Mayland the Bohemians set to work eagerly, clearing the wooded terrain for farming and soon growing corn, potatoes, and several kinds of fruit. Local residents interviewed years later mainly remembered the colonists as extremely hard workers, toiling seven days a week and resting only two days per year—Christmas and New Year's. They stayed relatively isolated from their neighbors, probably in large part because they were not fluent in English, and their apparent standoffishness soon aroused suspicion among their neighbors that untoward things were happening in the colony—even, in one case, suspicion that the colonists were on the verge of murdering a boy on grounds that he had become useless because his broken leg had refused to heal properly. Mainly, the story was one of incessant hard labor. Residentially, the settlers followed a European pattern, grouping their homes in a village and going out by day to work the land. They held their money and provisions as well as their land in common.

The kinds of dissension familiar to students of communal history plagued the colony throughout its life, in this case focusing at first on authority and leadership and on the fact that those who worked the hardest got no more for their efforts than the less diligent. After a year the conflict seemed insoluble, so the colonists split their land in half and established a second village, but discord simply continued within both villages. Finally,

things degenerated to the point that an armed conflict erupted in which
one person was wounded—a finger of the colony president's daughter was
shot off. One of the two villages collapsed; the other did not last much
longer. The last two families left in 1916, and the land reverted to the mortgage holder for nonpayment.[79]

Secular Communities

Although prophets, saints, swamis, and deities of all kinds were in the
center of the religious communal stage, decidedly secular dissenters were
also establishing communal settlements early in the century. Sometimes
the only central ideology or goal for such communities was communal living itself, but most of the time those participating saw themselves as
working for a heartfelt cause in a communal context. The most common
center points of secular communes and colonies in the early twentieth century were socialism, anarchism, social reform, ethnic identity, self-sufficient agrarianism, and art; some of the communities combined two or
three of those threads. The artists' colonies have a chapter of their own in
this book, and the rest will be discussed here.

SOCIALIST AND ANARCHIST COMMUNITIES

Socialism and anarchism, seeming opposites on the political spectrum
that have been closely tied together in American history, have spawned a
good many of America's intentional communities since the late nineteenth
century. Socialism rode a political roller coaster in the turn-of-the-century
era, gaining a real following from time to time, but never decisive political
power. The historic temptation of socialists has been to try to illustrate
how a socialist society might work by creating it in microcosm—in a communal society. Anarchists, meanwhile, have banded together into communities to pursue their vision of a better world. Anarchy might seem
inherently inimical to such a structured lifestyle as that of an intentional
community, which inevitably has some kind of government, formal or informal, and many anarchists undoubtedly would never choose such an
arrangement; but most major anarchist theorists, though opposing gov-
ernments to which one is forced to submit, find voluntary arrangements
for mutual assistance quite satisfactory. Indeed, some would argue, such
voluntary cooperation would be necessary in a world without formal gov-
ernments. So anarchist colonies have emerged from time to time, and gen-

erally have been quite unstructured, providing individual freedom to the greatest extent possible while providing just enough of a communal focus to make daily life possible and pleasant.

Llano del Rio. The best known of the socialist communities of the early twentieth century was Llano del Rio, which was founded in California in 1914 and moved to Louisiana four years later where, as Newllano, it survived until 1938. Job Harriman, a prominent socialist attorney who had been Eugene V. Debs's vice presidential running mate in 1900, began to ponder communitarian socialism in the wake of his two unsuccessful campaigns for mayor of Los Angeles in 1911 and 1913. His motivation was like that of the Debsian socialists who had turned to colony building two decades or so earlier: because socialism was not doing well at the polls and not making satisfactory inroads on American capitalism, voluntary societies of socialists would demonstrate the validity and desirability of socialism to a skeptical nation. Harriman therefore organized the purchase of a tract of several thousand acres in the desert forty-five miles north of Los Angeles, the site of a temperance colony called Almondale that had been founded in the early 1890s but had been dissolved after three years. In 1914 he purchased a socialist magazine, the *Western Comrade,* and eloquently pushed the colony in its pages.

No one could fault the colonists for lack of high ideals, articulated by Harriman's masterful socialist rhetoric.[80] The "Declaration of Principles" that guided the colony throughout its existence was a ringing affirmation of the virtues of cooperation:

1. Things used productively must be owned collectively.
2. The rights of the community shall be paramount over those of the individual.
3. Liberty of action is permissible only when it does not restrict the liberty of another.
4. Law is a restriction of liberty and is just only when operating for the benefit of the community at large.
5. Values created by the community shall be vested in the community alone.
6. The individual is not justly entitled to more land than is sufficient to satisfy a reasonable desire for peace and rest. Productive land held for profit shall not be held by private ownership.
7. Talent and intelligence are gifts which should be rightly used in the service of others. The development of these by education is the gift of the community to the individual, and the exercise of greater ability entitles none to the false reward of greater possessions, but only to the joy of greater service to others.

8. Only by identifying his interests and pleasures with those of others can man find real happiness.

9. The duty of the individual to the community is to develop to the greatest degree possible by availing himself of all educational facilities and to devote the whole extent of that ability to the service of all.

10. The duty of the community to the individual is to administer justice, to eliminate greed and selfishness, to educate all, and to aid any in time of age or misfortune.[81]

On May 1, 1914, the colony was opened to settlers. Growth was rapid and substantial; the five initial colonists grew to more than 150 by January 1915, and to an astonishing eleven hundred during the summer of 1917.[82] Harriman and his associates described the colony in grand terms as a haven in which comfort and beauty were already abundant and would only increase in the rapidly developing future, and various plans for the socialist metropolis and its infrastructure were compelling in their attractiveness.[83] Indeed, great conviviality characterized colony life, which from the beginning featured lectures, readings, band and other musical concerts, sports, crafts projects, and weekly dances, among many other diversions.

In other ways, however, colony life was strikingly less beautiful than the images conjured up by the promoters. People lived in tents and poorly built adobe houses that could never be called comfortable, much less luxurious. The communal dining room served unappealing, monotonous food. Meanwhile, the economy of the colony was always teetering on the brink, sustained only by the money brought by new members. Harriman and other leaders had projected a rosy agricultural future based on irrigation, but sufficient water was never present and little produce was grown. A 1916 government ruling denying the colony the water it needed for its acreage doomed the original Llano plan.

The problems in living conditions, water rights, and the dismal economic situation were aggravated by other interpersonal disagreements that were probably inevitable, for socialists, despite their devotion to the common good, tended not to all think alike. At one point a group held a series of secret nighttime meetings in the sagebrush surrounding the colony, emerging to demand that every plan or action of any kind be voted on by the assembly of colonists as a whole before it was implemented. These dissatisfied democrats, who called themselves the Welfare League, took to wearing bits of sagebrush in their lapels; the other colonists called them the "brush gang," and thenceforth "brusher" was the colony name for anyone who was chronically or unreasonably disgruntled.[84] It is possible that some of the brushers were saboteurs planted by *Los Angeles Times* publisher Harrison Gray Otis, a classic robber-baron capitalist and implacable enemy of Harriman and Llano as well as anything else labeled "socialist"; if so, they performed their mission well.[85] Whether contrived or not, internal strife became endemic at Llano early on, and that plus the lack of irrigation water soon doomed the colony. Harriman could see the handwriting on the wall by 1916, and quietly began looking for a new colony site.

The following year Harriman found a suitable property. The Gulf Lumber Company was willing to sell some twenty thousand acres of cut-over Louisiana forest land and a small company town at the bargain price of $120,000 and on easy terms. Once again optimistic projections for a grand communal future were floated in the *Western Comrade* and elsewhere, and in October 1917 most of the colonists who had chosen to stay with Llano departed for the new communal town, a small vanguard setting out in an automobile caravan and the rest moving on a chartered train. (A few would stay behind and run a smaller original Llano colony, and some left the venture altogether.) By January 1918 the new colony, appropriately named Newllano, had about three hundred members, including one hundred or so new ones, mainly Texans.

Communal life in Louisiana turned out not to be any more problem-free than life in California had been. The colony was always poverty-stricken and riven by internal dissension, now aggravated by conflicts between Californians and Texans. Members steadily drifted away, and farming and industrial enterprises largely fared poorly. One might well have expected the colony to close its doors by 1920. The problems never did go away, and the colonists and their leaders often made decisions that in retrospect were hardly wise. The biggest disaster of all, one historian has argued, was one of the several expansion projects. In 1932 the colony purchased a large tract of land complete with a nineteenth-century hacienda in Gila, New Mexico, which was to be home to a thousand colonists and be one of a chain of Llano colonies spanning the American continent. The population at Gila never exceeded fifty, and the whole venture was simply another financial burden for an already desperately poor colony.[86]

However, new leadership and a few glimmers of better times ahead kept many members going through all the difficult years. George T. Pickett became the colony's general manager, and his decisive style and "begging trips" to gather support from socialists outside the colony managed to keep Newllano afloat. Farming operations improved somewhat, and printing and publishing became a profitable business. New projects periodically interrupted the tedium of hard times, as when in 1922 the colony bought a "rice ranch" seventy-five miles south of the colony, a farm much more productive than the main colony land and one that provided both food and income to the colonists for several years. New members continued to arrive. In 1923 the colony became the host to a new, radical educational institution, Commonwealth College, although before long it moved to a separate campus at Mena, Arkansas.[87] The colonists always had good schools of which they were immensely proud, and even a separate child-care facility called Kid Kolony. And perhaps more important than anything else, throughout their hard years in Louisiana the colonists always had a robust social life, with a swimming hole, many dances, sporting events, parties, and theatrical productions, and they maintained a surprisingly enduring sense of idealism.

But all of that put only a veneer on the inescapable fact that the colony was never economically viable and was forever split by factional fights. Newllano struggled on until it was finally, hopelessly bankrupt. It was thus liquidated in 1938.

The Nevada Colony. Llano del Rio, despite its problems and shortcomings, was for years a beacon for socialists. Politics had not been kind to American radicals, and the idea of building socialism in microenvironments, although not novel, had renewed appeal to not a few of them. Llano had a larger-than-life presence by dint of glowing publicity right from its founding in 1914, and few socialists would have been surprised had dozens of Llanos sprung up around the country.

The fiscal agent of the original Llano was C. V. Eggleston, a honey-tongued promoter who, as a frequent contributor to the *Western Comrade,* Llano's paper, and as a public speaker had much to do with the rosy Llano image. For reasons that are not entirely clear, he left Harriman and Llano in August 1915, heading for Nevada and a projected new colony there. That fall he put together a Llano-like interlocking pair of corporations, the Nevada Colony Corporation and the Union Security Company, the latter a nominally independent firm set up to handle real estate and financial services for the colony. At first the Nevada project had legal ties to Llano, but in April 1916 the two colonies went their legally separate ways, although they remained associated in the popular mind.

In the meantime Nevada political and business leaders had set out to revitalize the economy of a state whose once-lucrative mines had played out and which had not yet discovered gambling and prostitution. Irrigation projects were inaugurated, and colonization plans seemed ideal as vehicles for bringing in the desired new settlers. Moreover, Churchill County, where the colony would be situated, had the heaviest per capita concentration of socialists in the state (among whom Eggleston would promote the colony as the Washington socialist colonies had been promoted—as constituting the foundation of a program to socialize the state). So the omens seemed to be lining up in promising fashion, and in the spring of 1916 Eggleston began promoting his colony with the same flair he had shown at Llano.

The first settlers arrived at the main colony site, Nevada City, in May 1916; slow but steady growth followed until the colony peaked at forty-eight stockholders (i.e., families—about two hundred persons) early in 1918. As of September 1916, the colony comprised about 1,540 noncontiguous acres of land. But dissension set in as early as that fall; when the first annual meeting was held in November 1916, disgruntled members— many of them local ranchers who had traded their land for colony stock— ousted three of the five members of the board of directors. More turmoil quickly followed, and by the end of the month five discontented members had been expelled from the colony. After a complex series of maneuvers and recriminations, Eggleston finally resigned from the colony board in June 1917. Eventually, the problems swamped the colony's ability to attract new members, and the decline throughout 1918 and after was punctuated by lawsuits and the exposure of deception and shortcomings in the various colony industries, which included farming, a print shop, a mill, a hotel, and a furniture store. The colony went into receivership on May 1, 1919, and the remaining few families departed a few months afterward. Today Nevada City is simply one of Nevada's many ghost towns.[88]

The Army of Industry. Job Harriman and C. V. Eggleston were not the only socialists in the Southwest to turn to communitarianism. Their contemporary, Gerald Geraldson, of Auburn, California, in the foothills of the Sierras, also started a commune of socialists in 1914. The Army of Industry, located in Geraldson's father's old fruit orchard west of Auburn, was smaller than Llano but just as earnest; Ernest Wooster, Newllano's chronicler of American communities, wrote in 1924 that its contribution "to the experimental work of community living is worth considerably more than its numerical importance indicates."[89] Among the thirty or forty original settlers were socialists, Wobblies, and others with a great variety of philosophies; the mix guaranteed plenty of internal conflict. From the beginning the colony was open to the poor; as policy it rejected the buy-in fees theoretically required by many socialist communes, including the Kaweah Cooperative Commonwealth (of which Geraldson had once been a trial member) and Llano. Thus it became, as Geraldson described it, a community of "'losers' in the property game," a "little group of 'broke' people" who eventually demanded poverty as a condition for entry: "Each member entering must certify that he or she is without property [and] must be willing to give up the idea of getting rich."[90] For several years the poor people's colony managed to survive, hosting a motley array of visitors and keeping the common table spread; by 1920 or so, however, little of the experiment seems to have been left. In 1922 Geraldson moved to New York, where he opened the Brotherhood House, a social-service facility, on the East Side and continued for decades to hope that it would eventually develop into a community that would finally achieve the ideal of the Army of Industry.[91]

Ferrer Colony. Although socialists dominated the secular communal scene from 1900 to 1912, anarchists did manage to claim a small piece of the action as well. In 1915 the Francisco Ferrer Association, named after a recently executed Spanish anarchist and closely associated with the radical magazine *Mother Earth,*[92] opened a colony focused on an alternative school on 143 acres near Stelton, New Jersey. Rural romanticism was an important force motivating the founders, who included such prominent anarchists as Leonard Abbott, Harry Kelly, and Joseph Cohen (the same Joseph Cohen who would found the Sunrise colony in Michigan during the depression[93]), but the site was carefully kept within range of New York City, the ongoing capital of radical anarchism—the colony was not far from the main line of the Pennsylvania Railroad, and many colonists commuted daily to jobs in the city.

Ferrer Colony was financed in what might be characterized as a businesslike fashion. The organization paid about $100 per acre for its land and then sold one- and two-acre lots to colonists at $150 per acre. The surplus was used to reserve nine acres for the school plus land for other amenities, such as roads and a water system. Thus individuals were allowed to build and own homes at Ferrer, but land was held in common as well—a pattern of ownership that would become more popular in land-trust communities two decades later. For Ferrer colony this development formula worked; the colony rapidly paid off its land purchase with lot sales and never had to struggle with severe debt in the way that many communities—Llano, to name a prominent example—did. Although the colony and its members were never rich, the necessary building projects were undertaken with considerable hardship, and members lived in primitive conditions for some time.

The Ferrer Modern School became known for its unstructured approach to education. It attempted to stay free of any dominating point of view, although anarchism and socialism were the context in which its students and their parents lived. At first it was truly anarchic, undisciplined, and chaotic, and after three or four years seemed doomed. But Elizabeth and Alexis Ferm arrived in 1920 and, plunging into the educational task with great energy, managed to combine apparent free choice by the young students with firm adult guidance, creating a sort of oxymoronic dictatorial anarchy. Manual labor and field trips were emphasized.[94] The success of the post-1920 school lay clearly in the genius of the Ferms, and by such measures as its students' moving on into college it was indeed a success.

Almost from the beginning the colony experienced steady growth. In September 1918 Ferrer counted fifty-one houses and about twenty year-round families resident. Improvements in the physical plant progressed slowly but steadily, and with them came more residents. At its peak in the early 1920s the colony had eighty to ninety houses and more than two hundred residents. It enjoyed a heady intellectual atmosphere, with vigorous discussions on all the topics of the day, especially political ones, and a vibrant social life with weekly communal meals. Even though the underlying principle of anarchism meant that the homes were privately owned and persons could go about their private business, the spirit of community reigned, with much mutual support and concern. Not surprisingly, the enclave attracted more than its share of eccentrics, including, especially, quite a few health and food faddists, who seemed to fit into the social fabric well enough.

The colonists inevitably had some struggles with their neighbors; rural Americans then as now tend not to think highly of anarchists and socialists, at least when they use those labels to identify themselves. When colonists hung a red flag from their water tower to applaud the German revolution in 1918, armed vigilantes removed it after a heated discussion with Joseph Cohen. But such struggles were not as severe as they have been at a good many other intentional communities, and at Ferrer, as elsewhere, as the colonists became a familiar part of the local scene, opposition to their presence faded away.

Although never prosperous and always somewhat disunified—a split between Communists and anarchists caused factional strife in the early 1930s, for example—the colony survived well enough until the sudden establishment of Camp Kilmer immediately adjacent to the colony during World War II brought drastic changes to the human and natural environment and, in essence, did in the outpost of anarchism. Many of the colonists were reaching retirement age anyway, so they began to move out. Given the anarchic basis of the colony, they could simply sell their homes to any buyers, and the soldiers were a ready market. By the end of the war the colony was history. Its influence, though, continued to be felt for decades as some of its participants—most notably Will Durant—went on to intellectual prominence in the larger culture.[95]

Freedom Hill. There were other, usually smaller, anarchist colonies as well. One about which information is sparse was Freedom Hill, opened by J. William Lloyd at Roscoe, California, at the edge of the San Fernando Valley. Lloyd, born in 1857 in New Jersey, took to anarchism as a young man and developed a philosophy that was fairly typical for radicals of his day in combining socialist-anarchist politics with a crusade for individual and sexual freedom, but was decidedly unusual in that he also was involved in the Vedanta Society and stirred its we-are-all-one cosmology into his intellectual stew. About 1900 he took over editorship of the *Free Comrade,* an anarchist paper that was especially known for its advocacy of sexual freedom. At least since the 1890s Lloyd had advocated rural colonies for anarchists, and his ideas seem to have influenced the founding of the Ferrer Colony, for Lloyd was a close friend of Leonard Abbott, one of the principal persons active there. Lloyd wrote many books, including at least two utopian novels and many other pieces of romantic prose.[96] Early in the century he had some association with George Littlefield of Fellowship Farms; his second utopian novel was published by Littlefield's Ariel Press, and he was for a time a regular contributor to Littlefield's periodical, *Ariel.* In 1908 he was reported to be living at Westfield, New Jersey, with his sister and his son,[97] so the colony at Roscoe must have been founded between then and 1913, when Freedom Hill is reported to have been in existence.[98]

In New Jersey, Lloyd's daughter had at one time run a print shop, publishing the work of William Morris as well as that of her father, which may have had something to do with the fact that there was a print shop at Freedom Hill. There the publishing operation was run by LeRoy "Freedom Hill" Henry, a colorful local sometime physician who became enamored of the ideas of Jacob Beilhart, the founder of the Spirit Fruit Society. Beilhart had died in 1908, but his group continued its communal life in the hills above Santa Cruz, California. Over several years Henry reprinted large portions of *Spirit Fruit* and *Spirit's Voice,* that group's periodicals during its turn-of-the-century halcyon days, as well as other of Beilhart's writings and his own homespun philosophy, possibly continuing his work into the 1940s. Thus Freedom Hill appears to have outlived Lloyd, although it never became large or influential.

LITTLE LANDS AND SUBSISTENCE FARMING

Some of the new twentieth-century communities resembled those of times past, chiefly in being dedicated to the promulgation of a particular religious or political philosophy, but new thrusts were appearing as well. One innovation during the period 1910 to 1929 was a surge of communities of small acreages on which residents would try to achieve self-sufficiency through subsistence agriculture and occasional cottage industries. Among the early examples of the genre were the Fellowship Farm Association, the Little Landers, and the Los Angeles Fellowship Farms Company.

Fellowship Farm. The first Fellowship Farm group was inaugurated in 1908 when about forty persons under the leadership of George E. Littlefield pooled their savings and purchased seventy acres near Westwood, Massachusetts. As a Unitarian minister in Haverhill, Massachusetts, Littlefield had been an ardent reformer, publishing a reformist magazine, the *Ariel* (which eventually would become the Fellowship Farm organ), running for Congress, and finally resigning his church position when his congregation rejected his plan to reorganize the parish as a "cooperative church" that would, among other things, operate a cooperative store.[99] After leaving his church, Littlefield continued to publish the *Ariel,* expounding therein his mild economic radicalism, which mainly advocated cooperative enterprises, until eventually he pulled enough like-minded fellows together to buy the land at Westwood. Littlefield was possessed of a great sense of immediacy, as his credo proclaimed:

Get up and get.
Get an acre and live on it.

Get a spade and dig.
Get off the backs of the workers.
Get the shirkers off your back.
Get honest.
Get busy.[100]

Each member was given one acre to cultivate; the thirty common acres were worked collectively. Never, however, did the whole colony manage to earn its living from farming, printing, or crafts; many members commuted to work in Boston, and some lived at Fellowship Farms only in the summer. Nevertheless, most participants seem to have been happy with the experiment. A press account published in 1912 depicted the project as thriving, with many residents living in self-built tidy houses and earning respectable livings from gardening and poultry; a satisfied member, in fact, was reported as having just purchased another seventy acres a few miles away to replicate the project.[101] Just how cooperatively and long it operated is unclear. Ralph Albertson, in a survey published some years later, reported that the experiment was discontinued in the year of its founding[102]; Eileen Boris writes that the cooperative association was dissolved when the last tracts were paid for in 1918, implying that many continued to live on their plots[103]; Robert Fogarty asserts that it was still operating in the 1920s.[104]

In the meantime, however, the Fellowship Farm idea had spread. Littlefield reportedly founded offshoot communities in Kansas City and Independence, Missouri, and in Norwood, Massachusetts, in 1911.[105] Little seems to have come of the satellite efforts; about all that seems to be known about Fruit Crest, for example, as the Independence venture was known, was that Littlefield and C. B. Hoffman (previously a major player in the stateside supporting cast of the Topolobampo Colony in Mexico[106]) purchased thirty-five acres for it.[107] Others, however, took up the torch more successfully. Inspired by Littlefield's work, Kate Buck, a Los Angeles dentist, acquired seventy-five acres in the Los Angeles area and enlisted Littlefield to help her get a similar enclave started. Twelve families moved to the farm in the winter of 1912–13. Again each colonist got about an acre of land and a share in the central communal property, and soon membership reached fifty to sixty, including a sprinkling of eccentrics, among them one who hiked into Los Angeles each weekend to do street preaching. As they and other microfarmers eventually discovered, however, one acre is not much land for making an agricultural living, and those who stayed gradually bought out those who left. The cooperative, egalitarian spirit disappeared, and the project was formally dissolved in the 1920s.[108] Altogether, however, the various Fellowship Farms had a substantial following; some three hundred families lived at them for various lengths of time.[109]

The Little Landers. A similar but larger-scale venture was begun in San Ysidro, California, a year after Littlefield's farm opened. William E. Smythe, a prominent authority on irrigation and land reclamation, was a San Diego historian and booster who found his inspiration for a small-acreage cooperative farming enclave in the then-popular country life movement and especially Bolton Hall's country life tract, *A Little Land and a Living,* which outlined specialized strategies for microagriculture.[110] Convinced that a person, and even a family, could eke out a living on a one-acre plot, he established the first Little Landers colony in 1909 to demonstrate the validity of that premise. A corporation was formed to raise capital, and land—eventually 550 acres—was purchased south of San Diego in the Tijuana River Valley near the Mexican border. Smythe oversaw the development of necessary infrastructure—streets, sewage and water lines—and began to seek colonists who could pay $350 to $550 for their one-acre farms. He even created a colony flag, a white star on a blue field, described as a star of hope for those seeking self-sufficiency. Plenty of would-be settlers responded, and by 1912, 116 families were on the land, busily cultivating their tiny farms, raising crops and animals that ranged from head lettuce to pigs to Belgian hares. Articles in the popular press extolled life at San Ysidro as prosperous and healthy.[111] The idealistic settlers included many professional persons—teachers, doctors, lawyers—who gave the colony an engaging intellectual and social life.[112] By 1915 the Little Landers boasted five hundred settlers and two hundred homes, and by the following year four additional Little Landers colonies had been established at various locations around California. One of them was within the current city of Los Angeles, now known as the neighborhood of Tujunga; its community building, called Bolton Hall, now functions as the Bolton Hall Museum.[113]

But all was not well in San Ysidro. As early as 1910 financial and management problems had cropped up. Some settlers had never gardened before and could not readily make their plots produce as intensively as the colony's plan envisioned. Smythe's great expertise notwithstanding, the irrigation system did not perform adequately. Reorganization and physical improvements, including further irrigation work, saved the colony from an early demise, and indeed helped it grow through hard times, but underlying problems persisted as well.

What might have happened in the long run will forever remain unknown, for on January 18, 1916, a flood devastated the colony, and it never recovered. A hundred families were utterly wiped out, and two colonists drowned. In a sense the colony survived, and leaders continued to talk about the future, but the end was in sight. It had turned out, in the estimation of many participants, that producing a living from a single acre was not easy, so some chose not to reestablish their holdings. The experiment gradually played itself out. What now remains to commemorate the project, apart from the museum in Tujunga, is a street name in San Ysidro —Smythe Avenue.[114]

Durham and Delhi. One of the more ambitious projects to get people back to the land on small holdings was sponsored by the State of California through a state agency called the California Land Settlement Board, created by the legislature in 1917, which sought to sustain some movement of people to rural land at a time when the state had run out of free homestead land. Two colonies of note resulted from the program, Durham and Delhi.

Durham was started with a $260,000 loan from the state that was to be paid back over fifty years. The Land Settlement Board, chaired by Elwood Mead, like his Little Landers counterpart, William Smythe, a leading expert on irrigation and water rights and at this point in his life a vocal advocate of rural resettlement, purchased 6,239 acres near Chico in inland northern California and soon had about a hundred families settled there.[115] In what was becoming the standard pattern for cooperative homestead projects, a central acreage was set aside as a community center with recreation facilities, and each family was allotted a small acreage to farm; settlers socialized at the community center, built homes cooperatively, and developed a joint purchasing program for farm and building supplies. Solid preparation was done before the first settlers moved in—an irrigation system was installed, for example, and the backing of the state treasury meant that attractive loans were available for land purchase and home construction—and contemporary reports on the first year or two of colony life were glowing. A particular point of pride was the dairy operation; extensive orchards were also established. Other crops thrived as well, and the homes had electricity and running water. The settlers, one admirer of the California projects wrote, represented "the kind of citizen or family that could not wisely attempt farming or land ownership except as a member of a neighborhood group which, while not communistic or socialistic in any bolshevik sense, is coöperative in many of its activities (especially those having to do with buying and selling) as well as in its educational and social life."[116] Things went well enough at Durham that by 1921 the Land Settlement Board was pressing on with the second in what it projected would be an extensive string of colonies. Delhi, created on eighty-four hundred acres in the San Joaquin Valley, was advanced a million dollars by the state to be relent to settlers (all of whom in this case were to be veterans), who could acquire tracts of up to forty acres each.

The good early news from both colonies did not last for very many years. The 1920s saw a serious agricultural depression in the United States; by middecade many of the Durham settlers, like legions of conventional, private farmers, were delinquent in their loan payments. And things were much worse at Delhi, which by mid to late decade was a virtually total financial failure. Elwood Mead's vision for Delhi had expanded with the apparent early success of Durham, and expensive common improvements—a factory, a community building—put land prices out of reach for many poor would-be settlers. By 1928 nearly half of the Delhi acreage remained unsold.

Even before the colonies' situations had become hopeless, some California politicians wanted to get and keep the state out of the land business, so ongoing controversy swirled around the problem-laden colonies. After tedious political recriminations and litigation, the state reached a financial settlement with the colonists in 1930. The experiment was over—at least in California.[117]

Despite their problems, however, these California colonies directly influenced what the federal government would do on a much larger scale nearly two decades later as the Farm Security Administration and then the Resettlement Administration organized cooperative farm colonies to help displaced industrial workers support themselves and thus survive the depression. Some private efforts for cooperative homesteading would emerge as well, most notably under the aegis of Ralph Borsodi, who would become the depression generation's leading prophet of back-to-the-land idealism. Cooperative small-acreage farming was to get its most extensive trial yet. Those depression-era efforts will be discussed later in this volume.

Much of the housing college students have occupied since the rise of the modern university has had communal features. Dormitories, rooming houses, fraternities, sororities, and shared apartments and houses all have some cooperation about them, but their transient population and lack of purpose larger than that of simply providing low-cost housing make them unlike the communities within the scope of this volume. One special type of student housing, however, does merit inclusion much more than the rest do. In this century hundreds of organized housing cooperatives have arisen to offer college students (and sometimes nonstudents) not only inexpensive room and board but also a sense of common purpose and, in many cases, centers for social change activism.

Nonprofit cooperative student enterprises began to emerge in the latter part of the nineteenth century, notably with the opening of the Harvard Co-op bookstore in 1882. Some organized cooperative housing owned and operated by its residents seems to date from that era, but the first well-documented projects appeared later, from 1910 and after. Early among them was a co-op at the University of Wisconsin founded in 1915; co-ops for women followed at the universities of Michigan (1917) and Kansas (1919), providing residential facilities whose low cost of living enabled some women to attend college who otherwise would have been denied that opportunity.

The movement boomed with the depression in the 1930s.[118] Needing to conserve every penny, students in several cases repaired dilapidated houses and found other creative ways to live on remarkably little money. The social ends of cooperative housing were important as well; in several college towns student co-ops became the vanguard of racial integration, offering equal-access housing in defiance of long-standing local mores. In Lawrence, Kansas, for example, the women's co-op that had provided the first racially integrated housing in the city was across the street from a café popular among students at the University of Kansas, and in 1948 the co-op started an eventually successful campaign to get the café to serve African American diners. Some co-ops went so far as to embrace socialist politics, as at the University of Michigan, where the Michigan Socialist Co-op House was founded in 1932.

The co-op movement waned during the 1950s, but since then has emerged stronger than ever. At one recent count the Inter-Cooperative

Council at the University of Michigan embraced nineteen houses with some 550 residents. The North American Students of Cooperation hold annual conferences that attract students from across the United States and Canada. Student housing with a purpose seems a well-established presence in communal America.[119]

Yet other intentional communities do not fit very well into the above categories. These unique ventures ranged from bizarre group adventures under charismatic leadership to idealistic political activist projects. The American Woman's Republic, Helicon Hall, and a few other unusual communities round out the story of the communal early twentieth century.

Bride of Christ. The world always has a few scoundrels—or, more charitably, seriously misguided dreamers—among its inhabitants, and the intentional community movement, like every other venue populated by human beings, has had its share of them. One of them was Franz Edmund Creffield, who for three years reigned as the most flamboyant and outrageous religious leader Oregon has ever seen.[120]

Creffield was said to have been trained for the Catholic priesthood in his native Germany, but his first known religious affiliation in the United States was with the Salvation Army, which he joined shortly after arriving in Portland in 1903. He was sent from there on a mission to Corvallis, where he struck out on his own, soon proclaiming himself the second Christ—"Joshua." His charismatic powers must have been great, for a female following numbering several dozen coalesced around him almost immediately. In short order he had denounced evening religious meetings and instituted afternoon meetings in homes, a convenient time for his female followers to gather while their husbands were at work, and condemned that vehicle of beastly vanity known as clothing. It was not long until nudity prevailed at Creffield's meetings, and then it was a short step for him to select special wives who would be entitled to special status in heaven by copulating with the master on earth.

The early meetings of the Holy Rollers, as Creffield and his followers were soon popularly known, were held in the home of businessman Victor Hurt, whose wife and two daughters were early and devout believers, but Hurt soon threw the group out. A secluded location for the work now seemed in order, and soon the faithful had established a colony outside town near the Willamette River. A photograph of a group of the believers, all naked, suddenly appeared in Corvallis, however, and the prophet was tarred and feathered and advised to make himself scarce. Undeterred, he soon managed to sneak back into town, only to be caught in a compromising position with a woman whose husband swore out a warrant for adultery. Creffield immediately disappeared—to be found, three months later, hiding, naked, in the dirt under the home of Hurt, whose daughter, Maud Hurt, Creffield had earlier married (although she had later divorced him at her father's insistence). Creffield was sentenced to two years in the penitentiary. He served a bit over a year and, upon release, immediately began to acquire a new round of followers. With financial assistance from his brother-in-law (he and Maud had remarried after his release from prison), he acquired, in 1906, land near Waldport, Oregon, where he urged followers to come lest they be engulfed by the Lord's coming destruction of Corvallis—which had just been foreshadowed by the San Francisco earthquake and fire. Amazingly, they did turn out again, to resume back-to-nature life on the Oregon coast.

The Corvallis men whose wives and sisters had flocked to Creffield's side had had enough. One George Mitchell, whose sister Esther was one of Creffield's most devoted followers, found Creffield in Seattle on May 7, 1906, and shot him dead. Mitchell was duly arrested, but at his trial was quickly acquitted—not surprisingly, given the district attorney's observation that he had done "a very laudable act in eliminating that miserable animal Creffield from the face of the earth."[121] Esther, avenging her prophet, shot her brother in the head at the railroad station as he was preparing to leave Seattle.[122] This time the court was less sympathetic, committing Esther to the state hospital. Only several weeks later did the naked female followers out on the Oregon coast learn of their leader's demise and make their way back into conventional society.[123]

The American Woman's Republic. One early-twentieth-century communal settlement was related to the woman's suffrage movement then burgeoning throughout the country, although, ironically, the motive force behind it was a man whose interest was probably as much commercial as ideological. At the beginning of the century, Edward G. Lewis was the successful publisher of several magazines and even a daily newspaper, the *Woman's National Daily,* for women. In 1908 Lewis announced the formation of the American Woman's League, which, he thought, could increase his business and at the same time uplift women by, among other things, helping them win the right to vote. Under his plan a woman (or a man, for that matter) could join the League by selling $52 worth of subscriptions to his publications. The proceeds would be split: half would go to the publications operation, and half to the League.

An extraordinary feature of Lewis's plan was the building of chapter houses for the local league chapters. A chapter could qualify for one of five classes of chapter houses based on local membership, which in turn was a function of newspaper and magazine sales. Records indicate that at least 180 of the League's more than 1,000 chapters qualified for houses and at least thirty-eight houses were built. The fact that many qualifying chapters never received their promised buildings seems to reflect the financial straits in which Lewis, a wheeler-dealer often deeply in debt, periodically found himself.[124] But the plan attracted much interest; Lewis claimed in 1910 that the League had nearly one hundred thousand members, which would have made it one of the most substantial women's organizations of its day.[125]

Meanwhile, to prepare women for their liberated collective future, Lewis in 1906 had chartered a large tract of land he owned just west of St. Louis as University City and there began to build a People's University. Several grandiose buildings were erected to house his publications and the courses of the university, the main component of which was an Art Academy. Lewis hired a distinguished art faculty and offered courses by correspondence as well as in residence. The Art Academy evolved into the University City Pottery Works, which became a major American center for art pottery.[126] Several of the impressive buildings still survive, including the former Woman's Magazine Building that is now the city hall of University City (the city's name has survived, although the school did not).

In 1912 the League was reorganized as the American Woman's Republic, which promulgated a Declaration of Equal Rights, and it was here that the movement became communal. The Republic would be a separate nation for women in which they would have the vote denied them in the United States; when the United States finally granted suffrage, the Woman's Republic would reunite with the rest of the country. The Republic was headed by Lewis's wife, Mabel Wellington Lewis, and soon after the grand events of the Republic's founding, the president and her husband set out to find a location for a cooperative colony dedicated to women's rights. Later that year Lewis purchased a California estate called Rancho Atascadero. Official founding ceremonies were held on July 4, 1913, and colonists began to purchase lots and build homes. During World War I the colony prospered, its economy based largely on a dehydrated food products company that secured wartime government production contracts. The women steadfastly worked at creating their model women's nation, adopting a flag (with six stars, representing the states in which women had by then achieved full voting rights) and even opening at least one foreign consulate, in Scotland. The population grew steadily, eventually reaching up into the thousands, female and male. After the adoption of the Nineteenth Amendment, the Republic faded away as planned, and Atascadero became another booming California city.[127]

Helicon Home Colony. Upton Sinclair lived his long life as a thoroughgoing utopian, and it should surprise no one that in his quest for a better society he dabbled in communitarianism. The experiment to which his name is indelibly wedded was the Helicon Home Colony, or Helicon Hall, which attracted much attention in its tragically short five months of life.

Sinclair became a socialist early in life and rejected bourgeois comforts to write novels that promoted his ideas. As a voracious reader of socialist literature Sinclair became familiar with the work of Charlotte Perkins Gilman, who sought ways to liberate women from their onerous domestic responsibilities, and Gilman's theories about the rationalization and minimization of housework led directly to the Helicon colony,[128] even though Gilman herself rejected this specific application of her ideas.[129]

What made the experiment possible was *The Jungle.* This most influential of the plethora of reformist and muckraking novels of the progressive era excoriated the revolting villainy of the meatpacking industry, becoming an instant best-seller and inspiring governmental oversight of the packinghouses. The book's success also brought the previously impecunious Sinclair and his family some real income, enough to pursue his dream of establishing an intentional community. In June 1906 Sinclair published the manifesto for his colony in the influential intellectual magazine *The Independent,* outlining the physical facilities and options for living that the new colony would have.[130] The colony would be democratically governed and would provide comfortable, even elegant, living for professionals and intellectuals at a fraction of the cost of single-family housing. Common child care and meal service would be especially attractive features of the colony.

Sinclair had no trouble attracting applicants, and more than seventy-five persons in all lived at Helicon.[131] A fair contingent consisted of writers, one of them the young Sinclair Lewis. Soon they found a property ideal for their purposes—Helicon Hall, a large building that had housed a private boys school in Englewood, New Jersey, just across the Hudson from Manhattan. It had extravagant amenities, including an indoor swimming pool and a pipe organ, and sat on nine and a half acres. The aspiring colonists purchased it all for $36,000.

The members generally remembered Helicon life as mostly positive. The predictable clashes of strong personalities were there; life was easy in part because the colony hired domestic help. Dinner, especially, was the scene of elevated conversations, and well into the evening colonists gathered around the massive fireplace for camaraderie. Among the legions of guests were many renowned political and intellectual figures of the day: Emma Goldman, William James, Lincoln Steffens, John Dewey. Like intentional communities everywhere, the experiment caused raised eyebrows in its own neighborhood, in this case an upscale suburb; rumors, quite unjustified, that Helicon was a nest of free lovers circulated widely. The New York press was largely caustic and baiting in its steady coverage of the situation at Helicon, which flabbergasted the perhaps naive Sinclair:

It was generally taken for granted, among the newspapermen of New York, that the purpose for which I had started this colony was to have plenty of mistresses handy. They wrote us up on that basis—not in plain words, for that would have been libel—but by innuendo easily understood. So it was with our Socialist colony as with the old-time New England colonies—there were Indians hiding in the bushes, seeking to pierce us with sharp arrows of wit. Reporters came in disguise, and went off and wrote false reports; others came as guests, and went off and ridiculed us because we had beans for lunch.[132]

What might have happened in the long run can only be guessed. At 3:00 in the morning on March 16, 1907, a fire destroyed the building, killing one person and leaving the rest homeless. Sinclair and several other members for several months insisted that the fire was only a temporary setback, that the colony would be reconstituted elsewhere. But no such plan ever came close to fruition, in part because the insurers of the property were less than forthcoming in compensating the Heliconites for their loss.[133] The property was finally sold for residential development in the summer of 1908. Helicon Hall had taken its place as an unusual chapter in the American communitarian tradition.[134]

Sinclair rued the fact that the experiment had ended. As he reflected a dozen years later,

I look back on Helicon Hall to-day, and this is the way I feel about it. I have lived in the future; I have known those wider freedoms and opportunities that the future will grant to all men and women. Now by harsh fate I have been seized and dragged back into a lower order of existence, and commanded to spend the balance of my days therein. I know that the command is irrevocable, and I make the best of my fate—I manage to keep cheerful, and to do my appointed task; but nothing can alter the fact in my own mind—I have lived in the future, and all things about me seem drab and sordid in comparison. I feel as you would feel if you were suddenly taken back to the days when there was no plumbing and when people used perfume instead of soap.[135]

The Altruist Community. Few idealists were as committed to intentional community as Alcander Longley, and few had less success at establishing flourishing, enduring actual communities. Inspired by the Fourierist phalanxes and other utopian colonies of his youth (he was involved with the North American Phalanx in New Jersey from 1852 to 1854, and with the Icarians in Iowa briefly in 1867), he began opening intentional communities in 1868, eventually founding five communes at as many locations in Missouri: the Reunion, Friendship, Principia, Mutual Aid, and Altruist communities. Most of the scholarship on Longley focuses on the earlier groups, but at least sketchy information is available on his last gasp, the Altruist Community, founded in 1907. A 1908 report says that the Altruists owned eight and a half acres near Sulfur Springs and were engaged in gardening and a poultry business, and that they also maintained a headquarters in St. Louis.[136] One surmises that Longley was experiencing devolution of fortune; three and a half decades earlier his second community had 280 acres and a greater air of prosperity than can be discerned at the Altruist.[137] He had certainly been productive as a propagandist, publishing hefty tomes advocating the collective lifestyle, not to mention phonetic spelling, speed writing, and new systems of musical notation.[138] He was excellent at writing manifestos, lists of rights and obligations of members, and constitutions and bylaws. He was not apparently so skilled, however, at working with people; none of his communities had been large, and the Altruist Community, the "smallest and most pathetic of his many utopian ventures," as historian H. Roger Grant puts it, went virtually nowhere.[139] A rare extant account of the actual circumstances of the community depicted it as consisting of "himself and an elderly woman stricken with paralysis and rheumatism, bed-ridden but enthusiastic." She and Longley lived in "an ancient weather-boarded house of two rooms, one upstairs, one down."[140]

The Farm (Massachusetts). The story of the Christian Commonwealth Colony, the idealistic social gospel commune that collapsed amid poverty, illness, and death, was recounted earlier. A few years after its demise, however, its guiding light, the Congregational minister Ralph Albertson, surfaced as the central figure in another intentional community, this time one that grew up almost accidentally and without a specific religious focus, although Albertson's Christian reformist outlook colored his whole life.

In 1909 he and his second wife, Hazel, purchased a run-down old farmhouse in West Newburyport, Massachusetts, on the Merrimack River. Others quickly joined them—many just to visit, but some to live. Whatever the status of the residents at any given moment, the house was full much of the time. Among the visitors and short-term residents in the early years were Walter Lippman (then a Harvard student), Lincoln Steffens, and dozens of less prominent but creative persons. Albertson, ever the thoroughgoing altruist, never tried to make the others pay anything like a fair share of the expenses, and as a result spent his life in debt.

The idyll dwindled somewhat over the years. Ralph Albertson, never able to confine his affections to a single woman, eventually left Hazel and moved to New York. Hazel kept the place together somehow, and by the 1940s a younger generation of residents who had grown up on the Farm (the place always had a full contingent of children) returned and kept the loose community alive. And thus things went, quietly, for many more years. As late as the 1980s, at least, some with long-standing ties to the Farm were still living there, and others were frequent visitors.[141] An informal and thoroughly obscure bit of the history of the communitarian spirit had turned into one of the longest-lasting communities of all.[142]

How many more? Any survey of intentional communities in any age is bound to be incomplete. Many groups deliberately shunned publicity for a variety of reasons—they did not want to become magnets for cranks and misfits, or they did not want their neighbors to know much about their beliefs and practices, or they simply rejected the decadence of majoritarian society. Others were not so reclusive, perhaps, but records about them are fragmentary or nonexistent. There seems, for example, to have been a Gibbs Co-Operative Colony founded by one A. W. J. Gibbs that was substantial and long-lived enough to have had several buildings in 1901 and to have changed its focus from agriculture to operating a summer resort in 1903, but that closed in 1906 or earlier, considered a "rank failure" by its founder, who was disgusted at the unwillingness of some members to work hard. However, little else, including the colony's location, is known.[143] One can only wonder just how extensive the communal presence was at any given point in American history.

For that matter, communal dreaming has vastly exceeded communal actuality. For every community founded there were undoubtedly dozens envisioned. In 1907 and 1908 the freethought magazine *To-Morrow* published a feature entitled "Bureau of Group Organization" that listed "cooperative and group movements." The lists were not comprehensive (the Shakers, for example, then still quite alive, did not appear on the earlier ones) and not entirely accurate (there is a listing for Martha McVister of Washington, D.C., throughout the run; surely the reference means Martha McWhirter of the Woman's Commonwealth). However, every month dozens of groups were listed as active. Many well-known communities were named (the Amana Society, Freedom Colony, Helicon Hall, Home, the Koreshan Unity, the Roycrofters, Ruskin, and others), but there were even more whose places in history are obscure, at least. There seems to be little independent documentation of the Beacon Company of Aberdeen, South Dakota, or the Alamo Colony of Bonners Ferry, Idaho. Other listed groups were not communities but organizations working for certain progressive causes (the Chicago-based Right Relationship League, one of those listed, promoted the establishment of cooperative retail stores, for example). Quite a few (the Bureau of Helpfulness of Collinwood, Ohio, the Materialist Association of Brooklyn, and the University of the People of Chicago, to name only three) would seem to be, perhaps, study groups at best, for they do not turn up elsewhere in the historical record. But ultimately, the lists, which typically contained names of about fifty organizations, demonstrate the existence of much communal energy, in both talk and action, early in the century.[144]

4

The Quiet Twenties and the Roaring Thirties

Little organizing of communes seems to have taken place during the War to End War or in the decade or so after it. Although such established groups as the Hutterites, by now almost exclusively in Canada, continued their isolated proliferation, only a handful of new communes saw the light of day before the depression. Thus the communal story of the 1920s consists more of the ongoing activity of existing communes than of the founding of new ones. When new communities did crop up, they often did so in the context of commitment to a special mission, most frequently a religious or educational one.

The 1930s, on the other hand, saw hundreds of new communities emerge, many of them the fruit of government depression-fighting programs. In addition, the socialists, anarchists, cranks, visionaries, and other idealists who had started up so many communal settlements in the American past had not entirely disappeared from the scene and continued to make their contribution to the fabric of community. As ever before, intentional communities were centers of political agitation, social reformism, the creation of art, and cooperative homesteading. Thus the 1920s and 1930s taken together made a solid contribution to the progress of the communitarian ideal in America.

Communal Colleges

Many intentional communities have dedicated themselves to one mission or another, and for several that mission has been education. Innovative educational institutions go back in American communal history at least to Robert Owen's New Harmony, where progressive pedagogical experiments were considered central to the community's reason for existence. Most experimental communal educational ventures have been at the grammar school and high school levels, but an occasional college has emerged as well, two of the most important of them in the 1920s and 1930s. For both Black Mountain College and Commonwealth College communal operation was essential, both because community embodied the colleges' vision of egalitarian sharing and because resources with which to pay real salaries were not available, hence all involved were forced to live equally and simply. Intentional community and politically radical education have a natural affinity for each other, and communal education has often been held up as ideal by American socialists and other progressives and activists. The colleges considered here were neither the first nor the last experiments in communal higher education.

Many dreams of community-based education were never brought to fruition, and some that did get under way were short-lived. The Ruskin Colony, for example, envisioned a cooperative institution of higher education to be called the College of the New Economy, designed a grand building to house it, and raised money to start it, money that was somehow diverted into other projects after the laying of a cornerstone.[1] But the Ruskin spirit did eventually get embodied in a college, as we have seen in an earlier chapter, when former members of the Ruskin Colony and others launched Ruskin College at Ruskin, Florida, as the educational institution of the Christian Socialist Guild. The college enjoyed modest success, attracting some eighty students, although it met a premature demise when its largely pacifist student body scattered when America entered World War I. The vision, however, was not to die.

COMMONWEALTH COLLEGE

Perhaps the most significant experiment in communal socialist collegiate education came a few years after the collapse of Ruskin College with the opening of Commonwealth College, a communal institution founded at Newllano Colony in 1923 that lasted until it was demolished by anticommunist zealots in 1940.[2]

The year 1923 saw the arrival of several new socialist settlers at New-llano, among them educator William E. Zeuch and prominent socialist publisher Kate O'Hare, both of whom had been at Ruskin College and wanted to continue the kind of alternative education that had been conducted there. Their mission was clear: Commonwealth was established to produce labor leaders from the working class. The Commonwealth founders had a breadth of vision that embodied a great respect for individual and academic freedoms, and the college in its early years shunned any single ideological model, despite its prevailing socialist orientation. As an early pamphlet explained,

Commonwealth College is not a propaganda school. It holds no brief for any religious, political, or economic dogma. Its aim is to develop personality and the power for leadership among the sons and daughters of workers. . . . Commonwealth will attempt to make evident to its students that dogmas are a positive menace to a dynamic, progressive world, and help them to realize that intelligent experimentation carries the only hope of adjustment or solution of our personal and social problems.[3]

The original agreement between the educators and the other colonists specified that the students would work half days for the colony and in return be supported as the rest of the colonists were. But friction arose between the financially strapped colony and the backers of an ambitious college program, and within a year the college was seeking its own campus. By the spring of 1925, Zeuch, the college's first director, had settled on a tract in the Ozarks west of Mena, Arkansas. The original 80 acres (later increased to 320) had a few simple buildings and some overtilled but potentially useful farmland.[4]

The students and faculty at Commonwealth College had, predictably, diverse interests and commitments that ranged from organic food to the promotion of Esperanto. They all agreed, however, that education was the key to the improvement of the common people of America and that cooperation should supplant competition. They farmed, built buildings, cooked and ate meals, and studied together, with classes in the morning and work after lunch. They communicated with their larger circle of supporters through the *Commonwealth College Fortnightly*. Financially, the college was always extremely lean; faculty and staff members were not paid, but lived in communal equality with the students and put in the same twenty to twenty-four hours per week of manual labor that the students did. Despite the reigning poverty and high-demand life, most of those who taught and studied at Commonwealth found it a stimulating intellectual experience in a beautiful natural setting. The library was surprisingly solid, considering that it, like the rest of the campus, essentially had no budget.[5] The college attracted several prominent trustees, faculty members, and students, among them novelist Upton Sinclair, civil libertarian Roger Baldwin (both trustees), poet Kenneth Patchen (student), folk singer Lee Hays (faculty member), and Orval Faubus (student and the son of a longtime Arkansas socialist who was to become famous as the 1950s Arkansas governor who resisted integration of the state's public schools). The student body never numbered more than fifty-five, but Commonwealth became a noted center of leftist thought and action.[6]

The Commonwealthers were careful not to offend southern sensibilities unnecessarily, keeping African Americans, for example, away from the campus, and relations with their neighbors and other Arkansans were at first reasonably good. A nice guest house was built and made available to all visitors. Nevertheless, the campus was undeniably a radical place. As early as 1926, shortly after the campus had been established at Mena, the state American Legion chapter demanded that the state shut the college down, proclaiming that Commonwealth was receiving money from the Wobblies and from Russia and teaching "bolshevism, sovietism, communism, and freelove."[7]

The college managed to shrug off those early hostilities, but by the 1930s the campus situation had changed and outside pressure mounted accordingly. Under Zeuch the campus had exuded a freewheeling, nondoctrinaire atmosphere and was dedicated to true academic freedom, but Zeuch was deposed while away from the campus in 1931 and replaced with the more militant Lucien Koch, under whose leadership members of the campus community became directly involved in depression-era labor struggles. Koch in turn was replaced by Richard Whitten in 1935, and the college moved yet further from its earlier liberal diversity toward identification with the Communist Party.

By 1935 the state was investigating Commonwealth in earnest, and 1936 saw vicious, ill-informed attacks on the college by several Arkansas preachers. A sedition bill aimed at Commonwealth was introduced in the legislature in 1937.[8] The end came in 1940, when the college was convicted of such "crimes" as failing to display an American flag. Commonwealth College was finished. Its livestock, land, buildings, and even the impressive library were auctioned to pay the fine the court had levied.

BLACK MOUNTAIN COLLEGE

While Commonwealth College was clinging tenuously to life in Arkansas, another experiment in higher education dedicated to the common life—and one even more poverty-stricken than Commonwealth—was inaugurated in North Carolina. John A. Rice, a young and iconoclastic professor, had been fired from the faculty of Rollins College in Florida for his unconventional behavior. Casting about for ways to do truly unconventional teaching, he, joined by a group consisting largely of other Rollins dissidents, rented the facilities, including several good buildings, of the Blue Ridge Assembly, a Baptist camp association that used the premises only during the summer. (In 1941 the college moved a few miles, across the valley to Lake Eden, to a campus it had managed to purchase in the meantime.) After a few frantic months of raising a pitifully small bit of money and recruiting students, Rice and his comrades opened the college doors in the fall of 1933.[9]

A vision of cooperation was present at Black Mountain College from the beginning, but in any event stark economic necessity dictated that poverty would be the common lot of students and faculty alike. In the beginning the faculty members received nothing but room and board. Thereafter they did manage to earn a pittance, which two years later had advanced to an average of a miserable $819 per year. As Martin Duberman, the foremost historian of Black Mountain, has put it, "The guiding principle had to be modified Marx: from each according to his ability, to each according to his (bare) needs."[10] Individual assets and incomes were not pooled, but it was made clear that a person's economic status had nothing to do with his or her standing in the community of scholars. Students had to pay tuition, but scholarships and work opportunities were always available. And sharing went well beyond economics: students were guaranteed the right to form their own student government, its chief executive receiving a seat on the college's Board of Fellows; all records of the corporation were declared open; students were invited to sit in on faculty meetings and on administrative committees; all shared in the physical maintenance of the campus as well as the work of the sideline businesses, including a dairy farm and a timber operation, that helped finance the venture. A vigorous social life—music and dancing were daily pastimes—in this college colony of artists also provided social glue. Eric Bentley, who taught there for a time, reported that life at Black Mountain has much to commend it, especially in its omissions. There are no organized sports, no fraternities or sororities, none of those institutions or *mores* that on so many campuses serve to prolong adolescence and fortify Philistinism. . . . Black Mountain knows few hard-drinking, hard-whoring, jaloppy-driving hearties and even fewer giggling, over-painted, movie-starrish, jitter-bugging girls who spend the week waiting for Saturday night. The Black Mountain "way of life" is a way of endless activity scheduled morning, afternoon, and evening, weekday and weekend. Instead of sports there is farmwork, maintenance work, building, typing, entertaining. These things go on every afternoon, and in the evenings a steady stream of lectures, concerts and meetings takes place.[11]

Communal equality was simply a necessary means to Black Mountain's end of creative, undoctrinaire education in a setting in which learning would not be separated from living. And for that it became deservedly famous. Several who were, or would become, leading cultural lights of the twentieth century taught or studied there, among them John Cage, Robert Creeley, Merce Cunningham, Anaïs Nin, Alfred Kazin, Willem de Kooning, Robert Motherwell, Charles Olson, Paul Goodman, Robert Rauschenberg, and Buckminster Fuller (whose students helped him construct the first geodesic dome there). Campus visitors were similarly distinguished—John Dewey, Thornton Wilder, Fernand Léger, Henry Miller, Aldous Huxley, Walter Gropius. Some of the distinguished visitors ended up providing more than inspirational words for the college; Gropius, for example, joined the team that designed a complex of buildings for the new campus to which the college moved in 1941. As a center for cutting-edge art and literature Black Mountain became, deservedly, a legend in and after its own time.[12]

The big names were only icing on the cake. As erstwhile student Fielding Dawson wrote in later years, "The list of famous names of students and faculty (that I am sick of), gives a false—wrong—impression, that leaves, however, a lasting mark. Too bad, because there were all kinds of people there."[13] Black Mountain was definitely a college, one with a wide range of offerings outside the arts; standard educational achievement was substantial enough that, according to one survey, most Black Mountain alumni earned advanced degrees, and many ended up teaching in other colleges.[14] Several alumni credit their artistic success to their work at Black Mountain, as in the case of Francine du Plessix Gray, who studied there for two invigorating summers under Olson.[15] Although students were not given letter grades for their course work, to graduate they had to pass comprehensive examinations administered by outside examiners.[16] Dawson again:

We had to go to classes or face the wrath of the teacher: there wasn't any kidding around. The other prevailing faculty attitude was if you missed class fuck you—classes were tough, we couldn't miss them—homework, heavy as it was, then doubled . . . it may have been free of academic rules and regulations, but that made it worse, the whole burden on us, and the faculty maybe getting plastered with us the night before no matter, we had to produce.[17]

Black Mountain was a community of free spirits and of artists; especially in its last few years, when student count was down but creativity greatly valued, it resembled the artists' communities that had flourished earlier in the century. As one might guess, the rude, anarchic atmosphere of the campus, the eccentricity of many members of the community, and Black Mountain's endemic economic poverty for some residents quite thoroughly overcame the sense of history making and ecstasy that has dominated the written memories of many who were there: Mildred Harding, a faculty wife for a year in the 1950s, for example, later published a memoir that depicts life at Black Mountain as grim, chaotic, and filled with serious privation.[18] In any event, declining numbers of students and faculty members and an ever-larger financial crisis finally caused the college to close in the fall of 1956.[19]

An Early Feminist Commune: Community House

Small, inconspicuous urban communal dwellings have long been a mainstay, and an underappreciated one, of the American scene. One commune of women that has only recently been exhumed by the scholarly world was founded in 1921 in New York City and provided housing and an organizing base for a population of radical women that averaged more than half a dozen. The group, spearheaded by Anna Rochester and Grace Hutchins, referred to itself tongue-in-cheek as the "Sisterhood of the Smiling Countenance and the Merry Laugh," but was more commonly called "Community House" or simply "352" for its location at 352 West Twenty-seventh Street. The leftist reformers and writers who lived at 352 apparently spent about three years in their communal household, which appears to have disintegrated in 1924, and thus anticipated the wave of feminist communes of the 1970s by half a century.[20]

The Depression Era: Fighting Poverty Communally

Although the 1920s saw little communal organizing, a veritable wave of cooperative living washed over the country as the depression settled in, forcing the rural poor, especially, to find new ways to supply life's basic necessities. Michael Barkun has declared the 1930s one of the cyclical high points of communal activity in America, with hundreds of ventures founded, many of them with the assistance of the New Deal.[21] Many cooperative and communal projects grew directly from hard times, offering the hope of a decent future to individuals and families whose outlook was inescapably bleak. Others held up a model of social justice as well—several communities were influenced by the new wave of Christian socialism that arose in the 1930s—and specifically, in a few cases, promoted racial equality through interracial communal living, thus helping cultivate the ground for the civil rights movement two decades later.

RALPH BORSODI AND THE SCHOOL OF LIVING

In the 1920s and 1930s a new version of small-scale subsistence farming in colonies appeared with the work of Ralph Borsodi, who preached self-sufficiency for families living in focused communities with adjacent leased homes on commonly owned property—a concept reminiscent of the earlier work of George Littlefield, William Smythe, and others—and who worked harder than anyone else to put that vision into practice. Borsodi's first public impact was as a strong critic of American culture, but as his thought developed he began to advocate decentralization and self-sufficiency as elements of a solution to the growing problems of industrial society. The most influential force on him in his early life was single-tax thought; soon after he met Bolton Hall, the single taxer and self-sufficiency booster who founded the Free Acres enclave in New Jersey, he was dreaming dreams of his own small homestead. (Borsodi later distanced himself from pure single-tax doctrine, however, concluding that if applied in rural areas it would tend to force farmers toward high-level production rather than small-scale self-sufficiency.[22])

Borsodi represented one element in the broad decentralist movement of the 1930s. Other elements included the Nashville agrarians who published their manifesto *I'll Take My Stand*[23] in 1930, proclaiming their desire to keep northern industrial influences out of the South; persons involved in the Catholic Rural Life Movement, whose Jeffersonian agrarianism was buttressed by papal social teachings[24]; and the associates of Herbert Agar, who coauthored the decentralist manifesto *Who Owns America? A New Declaration of Independence*[25] and thereafter, from 1937 to 1946, edited the journal *Free America* (which Borsodi had helped him found), a back-to-the-land sheet that in some respects played a social role much like that played three or four decades later by *The Mother Earth News*.[26] Most of the American decentralists were influenced to a fair degree by the English Catholic distributists, notably Hilaire Belloc and G. K. Chesterton, who wanted to reestablish a preindustrial society that would embody tradition- al religious values. At first they tended to be supporters of Franklin D. Roosevelt's New Deal. By the mid-1930s many had judged it too moder- ate in its goals and programs, and in several cases believed that getting in- volved with the government in a program was tantamount to stepping into a swamp.[27]

In 1920 Borsodi and his wife, Myrtle Mae Borsodi, had their rented house in the city sold out from under them, and instead of looking for an- other rental left Manhattan for a seven-acre tract near Suffern, New York, with a small, older house and some outbuildings and fruit trees where they raised food, including animals, and made as much of what they con- sumed as possible—using, wherever they could, up-to-date machinery that would make their physical tasks relatively simple. Borsodi ever after- ward argued that that kind of life brought immense satisfaction.

In 1929 Borsodi published *This Ugly Civilization*, a stinging critique of American society and its factory-based economy.[28] Four years later he offered the beginnings of a solution to it all with *Flight from the City*, the story of his family's venture into "creative living on the land" at Suffern. If others would only follow in the Borsodis' footsteps, the social result would be nothing less than revolutionary:

Domestic production, if enough people turned to it, would not only annihilate the undesirable and nonessential factory by depriving it of a market for its products. It would do more. It would release men and women from their present thralldom to the factory and make them masters of machines instead of servants to them; it would end the power of exploiting them which ruthless, acquisitive, and predatory men now possess; it would free them for the conquest of comfort, beauty and understanding. [29]

In 1933 the city of Dayton, Ohio, invited Borsodi to start a demonstra- tion project for his ideas. The way had been paved the previous year with the organization of a series of "Cooperative Production Units," urban buildings in which groups cooperated to produce food, clothing, and oth- er basics, bartering their excess with other units and exchanging their products for raw materials. The dozen or so units involved between 350 and 500 families. But members of the coordinating agency overseeing the units sought to expand their program to include land colonization, and to that end brought Borsodi in as a consultant.[30] He quickly persuaded local leaders to support a Liberty Homesteads (sometimes called Dayton Homesteads) project, which was envisioned as ultimately encompassing two thousand or more families on tracts of three or so acres each. It began with the purchase of a 160-acre farm; several residents quickly moved into temporary housing (the original brick farmhouse plus several outbuildings) and some began to construct permanent residences on their homesteads. In all the Borsodi projects, land would be leased, not owned, by the occupants, to deter price speculation.

However grand its intentions, the project soon ran into serious difficulties. The temporary housing was unsatisfactory, and progress toward completion of permanent structures was slow. Some residents gardened on their plots, but the plans for rammed-earth houses turned out to be impractical, and no homes were finished during the first summer. Fundamentally problematic was the failure of Borsodi's plan for financing the project through the sale of "Independence Bonds" to small local investors. Faced with impossible financial circumstances, project leaders decided to seek federal money appropriated by the National Industrial Recovery Act, and Borsodi's work to secure that support at first appeared promising. No lack of vision afflicted Borsodi: his plan was to develop dozens of cooperative homestead projects for thousands of families, and he ended up seeking millions of dollars from Washington.

Before the money had finally been secured, problems erupted. Persons living near some of the planned projects began to complain about an influx of residents who would cause taxes to increase and overcrowd the schools. More important, a weekly paper in Dayton undertook a crusade against the homesteads, accusing Borsodi of hypocrisy, misrepresentation of facts, cronyism, promoting racial integration, financial chicanery, and, ultimately, dictatorship. The external complaints were mirrored by internal dissent; some residents accused Borsodi of domineering tactics that destroyed the freedoms of residents, and internal bickering grew apace. Finally, in May 1934 the secretary of the interior, Harold L. Ickes, in whose bailiwick the Division of Subsistence Homesteads, the federal funding agency, resided, simply federalized all subsistence homestead projects, in effect kicking Borsodi out.[31] As a community of small, self-sufficient producer/consumers, Liberty Homesteads ground to a halt, and by early 1936 the last homesteading families had departed.[32] The episode permanently sealed Borsodi's antipathy toward governmental solutions to social problems, and through the rest of the depression he remained convinced that small homesteads in cooperative settings would do far more to solve the country's economic and social problems than all the New Deal programs together ever would.

Even though Borsodi became vehemently opposed to any kind of federal control of decentralization projects, he did not lose his drive or breadth of vision. His ideas became more sweeping; he proposed a whole new kind of education that would prepare people for the way of living he saw as necessary for escaping the jungle of urban industrial civilization. As he wrote in 1935,

In the school of living, as I conceive it, there will be no sharp separation of life from reading and discussion. Each practical problem as it comes up from day to day will lead the student inevitably to the accumulated wisdom of the ages in an effort to solve that problem most intelligently. Reading will not be an exercise; it will be an integral part of the living process. If in the course of trying to find the best answer to the question, "Why does bread made with whole wheat flour fail to rise in the same way as that made with white flour?" one is inadvertently betrayed into the study of the whole question of nutrition and the chemistry of foods, it will be a fortunate but, in such a way of living, an inevitable accident.[33]

The school itself would consist of a cluster of "charming homes," residences with integral studios and workshops. Teachers—experts in the various practical arts of living—would help those learning new ways of living. Ultimately, those who had made great progress would go forth to establish similar schools elsewhere. And so would the human race be reoriented.[34]

In 1936 Borsodi started, according to the model he had outlined and without government assistance, his School of Living, and with it a private community of sixteen leased two-acre homesteads plus several acres of common land, known as Bayard Lane, near his homestead at Suffern. The school taught a wide range of practical skills—from weaving to carpentry to food storage—useful to the small-acreage homesteader, and also taught the larger Borsodi philosophy. A parallel organization, the Independence Foundation, was formed to help depression-era would-be homesteaders purchase their plots and buy materials for getting started in the business of self-sufficiency; its role was crucial, for credit was hard to come by and in any event banks were hesitant to lend money for an unconventional project, especially one in which homeowners did not have fee-simple title to the land on which their houses sat. Soon another homestead community followed, Van Houten Fields at West Nyack, New York, along with various cooperative support groups, such as purchasing clubs and bartering associations. Still others were planned (at Ringwood, New Jersey, for example, and in northern Westchester County, New York), although some of them apparently never got completely off the ground.[35] Even the capitalist *Fortune* magazine was impressed with Borsodi's achievements, marveling in 1938 at the plan that enabled urban refugees to obtain land at a third what it would cost in a subdivision and build homes at 10 to 15 percent less than prevailing prices.[36] Construction costs were low because Borsodi persuaded workers to accept lower-than-normal wages in return for guaranteed year-round work; the workers nevertheless made more money in a year than those who worked in the normal cyclical pattern.[37]

Borsodi's strong personality endured, and the conflicts that first appeared at Dayton were replayed from time to time—indeed, would recur throughout his life. There was major blowup in 1940 involving the Independence Foundation. Some homesteaders revolted against Borsodi, claiming that they were being made to help pay for the School of Living's research and teaching activities as well as for their land and homes, and that at any rate Borsodi was simply too heavy-handed an administrator. As a result of that fracas, he withdrew from the administration of the Foundation.[38] The following year he resigned as director of the School of Living as well.[39]

Despite Borsodi's emphasis on interdependence within the communities of homesteaders, privatist sentiments were strong among settlers who, after all, had their roots in an individualistic American society whose citizens virtually defined their worth in private property ownership. Against Borsodi's wishes they switched both Bayard Lane and Van Houten Fields from cooperative leasehold ownership to privately deeded plots. At that time the American factory system was gearing up to fight a mighty war, and few believed that decentralism could contribute much to smashing the Axis powers.[40] The land-ownership controversy, the war, and Myrtle Mae Borsodi's battle with cancer combined to force the Borsodis to sell the school property to one of the homesteaders in 1945.[41]

After the war, however, the work was picked up again under new leadership, that of Mildred Loomis, who opened a new School of Living at the Loomis Lane's End Homestead near Brookville, Ohio. Loomis's work eventually became a major link between communal generations, providing continuity between the depression-era experiments and the new communitarianism of the hippies, and as such it will be described in more detail in the successor volume to this one. Borsodi's influence also continued through other channels. Among the many visitors to Bayard Lane, for example, were J. I. and Robert Rodale in 1940; they were stimulated by the Borsodi family's self-sufficiency as well as its commitment to organic farming techniques and its healthy diet. The Rodale magazines *Prevention* and *Organic Gardening* (founded in 1948 and 1953 respectively) spread the decentralist message much farther than Borsodi had ever managed to.[42]

The early-twentieth-century's fascination with clusters of small, self-sufficient holdings melded into communities by a sense of common purpose and extensive sharing amounted to the creation of a new branch of the American communitarian tradition. Some of the basic ideas that emerged from the Borsodi projects and other cooperative homestead ventures survive; many intentional communities today operate as land trusts, each with a hybrid public/private ownership structure and a sense of common purpose, most often one centered in helping preserve the environment and pointing the way toward a sustainable future.

THE GOVERNMENT GETS INVOLVED

Ralph Borsodi may have fought tooth and nail, after his experience in Dayton, to keep decentralized homestead settlements in private hands, but others saw government as the only source of the extensive resources needed to build homestead villages on a wide scale, and in the end the federal government's rural semicommunal resettlement programs were far larger than any private efforts for several depression years. At least twenty-five cooperative group-farming projects, with varying levels and types of communitarian features, were organized between 1937 and 1939 by the Farm Security Administration in the hope that through cooperation and sharing some indigent farmers could at least survive until the economy improved. The FSA farms were in turn part of a larger effort on the part of a variety of New Deal agencies (including the FSA's predecessors, the Division of Subsistence Homesteads and the Resettlement Administration) to establish cooperative agricultural and industrial settlements, garden cities, and other innovative, nonindividualistic approaches to the economic crisis. Depending on how broad one's criteria for inclusion are, one could count in all upward of a hundred residential projects ranging in scope from mildly cooperative to substantially communal.[43]

Federal officials did not invent the idea of government-sponsored farm communities. California, as we have seen, had inaugurated such a program in 1917, when its legislature appropriated $250,000 for the purchase and development of the Durham farm colony, and later expanded it with a $1 million appropriation for a second colony, Delhi. In the end the colonists fell victim to the agricultural depression of the 1920s and to managerial misjudgments, and by 1930, well before the advent of federal colonization programs, the California experiments were history. Nevertheless, when the Great Depression devastated rural America the various land-colony experiments—not only those in California but also such earlier ventures as the Little Landers, Fellowship Farms, and the Borsodi projects—provided models for attempts at saving the day.

LAND COLONIZATION UNDER THE NEW DEAL

The first stirrings of land-colonization sentiment in Washington predated the depression by more than a decade. In 1916 representative Robert Crosser of Ohio introduced a bill that would have paid for the development of a series of cooperative colonies in which families could eke out subsistence livings; the bill never reached the floor of Congress for a vote, but the idea was debated for years afterward.[44] With the arrival of the depression-fighting Franklin D. Roosevelt administration the idea came off the back burner, and the National Industrial Recovery Act, passed by Congress in May 1933, included $25 million for self-sufficient homestead programs. The following month interior secretary Harold Ickes was appointed to head up what soon became the Division of Subsistence Homesteads. Milburn L. Wilson, a prominent agricultural economist who had been promoting the concept for years, was put in charge, and plans were drawn up for forming several types of rural colonies that would typically involve twenty-five to a hundred families on one to five acres, each working toward cooperative self-sufficiency. The first loan went to Ralph Borsodi for his Liberty Homesteads project in Dayton. The second was for a community for "stranded" coal miners (so called because they had been left stranded, jobless, when their mines closed) called Arthurdale near Morgantown, West Virginia. Several others soon followed. In the less than a year that Wilson presided over the program, some thirty-one projects were authorized.[45] Times were heady; Wilson was certain that the group-settlement concept would prove to be enormously successful, a red-letter entry in the list of communal and cooperative settlements in American history.[46]

Just as the Subsistence Homesteads program was being cranked up, the Federal Emergency Relief Administration became the second New Deal agency to undertake the development of cooperative colonies. The agency began to work out its plans in 1933, and in the following January a group of farmers who had gone on relief began to build Woodlake, a colony designed for a hundred families north of Houston. There each family received a three-acre subsistence plot with a house and outbuildings and a share in one of two large cooperative farms. By the time the FERA homestead program was taken over by the new Resettlement Administration in May 1935, about twenty-five communities had been started or planned.[47]

The largest of the New Deal government colonization programs was that of the Resettlement Administration, which upon its founding in 1935 took over the Division of Subsistence Homesteads. The Resettlement Administration was headed by Rexford G. Tugwell, one of the most controversial of the leaders of the New Deal. Tugwell, a sometime critic of capitalism itself and a firm believer in collective enterprise, oversaw assistance to cooperative industries, cooperative farms, greenbelt cities, and other kindred projects with a budget enormously larger than the budgets of its predecessor agencies. Although he had some specific reservations about the Subsistence Homesteads program's ability to provide productive employment for colony residents, he did implement the plan vigorously.[48] By June 1937 the Resettlement Administration had opened thirty-eight communities and had eighty-four more under construction. Congressional opposition and other problems, however, kept its successes limited. In September 1937 the RA was absorbed by the new Farm Security Administration, a division of the Department of Agriculture, and the growth phase of the homestead projects was over. The FSA remained committed to cooperatives, but many of the settlements had serious economic problems (the ongoing depression, poor management, members unaccustomed to cooperation, bureaucratic tangles, and other things all contributed to them) as well as continued public and congressional opposition.

Although a basic goal of the RA under Tugwell was the establishment of cooperative industrial enterprises, some resettlement communities met that goal more fully than others. Some colonies never filled up because occupants interested in cooperative projects could not be found. In other cases, however, collectivity was substantial. In Terrebonne Parish, Louisiana, for example, the RA purchased a large sugar cane plantation and turned it into a twenty-eight hundred-acre collective farm. Each of the seventy-one resident families had a six-acre subsistence tract, and collectively they grew cane and truck crops and raised livestock.[49]

As conservative opponents of the New Deal—and of its forthright Rooseveltian liberal advocates and technicians, of whom Tugwell was a prime example—began to increase their presence in Congress after 1936, the communities offered perfect cannon fodder for champions of individualism, some of whom began to attack the FSA farms on the grounds that any kind of cooperation amounted to something close to communism, at that time the most devastating epithet in the American lexicon. Beneath that allegation lay commercial interests interested in stifling competition for their wares. The FSA's goal of trying to lift the poorest farmers was, as Russell Lord has written,

a purpose Thomas Jefferson would surely have understood and backed with all his heart. But big commercial farmers and landlords of the middle 1930s, Democrats or not, were of a different breed and temper. They howled and whined that the whole idea of Farm Security was un-American; that the rehabilitation of the Okies and other migrants was but a misguided impulse of social workers and do-gooders to pamper worthless white trash and run up taxes; that the co-operative farm projects and Subsistence Homestead Colonies were dangerous and Communistic in intent. . . . The big boys argued flatly that even the inconsiderable amounts of garden stuff, milk, eggs, and meat these poorer farms would be led to produce in process of self-aid and a recovery of status in the community might overflow the slender larders of the have-nots and overburden the commercial market—*their* market.[50]

Eventually Congress undertook a major investigation of the FSA, and subsequently the agency's holdings were sold off. The FSA itself was abolished in 1946. As Paul W. Conkin wrote in 1959, "By the time of the Farm Security Administration investigation in 1943, any challenge to the old society was branded as treason, or at least heresy. The renewed popularity of the older, more established institutions doomed the experiments being carried on within many of the New Deal communities."[51] The attacks proved impossible to surmount, and all but one of the communities were liquidated in or soon after 1943. The exception was the Red Banks Mutual Association of Maxton, North Carolina, which was populated by American Indians and had the most thoroughly collective organization, as well as the highest communal spirit, of all the projects and which survived at least into the latter half of the 1950s.[52]

NONGOVERNMENTAL RESETTLEMENT COMMUNITIES
DURING THE DEPRESSION

Penn-Craft. Most communities founded during the depression, private as well as governmental, sought to provide direct assistance to people in dire need. Penn-Craft, founded by Friends (Quakers) in western Pennsylvania, exemplifies this tendency well. Penn-Craft was a resettlement colony of unemployed coal miners near Uniontown, Pennsylvania, named for the state and for the Craft family farm whose land became the community site. It had close ties with Norvelt, a nearby Division of Subsistence Homesteads colony that had been started in 1934, two of whose key managers, Clarence Pickett and David Day, left the government to work on the private Penn-Craft project.[53] The American Friends Service Committee, a leading Quaker charity, raised seed money (including a large gift from the U.S. Steel corporation, the decline of whose mining operations in the area had been a prime source of its economic distress) for the self-help project, and families began moving in in 1937. Penn-Craft would not simply provide its residents with a handout; the carefully selected participants would be given job training and opportunities and would gradually buy their own homes. Much of the two hundred-acre tract was divided up into fifty homesites, and modest stone homes were soon erected. From the beginning the village was cooperative; it had a cooperative store, a knitting mill was opened as the first of what was projected to be a series of cooperative industries, and many clubs, social organizations, and service committees were soon established. Residents worked together to build their houses, using native stone and other materials as much as possible. By most measures it all was a solid success, so much so that in 1946 the sponsoring Friends expanded the project by adding fifteen new homesteads on adjacent land. Although the return of better jobs with World War II undermined the basic point of the community and in essence moved the residents toward private living, Penn-Craft provided a good example of a cooperative route to survival in tough economic times. Half a century later many of the original Penn-Crafters and their descendants still lived in the community.[54]

Delta and Providence. Another private program, again seeking to alleviate rural impoverishment during the depression, was begun in 1936, when several religious leaders, including social activist Sherwood Eddy, theologian Reinhold Niebuhr, and Episcopal bishop William Scarlett of St.

Louis set out to assist black tenant farmers in dire straits—specifically, impoverished sharecroppers in northeast Arkansas who had joined the Southern Tenant Farmers' Union and had been subjected to a reign of terror by planters as a result. They purchased 2,138 acres near Hillhouse, Mississippi, upon which they established Delta Cooperative Farm, an interracial community of twenty-four families who farmed and ran a sawmill. Later a second tract of 2,880 acres was purchased near Cruger, Mississippi, and was named Providence Farm; its major business was dairy farming. Both Delta and Providence were enormously successful in assisting their residents, although they owed most of their economic success to support from northern white liberals. Both projects lasted several years; Delta was eventually sold so that the backers could concentrate on a single enterprise. The demise of Providence came in 1956, after about a year of severe harassment at the hands of local white racists. The Supreme Court decision in *Brown* v. *Board of Education,* directing that public schools be integrated, set off a wave of resistance to integration throughout the South, and threats and intimidation directed at those living at the farm ultimately ended the project.[55]

Diga. One of the most completely communal of the depression relief colonies was founded on the outskirts of San Antonio, Texas, under the leadership of Maury Maverick, the tax collector of Bexar County. As soon as the depression hit, Maverick became active in various protest activities and relief projects. Seeking something more substantial than pleas to Congress for assistance, he persuaded the Humble Oil Company to let him use a thirty-five-acre site for an experimental settlement and then rounded up old railroad cars and salvaged building supplies with which to remodel them into living quarters. Maverick called his project Diga, a backward acronym for Agricultural and Industrial Democracy.

The first settlers, who had been living at a relief camp for military veterans, arrived in November 1932. By January they had remodeled several boxcars into decent living quarters and had established several service businesses, a medical clinic, and a kindergarten. Plans were laid for agricultural and livestock operations to help the colony become self-sufficient.

What distinguished Diga from most other depression-era relief colonies was its rigid economic communalism and social restrictions. All money, including veterans' benefits, had to go into a common fund, and various restrictive rules were promulgated, including one that forbade anyone from speaking negatively of the colony to visitors and another that no one could leave the premises without permission. Such strictures naturally raised the hackles of many residents, and in several cases those who did manage to get some money refused to hand it over to the common purse. Diga provided good food, medical care, and relatively good housing, but those benefits came at a social cost that most residents ultimately found unacceptable. Many voted with their feet; the peak population of 171 in January 1933 dwindled to 86 by August. Two months later the colony was disbanded by fiat of a county official responding to the many complaints members had lodged against Maverick and other colony managers.[56]

The Cooperative Farm. Idealism among college students has generated many experiments in cooperation and community; one of that type, but about which little is known, was the Cooperative Farm, established in 1931 by students and alumni of the University of Oregon. The nine founders (by the beginning of 1933 their number had grown to fourteen) farmed 185 acres, raising truck crops for the Eugene market and grain that the members ground, baked, and sold. For almost two years the Cooperative Farm seems to have been prosperous, and its communitarian features were substantial, with common ownership of the property, a common treasury, and meals at a common table. However, things apparently fell apart by the summer of 1933; all but two members were reported in June to be laying plans to leave, and little news of the project appeared thereafter.[57]

And there were others . . . Other rural communities were similarly established in the hard times of the 1930s; most were small, many were undoubtedly short-lived, and no one has undertaken a comprehensive survey of them. Where their existence is known, information is often sketchy. One intriguing example of a little-known community is Saline Valley Farms, founded in the 1930s by Harold S. Gray in Michigan, which reportedly had sixteen resident families by the end of the decade. Apparently it was economically successful; with prosperity its cooperative features seem to have dropped quietly away.[58] There is probably a hidden grassroots communal history that, were it brought to light, would surprise us all.

Ethnic and Jewish Colonies

At least three colonies founded in the 1920s and 1930s were bound by ethnic ties. The Wayne Produce Association, one of the few communes

founded in the 1920s, was the enterprise of a group of Finnish immigrants. In the following decade two colonies populated mainly by Jews
were inaugurated—both named Sunrise, but not otherwise related and
hundreds of miles apart. Like nearly all communities started in the 1930s,
the two Sunrises were centrally concerned with making life tenable for
their members during hard times.

THE WAYNE PRODUCE ASSOCIATION

In the late nineteenth and early twentieth centuries, several groups of
immigrants from various countries banded together as communal ethnic
entities to make the task of settling in a new land easier. Several English
colonies and the two Bohemian colonies discussed earlier, among others,
fit that pattern. By the 1920s the ethnic cooperative communities were
largely on the decline, but one more emerged early in that decade when a
group of Finns led by Isaac Ahlborg founded a collective settlement on
about eight hundred acres at McKinnon, Georgia. The basic structure involved a land trust arrangement in which members were allotted half-acre
plots of communally owned ground on which to build houses. Members
received cash wages for their work, but all were paid equally at the rate of
$2.50 per day. In 1924 the colony was reported to have about seventy-five
members, a number that counted adult males only, although most of
them had families. The colony appears to have been productive, with
much livestock and crops ranging from cabbage to cauliflower to potatoes. Productivity was enhanced by a membership policy that restricted
admission to able-bodied men between eighteen and forty-five years of
age, and laggards were subject to expulsion.

American immigrant Finns were often a radical lot, and the Wayne
colonists were no exception. Most of the colony members were Communists, Wobblies, or members of the Workers' Party, and the colony was deliberately designed to implement the colonists' convictions about working
for the common good and rejecting private gain. Some members wanted
to abolish wages and strive for even greater equality, but the limited equality of the system under which the colony operated apparently served it
well. Just how long it lasted seems to have gone unrecorded; Ralph Albertson, writing in 1936, included it in a list of then-active communities,
but the material from which he was working may not have been current.[59]

Sunrise (Michigan). The depression-era communes were typically
small, and their life spans varied considerably. One of the more substantial

ones, and certainly among the most colorful, was the Sunrise Co-operative Farm Community, a colony of anarchists at Alicia, Michigan. Joseph
J. Cohen, the principal founder of Sunrise, had been active in the Ferrer
Colony in New Jersey a few years earlier. During the fall and winter of
1932 he put the finishing touches on a new vision of community that
would involve more collectivity than Ferrer had known, with common
ownership of land and tools and communal labor and meals, and began to
promote it among urban Jewish immigrants. By the following year he had
managed to put together a down payment on a nine thousand-acre working farm, and the birth of Sunrise was announced. Many settlers, including a disproportionate number of anarchists and radicals, flocked there
quickly, giving Sunrise three hundred members by its first autumn. The
membership was not restricted to Jews, and indeed a few Gentiles joined,
but culturally Sunrise was always substantially Jewish.

Because Sunrise already had many buildings, schools, a communal
dining room, housing (not enough, as it turned out), and other facilities
were soon in place. Life at the community was a steady counterpoint of
progress and problems. On the positive side, Sunrise had a rich cultural
life, with lectures, musical programs, and a library. The labor force was
well organized into Work Units, each of which had a fair amount of au-
tonomy in developing schedules and procedures. On the negative side,
however, Sunrise suffered problems ranging from several destructive fires
to a shortage of living quarters for the hordes of would-be colonists to a
major dispute over a proposal that Yiddish be the sole language permitted
on the premises. At one point a group of young members proposed to set
up a sort of subcolony in which they would be in charge of their own operations, and when they were rebuffed they left, depriving the colony of
many of its most able workers.[60] Financial programs always dogged the
settlers, and factionalism was a fact of life as early as the first autumn, as
the wide diversity of national backgrounds and political philosophies of
the residents fueled mutual suspicion and endless arguments. Vicious outside agitation against the colony by disillusioned former members soon
took a toll as well.

The problems prevailed, and in 1936 the property was sold to the
Resettlement Administration for use in its rural depression-fighting programs. Despite the problems the community had experienced, many Sun-
risers, including Cohen, stuck by their ideals and purchased a new Sunrise
property, a 642-acre site in Virginia. But interpersonal and financial prob-

lems continued to plague the project. Cohen left in 1938, and the Virginia property was sold in 1940.[61]

Sunrise (New Jersey). The other Sunrise, also predominantly Jewish but comprising a smaller chapter in American communal history than its Michigan counterpart, lived out its three-year life near New York City. Sunrise Co-operative Farms was founded in 1933 near Hightstown, New Jersey, on a thousand acres purchased by a group of Jewish philanthropists intent on resettling poor, urban Jews in farm country. The first settlers were workers from the garment trade; their political and social radicalism set the tone for subsequent settlers, who eventually consisted of about a hundred families.

Sunrise was more seriously cooperative in structure than the earlier Jewish colonies had been. Each family was to have a private home and a one-acre tract for gardening, but all other work—gardening, dairy, light industry—was to be undertaken in common. The first industry was to be, appropriately, a clothing factory, although the record does not indicate whether it functioned or not. In any event, within a few years most of the settlers drifted away and about 1936 the colony was closed. The site, however, had some good communitarian times yet to come: after the Jewish settlers had departed, the property became the location of a Resettlement Administration colony that housed two hundred families and operated a cooperative factory.[62]

Religious Communities in a Time of Breadlines

Not all who entered some kind of communal or cooperative living during the depression of the 1930s did so for purely secular economic reasons on rural subsistence farms. Several communal religious groups (some urban, some rural) appeared as well. In a few cases they embodied a stinging critique of the capitalist system that they saw as responsible for the economic debacle. In others they avoided such pyrotechnics, choosing instead to create little lifeboats that would amount to idiosyncratic Edens in a sick world.

THE CATHOLIC WORKER

The most influential community-oriented urban religious organization to emerge in the 1930s was the Catholic Worker movement. In its structure the Worker was and is a network of cooperative houses and farms, and communal ideals are basic to its life. From its founding in 1933 the Catholic Worker movement has been devoted to sharing, voluntary poverty, helping the down-and-out, and radical social reform. Although members do not pledge to stay with the movement for life, the lifestyle practiced in the hundreds of houses of hospitality opened in dozens of American cities since the 1930s is decidedly simple and communal. The needy who show up are sheltered and fed simple fare to the extent that resources are available. The Workers also developed a network of dozens of rural communal farms that served the movement as retreat centers and producers of vegetables for the feeding of the hungry.[63]

Dorothy Day was a New York bohemian and radical who became converted to Catholicism in 1928 and, building on a basis of deep commitment to the church, created a movement at once pious and politically radical. While searching for a way to live out the commitment she deeply felt, Day met Peter Maurin, a radical French Catholic, in 1932. Maurin, in pushing his social Catholic agenda, proposed early in 1933 that Day start a Catholic newspaper for the unemployed. Day, an experienced journalist, accepted the suggestion, and also accepted Maurin's "Three-Point Program" of, to use his terminology, round-table discussions (conversations to promote thought), Houses of Hospitality (providing services to the poor), and agronomic universities (in effect, rural communal farms). The paper, *The Catholic Worker,* promoted that program vigorously. It first appeared on May Day 1933, and came out monthly thereafter, selling for a penny a copy and addressing urgent social questions of the day from a distinctive Catholic and radical perspective. The Houses of Hospitality spread from New York across the country as Catholics and others became inspired by the new activist movement, providing food, coffee, and often sleeping quarters to society's outcasts. By the late 1930s the New York House of Hospitality, St. Joseph's House, was serving food to more than a thousand people a day.

A ruralist theme was sounded within the movement during its first year of existence. By April 1934 the paper was printing stories embodying the decentralist outlook that had already appeared in other depression-era social theorizing.[64] Peter Maurin's vision of decentralism was reminiscent of that of the art colonists of a few decades earlier, advocating essentially the re-creation of self-sufficient medieval villages based on craft work as well as agriculture. In April 1936 the fantasy took concrete form when the movement acquired its first farm on then-rural Staten Island. Several

Workers moved there immediately, and through hard work they created an agricultural success story.[65] Later that year a supporter donated another twenty-eight-acre farm near Easton, Pennsylvania; other similar outposts soon followed, and by the end of the decade the movement's program of helping the urban poor become productive small farmers was solidly under way. Preeminent among the Worker farms was Tivoli, north of New York City, which has been colorfully characterized by Rosalie Riegle Troester: "It's the one at Tivoli that stirred the senses. Crazy but beautiful Tivoli, high above the Hudson, with room for everyone—aging alcoholics from the Bowery, Catholic Workers who came up the river for a rest, and 'Catholic shirkers' who used and abused the buildings and grounds during the sixties and early seventies."[66]

In all, about a dozen farms were established; they functioned in a manner reminiscent of the Little Landers and other small-scale subsistence agricultural community projects. From February 1937 through May 1943 the larger Catholic Worker movement encouraged back-to-the-land thinking with a regular feature called "The Land" that comprised the entire last page of the paper. Many of the farms had turbulent histories, and most closed by the mid-1940s, although the rural vision continued to energize the movement, and several new Worker farms were founded as part of the new wave of American communalism in the 1960s. The paper and the Houses of Hospitality, as well as some farms, continue to operate as the backbone of the ongoing Catholic Worker movement.

Any stereotypes one might have about communal movements being inevitably escapist, romantically utopian, or authoritarian would be blown out of the water by the Catholic Worker. It was a decentralized grassroots movement run by those who participated in it and was deeply involved in the most nitty-gritty parts of life. Far from building up substantial assets, the Workers barely managed to keep the most essential bills paid. As a movement of committed Catholics it also posed a sober challenge to a Catholic Church that sometimes neglected to meet the needs of the least of its members as well as others in dire need. As a builder of community the Catholic Worker has had few peers in the twentieth century.

CONSERVATIVE PROTESTANT COMMUNITIES

People of the Living God. A leading Protestant community founded in the 1930s was the Pentecostal organization called People of the Living God. That there was some Pentecostal communitarianism at the time should not be surprising; as we have seen, a communal streak has been in Pentecostalism since the time of its modern founding in 1901 at the communal Bethel College and Bible School in Topeka, Kansas. The People of the Living God was founded in rural Kentucky in 1932 by Harry Miller, formerly a minister in the Assemblies of God, and soon expanded its work to Tennessee and Los Angeles; then, about 1950, the headquarters was moved to New Orleans, where it remained until 1985, when it was moved again to McMinnville, Tennessee. The Trinitarian Pentecostal group espouses both tongues-speaking Christianity and pooling of income, using the proceeds of its work to finance overseas missionaries. Since 1942 the movement has published a free periodical, *The Marturion,* that espoused strongly conservative and millennial Protestant theology, decried hypocrisy, and preached such doctrines as (Saturday) Sabbath keeping. In 1983 its membership was reported as about one hundred at three locations; the movement still adhered to total community of property, the private schooling of members' children, and a very active missionary program. It remains a leading evangelical Protestant intentional community today.[67]

Davidian Seventh-Day Adventists. The term "Davidian" broke spectacularly into American public consciousness in 1993, when the federal Bureau of Alcohol, Tobacco, and Firearms engaged in a brief gun battle with so-called Branch Davidians outside Waco, Texas, and then, failing to secure the group's surrender, mounted a seven-week standoff that culminated with a siege and fire that swept through the main Davidian communal building, killing seventy-four persons. (Six more members, as well as four federal agents, had been killed during the initial raid.) Recriminations — were the Davidians really dangerous? Should the government have mounted its attack in the way it did? — have filled the national political atmosphere ever since.

Had the raid not occurred, the group at Waco led by David Koresh in 1993 would have remained obscure as only one relatively small part of the larger Davidian story. The Davidian movement was and is a splinter group of Seventh-Day Adventists founded by Victor Houteff in 1934. Houteff, a Bulgarian who had immigrated to the United States in 1907, joined the Adventists in Los Angeles in 1918 and soon became active in his local church there. By 1929, however, he was publicly deviating from the official line on certain theological points, and after several quarrels with church leaders he and his followers went their own way, founding what was originally called Shepherd's Rod, and after 1942 the Davidian Seventh-Day

Adventists, reflecting Houteff's conviction that the Kingdom of David would soon be restored in Palestine. His theology remained heavily Adventist, but he believed that the denomination had lost its fervor and was in dire need of renewal before the return of Christ.

Houteff believed that his followers should live communally in preparation for the millennial events on the horizon, and in the center of the country to facilitate missionary work throughout the land. A search committee found a place to settle consisting of 189 acres (soon expanded to 377) just west of Waco, Texas. A dozen members at first went to Waco, with more following over the next few months. Buildings were constructed, and by 1940 a substantial community with sixty-four residents was fully functional at the site they called Mt. Carmel. The Davidians raised much of their own food, developed their own scrip money system, operated their own school, and held daily worship services and religious education classes. Life was short on creature comforts, and the community to a fair degree succeeded in cutting itself off from the decadent outside world. As much energy as possible was to be devoted to printing literature and sending missionaries out to convert the 144,000 believers necessary for the consummation of the millenarian scheme of things.

Houteff had expected the colony to last less than a year, for powerful eschatological events were expected imminently, but conviction remained high as the community continued its dedicated life for years, and then decades. Then the aging and ailing Houteff, who had been expected to be on hand for the ushering in of the Kingdom, died. His wife, Florence Houteff, assumed the leadership, but various splinter groups also emerged, among them one led by Benjamin and Lois Roden. The main body of Davidians sold their property, which was becoming surrounded by the city of Waco, and bought a new Mt. Carmel site east of the city, farther out, where, using the proceeds from the sale of their valuable former land, they built many homes and buildings on 941 acres.

In 1955 Florence Houteff stepped boldly into an arena from which her husband had shied away, predicting a specific date for the establishment of the Kingdom in Palestine—April 22, 1959. Some nine hundred persons arrived at the new colony to prepare for the dramatic events believed to be imminent. When nothing happened, hundreds left, and a year later only about fifty faithful members remained at Mt. Carmel.[68]

The failure of Florence Houteff's prophecy caused more factional strife between her loyal remnant and the Roden-led splinter group, occasionally referred to as the Branch. After exhausting court battles (and the departure of Mrs. Houteff from the area), the Rodens took control of Mt. Carmel. Things went well throughout the 1970s; Lois Roden became an effective leader who kept the believers on track after her husband's death in 1978. Into this situation came Vernon Howell in 1981, a committed Adventist and guitar player who immediately became close to Lois Roden and soon became her heir apparent, to the disgruntlement of her son George, who regarded himself as his father's proper successor as leader. After a series of conflicts, Howell took control of Mt. Carmel in 1988. By then he had taken the name David Koresh, David for the monarchy Davidian theology expected to be established in Palestine and Koresh, Hebrew for "Cyrus," for the messianic biblical Persian king.[69]

The controversies that preceded the raid on Mt. Carmel focused on sex and guns. Koresh took several wives as patriarch of Mt. Carmel (at least seven bore him children), and a few members of the group possessed a substantial arsenal—in part, at least, because they were licensed gun dealers and bought and sold weapons to produce income for the group.[70] Allegations of the arsenal led the BATF to launch the disastrous February 28, 1993, raid. Why Koresh was not detained on one of his regular trips outside Mt. Carmel has never been adequately explained, but he and his followers acted as many millennialists might have when attacked by gun-wielding agents—they fought back. Koresh had taught what is for most premillennialists a fairly standard doctrine—that when the catastrophic events of the end of the world arrive, some of the soldiers of the army of Satan will turn out to be existing civil authorities. As the party of God the Branch Davidians saw the end of all things at hand, and dug in for a long siege. After fifty-one days, on April 19, the Federal Bureau of Investigation, which had assumed command of the operation from the BATF, decided to force the defenders out by injecting gas into the buildings. Somehow a fire broke out, and most of those on the premises were incinerated.[71]

Some Davidians survive today. About fifty Branch Davidians survived the siege and fire, although at this writing they have not regrouped into a structured organization. Other wings of the movement that had broken off earlier continue to operate in low profile. The largest group, apparently, is the Davidian Seventh-Day Adventist Association, which operates a communal headquarters outside Exeter, Missouri, and engages in extensive missionary activity. Another group, the General Association of Davidian Seventh-Day Adventists, is headquartered at Salem, South Carolina.[72]

LATTER DAY SAINTS

In the early twentieth century the main body of the Mormons, head-quartered in Salt Lake City, moved decisively away from its history of en-couraging both intentional community and polygamy. Members of the church were forbidden to engage in plural marriages, and violators of that rule were eventually excommunicated. Polygamists and some other LDS dissenters, however, refused to abandon "the Principle" of polygamy, which, after all, had been proclaimed the will of God and as such could not be repealed. In the 1920s and 1930s they continued to retreat to isolat-ed communal enclaves where they could, under their own local leadership, continue plural marriage as far out of public view as possible. Several of those enclaves continue to thrive today.

Woolley: The United Effort Plan. Lorin C. Woolley was one of the most important figures in Latter Day Saint communitarianism in the twentieth century, founding his organization, formally known as the United Effort Plan, in a series of actions beginning in the late 1920s. Woolley claimed to have received direction to undertake his work from John Taylor, the presi-dent of the main Mormon Church in the late nineteenth century who, as a polygamist, spent much of his ten years in office hiding from the secular authorities who were leaving no stone unturned in their effort to arrest and incarcerate polygamists. Woolley spent the remaining years of his life (he died in 1934) gathering followers and organizing his church. Quietly, the fundamentalist movement, as it was soon informally known, spread in various parts of Utah and nearby parts of other states.

Seeking places inaccessible to public officials out to arrest them and eradicate their movement, fundamentalists developed several isolated res-idential enclaves. None would prove more popular than Short Creek, Arizona, where a substantial community developed. Short Creek was mar-velously isolated, cut off by the Grand Canyon from Arizona public au-thorities. It was also on the Utah border, which afforded a chance for a person being sought by law enforcement agents from either state to make a quick change of jurisdiction. Polygamists began to arrive in Short Creek in 1928, many of them excommunicated from the main church for their re-fusal to abandon plural marriage.

The settlers at Short Creek tried not to attract the attention of public officials, but their practices were always fairly widely known and eventual-ly several raids were conducted against them. In August 1935 Mohave County Attorney E. Elmo Bollinger, with the encouragement of the main

Mormon Church, arrested six leading fundamentalists of Short Creek and charged them with cohabitation. Two of them landed in prison and became within their community great martyrs of the faith. Another assault on Short Creek came in March 1944 when U.S. Attorney John S. Boyden decided to strike a knockout blow against polygamy by conducting simultaneous raids on United Order communities in Utah, Arizona, and Idaho. Some of those arrested were charged with federal crimes of mailing obscene literature (i.e., periodicals supporting polygamy), kidnapping, and violation of the White Slave Trade Act, which forbade the taking of women across state lines for "immoral purposes." Dozens of them were convicted, and several went to prison, although the United States Supreme Court eventually overturned the law on grounds of vagueness and the prisoners were released.

The last and most devastating raid took place on July 26, 1953. Governor Howard Pyle of Arizona orchestrated an expedition by dozens of police officers that wound its way through the desert to Short Creek, arriving at 4:00 A.M. The fundamentalists, warned of the raid despite the government's attempts to keep it secret, offered no resistance, and thirty-six men and eight women (those without minor children) were arrested. The mothers and children were taken by bus to Phoenix and dispersed to foster homes, where they were forced to stay for more than two years. In the end the raid backfired, as the government came under widespread criticism for its police-state tactics and the enormous financial costs of the raid and the maintenance at great public expense of the hundreds of persons in custody. Various legal procedures droned on for years, and in the end no one came out a winner.

Since the 1953 raid Short Creek, since renamed Colorado City, has been left largely in peace. With changing mores concerning private cohabitation and sexual activity, public officials have been less inclined than they once were to enforce laws against adultery and polygamy generally. In this spirit of toleration, or at least peaceful coexistence, Colorado City has thrived. In the late 1990s it had between four thousand and five thousand residents, making it by far the largest polygamous enclave in the country and probably the largest intentional community as well.[73] A satellite community of five hundred to six hundred operated at Lister, British Columbia, and other scattered pockets of the faithful brought the total United Effort population to an estimated seventy-six hundred in the early 1990s.[74]

The LDS tradition has always been marked by schismatic dissent, and the Short Creek movement has experienced at least two splits. In 1952 the group's governing Priesthood Council divided over the appointment of Rulon C. Allred to a leadership position. Allred, a physician, ended up leading his own organization that has become nearly as large as the Colorado City–based movement, although only about five hundred adults live at the movement's commune at Pinesdale, Montana, the rest dwelling as families in the Salt Lake City area and in other scattered locations. The movement has survived despite the murder of Allred by followers of Ervil LeBaron, the leader of yet another fundamentalist communal church (see below), in 1977. In the late 1980s another faction, originally led by Marion Hammond and Alma Timpson and now several hundred strong, withdrew over disputes with the United Effort Plan leadership and has been involved in legal battles over property rights and other matters ever since; members continue to live at Colorado City.[75] According to one recent report, twenty-one men were involved in a lawsuit against the United Effort Plan leadership, which they claim has tried to evict them from their homes—which happen to be on communal (UEP-controlled) land.[76] How the community will survive this latest challenge remains to be seen.

LeBaron. Alma Dayer LeBaron, a member of the main LDS Church, became involved with Mormon fundamentalism in the 1920s and took his large family to Mexico, where they settled at Colonia Juárez, an enclave founded in the 1880s by American Mormons seeking a haven for their unconventional marriage practices. Eventually, no fewer than six LeBaron sons—Joel, Ross Wesley, and Ervil, most successfully—announced that they were divinely appointed prophets and founded competing polygamous churches and their own intentional community, Colonia LeBaron, a few miles from Colonia Juárez.

The LeBaronites came most prominently to public attention with the criminal activities of Ervil. As a member of Joel's Church of the First Born of the Fullness of Times (founded in 1955), he became engaged in a disagreement with his brother that led to his excommunication in 1971. He thereupon founded his own Church of the Lamb of God, and the following year some of his followers, acting at his direction, murdered Joel. In 1977 Ervil's agents murdered Dr. Rulon C. Allred at his medical office. Ervil LeBaron is believed to have committed or ordered perhaps twenty killings in all. He was convicted of the murder of Allred and entered prison in 1980, dying there the following year.

Some members have carried on Ervil's work, including the murders;

the church apparently continues to have a small presence, mainly in Mexico. At least two other LeBaronite churches continue to operate in relative obscurity as well.[77]

The tradition continues. New LDS colonies continue to surface from time to time. Homosexual Mormons, whose sexual orientation is vehemently condemned by the main Mormon Church and thus, like polygamists, sometimes find security in group living, have founded communities in a few cases; among these was the United Order Family of Christ, founded by David-Edward Desmond in Denver in 1966.[78] One of the more public recent polygamous communes was founded as the Church of Jesus Christ in Solemn Assembly by Alexander Joseph at Big Water, Utah, in 1974; about 1977 it was reorganized as the Confederate Nations of Israel, a confederation of polygamous "patriarchs" whose families embrace an estimated four hundred members, many of them entirely outside the Mormon tradition. Joseph at last report had nine wives and, as mayor of Big Water, had temporal as well as spiritual power over his community in a manner reminiscent of the leadership of Joseph Smith Jr. at Nauvoo, Illinois.[79] Another movement emerged from the Reorganized LDS Church in the late 1980s under the leadership of Ronald Livingston. Outside Lamoni, Iowa, these fifty or so "Essenes," as they call themselves, have built two communal villages and live an Amish-like lifestyle that rejects most modern technology.[80] In short, the tradition of communitarianism among the Latter Day Saints in many of their branches is alive and well, even though the main body of Mormons has de-emphasized communal living for more than a century.

COMMUNALISM FROM ASIA:

THE FIRST AMERICAN BUDDHIST COMMUNITIES

One other religious communal story deserves mention, although relatively little has been recorded about it. Buddhist communitarianism first arose in the United States under the auspices of Dwight Goddard, who after his graduation from seminary in 1894 became a Baptist missionary to China. Goddard became intrigued with the religions he encountered in China, especially Buddhism, and after more travel in China and Japan he began to argue that Christians should drop their typically antagonistic attitude toward Buddhism and work for a convergence of the two great world faiths, because, as he became convinced, the two traditions had much in common and were simply divided over minor nonessentials, not fundamental principles.[81] Finally, Goddard converted to Zen, joining a Japanese monastery in 1925.[82] In 1934 he organized an American monastery, or, as he put it, "a cooperative home in the country quite apart from the tense life of the city where a few Brothers can live a quiet Buddhist life, to which a limited number of learners could come and stay for a longer or shorter period."[83]

The first monastic location, which featured a highly structured lifestyle for the brothers, was at Goddard's farmhouse in Thetford Hill, Vermont. Goddard soon opened a second center in Santa Barbara, enabling the monks to enjoy good weather most of the year, to interact with average Americans on their long road journeys between the two locations, and to avoid "routine and a tendency to lapse into easy going ways."[84] Goddard was committed to rigorous, celibate monasticism, and he never did attract a large contingent of monks. His periodical and book publications, however, did succeed in communicating Zen and Buddhist basics to a wider audience than they had previously reached in the United States. The American Brotherhood, as Goddard's organization was called, disintegrated after the founder's death in 1939, but by then non-Asian Americans had been introduced to Buddhism, and with the reopening of contact with Japan after World War II, Zen would become one of the first Asian religions to have a substantial presence in the United States.[85]

OTHER RELIGIOUS COMMUNITIES

Briggs and his devouts. Although most intentional communities observe conventional sexual mores, dissident Latter Day Saints are not the only communitarians to eschew heterosexual monogamy. One other group with rather unusual sexual arrangements consisted of followers of John Briggs, who founded one of the most obscure communal experiments of the early twentieth century, a community that briefly flourished in Arizona and practiced a unique mix of polygamy and polyandry inspired by, but distinctly different from, the "complex marriage" that had been practiced by the Oneida Community in the nineteenth century. Briggs, Richard Mathison relates, financed much of his venture with some $97,000 that he took in 1920 from the cash drawer of the bank in Chicago where he worked. Disappearing from Chicago with the cash, Briggs and his followers took the train to Arizona, where they settled in an isolated location west of the Navajo Indian Reservation. The architecture of the community featured homes with nine bedrooms, reflecting Briggs's unusual social arrangements: each woman would have nine husbands, who would sleep with her in rotation one night at a time; to keep numbers in balance, Briggs and his male inner circle each took nine wives under similar arrangements.

It all lasted for seven months. Some members tired of the structured sexual arrangements and began sneaking encounters outside their appointed circles of "marriage," and finally one disgruntled member left and related the story of the strange practices in the desert to law enforcement officials. Fearing a raid, the band of believers scattered. Briggs's odd experiment suddenly ended.[86]

Heaven City. Some communitarians want to live the good life, and Albert J. Moore of Chicago promised it to his followers in grand material terms. Disaster loomed, he told those who would listen in the early 1920s; 1923 would see a huge financial panic, 1924 would see crippling labor strikes everywhere, 1925 would see a reactionary worldwide revolution, and in 1926 a world war would wipe out three-quarters of the world's population. Those who wanted to see the "new dawn" thereafter had best get on board sooner rather than later; in return they would live in bliss, with everything in life available free.

Moore, a Welshman, first attracted notice in the early 1920s, when he founded what he called the Life Institute, which quickly spawned detractors as well as adherents for its promises of faith healing and resurrections from the dead. Moore was convicted of fraud in 1922, but the conviction was overturned on appeal and Moore and his twenty-eight followers went on to establish Heaven City. This paradise was founded in 1923 near Harvard, Illinois, on 130 acres. Private property was forbidden, and strict behavioral rules, including a ban on wearing jewelry, were imposed. Members operated a farm and a private school system and lived in family quarters, although they did most daily chores—cooking, laundry—in common.[87] Most of the community's cash income came from seven members who worked in Chicago as visiting nurses. Membership peaked at about seventy-five in the mid-1930s.

In the 1930s the group moved Heaven from Illinois to Mukwonago, Wisconsin, where they continued to observe strict community of goods, ran their own school, and enjoyed what have been characterized as fairly liberal sexual relationships—not surprisingly for a movement headed by a man who seemed to have a special way with women and was once quoted as calling the "sex instinct" the "creative force of the world."[88] For many years members ran a motel with a bar and a restaurant as their main business. A slow decline in the community was accelerated by Moore's death in 1963 at age eighty-two; the motel eventually was transferred to private ownership and was reported still in operation in the 1990s.[89]

Mankind United. Heaven City was not the only community to promise its members a virtual paradise and deliverance from earthly catastrophe. Another group preaching a similar message, this one springing up in the 1930s, was Mankind United, which first appeared in 1934 in California. A mysterious "Speaker" or "Voice of the Right Idea," finally in 1942 identified as one Arthur L. Bell, surfaced to warn of a massive plot to destroy human freedom. A group of mysterious Hidden Rulers had for decades been developing elaborate plans to enslave the human race, Bell asserted, but fortunately a heroic, top-secret countereffort had been in place since 1875. The virtuous leaders of the countereffort had finally determined that it was time to make their work publicly known and to put their own plan for the future of the world into action. The pioneers of Mankind United were to usher in nothing less than a Golden Age: as members of the movement, they would be provided with guaranteed employment featuring a four-hour day, a four-day week, and an eight-month work year, with a salary of at least $3,000 per year (in 1934 dollars) and retirement at full pay at age forty. Such largesse would be possible largely because of the incredible secret technological inventions already made by the secret saviors of the human race; members would produce bountiful food, clothing, and buildings, including a luxurious home for each member family. Thousands upon thousands of persons, mainly in California, were enraptured by the glowing promises of the movement, helping meet the tests imposed by the sponsors and communicated to them by Bell that necessarily had to precede the actual inauguration of the edenic program.

In 1942 the FBI arrested sixteen leaders of the movement for alleged efforts to interfere with the American war effort. The conviction of most of them in 1943 caused most members to leave the movement, but to the remaining faithful Bell announced a new program, a communal Christ's Church of the Golden Rule. Some 850 persons joined the movement in this new phase, formally organized in January 1944, giving up any claim of ownership of their personal property and real estate. For the communal church members, living conditions were Spartan and wages quite low, but there was a lively sense of purpose among the participants. Eventually, dissidents began to leave the movement, and from 1945 through 1951 bankruptcy and other legal skirmishes dominated the group's existence. At the end of 1951 Bell vanished.[90]

Christ's Church of the Golden Rule, however, survived the loss of its founder and the general disarray of the movement. A few members who remained devoted to the pursuit of the utopian vision regrouped and in the early 1960s merged their several scattered enclaves in California at a new communal site near Willits, California. In 1968 a visitor reported that the industrious members were operating several industries and maintaining large herds of livestock but keeping their focus largely inward and declining to admit new members.[91] By the mid-1990s the church campus included housing for more than a hundred residents, a dining hall, a school, a library, and a publishing operation. Elements of the utopian Mankind United program seemed still to speak through the community's vision statement, which conceived "a world free from want, with liberty and justice for all, and with understanding love toward God and one another."[92]

The Thelemic community. One of the most offbeat intentional communities of the twentieth century was the Thelemic Magick community at Pasadena, an enclave of followers of the renowned British ceremonial magician and occultist, Aleister Crowley. Crowley, famous (or infamous) for his unconventional ideas and behavior, including overt sexuality—"sex magick"—practiced ritually, developed an American and Canadian following in the early twentieth century. By the late 1930s, when the imminence of war curtailed European occult activities, the Agape Lodge of Los Angeles, under the leadership of Wilfred Smith, became the leading Thelemic center, reaching an active membership of more than eighty for a time, although unwanted media publicity with its implicit threat of costing members their privacy and perhaps their jobs caused many of them to drop out.[93]

Crowley had previously practiced sex magick in communal settings, notably at his Abbey of Thelema in Sicily, and a new Lodge convert, Jack Parsons, suggested that the California devotees start their own Abbey within metropolitan Los Angeles. In 1939 a handful of Lodge members moved into a large house on Orange Grove Avenue in Pasadena.[94] Parsons, a distinguished rocket scientist and cofounder of the Jet Propulsion Laboratory in Pasadena, who was characterized by a colleague as having "an uninhibited and fruitful imagination" and loving "the exotic aspects of life,"[95] led the group as it explored ritual sexual magick. The Abbey contin-

ued its work for several years, at least into the late 1940s. One of those
who was associated with Parsons and the rest during the Abbey's latter
years was L. Ron Hubbard, who later would found the Church of Scientology. Hubbard, according to an account later published in the *Sunday
Times* of London, eventually left with Parsons's girlfriend.[96] (The Church
of Scientology provides a different account of certain critical events: according to its version, Hubbard was never interested in Thelemic magick
but was engaged by certain unspecified government agencies to infiltrate
the Abbey, which he successfully did, rescuing a female member in the
process.[97]) It is conjecture whether the association with Parsons and company influenced Hubbard's development of Scientology, which he was
formulating about that time.[98]

The Future Beckons: Three Communities of the Late 1930s

The late 1930s and the 1940s were a time of communal transition, a period during which communal forms evolved in a direction that gradually
began to anticipate the exuberant new communalism of the hippies in the
late 1960s. Communities continued the long-standing, gradual shift toward less rigid governing structures and lifestyle regulations. In several
cases they further developed and refined the public/private property ownership systems that would eventually be called land trusts; and they self-
consciously held themselves up as countercultural, alternative institutions
populated by people unwilling to accept the norms of the prevailing culture. Mildred Loomis, who joined the School of Living in the 1930s and
became Ralph Borsodi's successor as its leader, embodied the transition as
well as any individual, overseeing the school's development of Heathcote,
in Maryland, which became a fairly classic hippie commune after 1965.
Meanwhile, three other communities founded in the second half of the
1930s also became harbingers of the American communal future, and fit-
tingly point this volume toward its conclusion.

CELO

In 1936 Arthur Morgan, the engineer whose promotion of small communities made him a leader in the intentional community movement for
several decades, founded what now calls itself the nation's oldest land trust
community, Celo, in the mountains of western North Carolina. The land
stewardship arrangement at Celo would prove attractive to many later

communities; individuals could own their own homes, but the land itself, including that under the homes, was and is held communally. Celo soon after its founding became populated largely by Quakers and like-minded pacifists, and as in the case of Macedonia, discussed just below, that caused headaches in wartime. Celo expressed its aspirations thus in 1959:

Details of the vision vary with individuals, but its broad outlines might be expressed like this: to live among like-minded people, striving for honesty in all human relations, with resulting mutual trust; to work with a group, even at some personal sacrifice; to pay allegiance to our common humanity overshadowing religious, racial, economic or political differences; to rear children in a wholesome environment where they can become acquainted with nature and be stimulated by intellectual freedom; to work for themselves—or in small organizations—at callings that will provide simple but adequate living; to raise some of their own food and in so doing to conserve rather than deplete the land; to grow from these roots a life that is full and integrated rather than shallow and fragmented.[99]

Celo was organized as a result of the philanthropy of industrialist William Regnery of Chicago. In 1936 he asked Arthur Morgan to suggest a project of substantial social value that he might underwrite; Morgan suggested that he bankroll a new intentional community. Why would a wealthy capitalist support a cooperative venture that would soon be dominated by Quakers? As George Hicks has explained it, Regnery, "a conservative businessman, a mild anti-Semite, a staunch opponent of President Roosevelt and the New Deal policies" nevertheless harbored "a nostalgic belief that people who lived in rural villages and earned their living by subsistence farming constituted the virtuous and self-reliant bedrock of republican government."[100] Together they and Morgan's son Griscomb selected about twelve hundred acres for the project and began helping families move there. A board of directors consisting of Morgan, Regnery, and Clarence Pickett, the executive secretary of the American Friends Service Committee, was put in place to oversee development. Recruitment went slowly at first, and the community, suffering from confusion about its identity and direction early on, at first amounted to little. During World War II, however, Arthur Morgan visited many of the Civilian Public Service camps where conscientious objectors were confined, and invited the men to bring their families to Celo when the conflict had ended. Several of them did, and by 1948 the community was well on its feet. Growth was gradual but steady until the community reached the maximum population its members deemed compatible with its goal of stewardship of the land. A visitor in 1966 counted sixty-seven resident members, twenty-nine of them adults,[101] and by 1993 the population had reached thirty-five families. Because the waiting list for the few openings that occur is long, many families sympathetic to the community's way of life have settled on its periphery.[102]

Although Celo has never provided jobs for its residents, cooperation has always characterized the community. It has a food co-op, a cooperative retail crafts store, and a program of sharing knowledge and skills (and organizing social events) called Cabin Fever University.[103] Families have run cottage industries, operated a summer camp, worked for local governmental agencies and school districts, and worked in the employ of the community itself. Physicians in the community for many years operated a clinic that served the surrounding area with medical care at relatively low prices. Within the community one group set up a common-purse arrangement for a time, pooling money and labor, but the experiment ended when most of those involved joined the Bruderhof.[104]

Secular idealists tend to believe in education as a key to achieving a better future, and in that spirit Celo established the Arthur Morgan School in 1962. Limited to the junior high grades, the school attracts students from outside the community, many of them from pacifist and activist families. The school operates several businesses and runs a summer family camp.[105]

Life at Celo is not elegant; its location has caused it to suffer the privations of the rest of the rural South. However, residents are generally committed to simple lifestyles, and the community has developed good camaraderie. Celo members continue their quiet life together and provide an ongoing good example of a working small community.[106]

THE MACEDONIA COOPERATIVE COMMUNITY

Another secular community devoted to the historic communal quest of promoting human fellowship and cooperation that opened just about the time Celo did was the Macedonia Cooperative Community, which operated near Clarkesville, Georgia, for about two decades. Macedonia was founded by Morris Mitchell, a liberal southern educator who believed that communitarianism could solve many of the problems of modern society. In the mid-1930s he began to purchase land for his colony; the first two families moved in in 1937, and Macedonia grew slowly thereafter. Officially, the group proclaimed, "Macedonia belongs to no ism. It is seeking with open mind a more effective pattern of community organization" through cooperation, planning, education, and conservation of human and natural resources.[107] The atmosphere was predominantly non-sectarian Christian, tending toward a Quakerly outlook, although there were secular liberals and radicals as well, most of them from Christian, typically liberal Protestant, backgrounds. One member in 1948 listed pacifism, disillusionment with modern industrial society, and distrust of arbitrary authority as central to Macedonia's outlook.[108] Such convictions, especially pacifism, constituted a public-relations problem for the community during World War II, when traditional southern conservatism reared its head in the neighborhood. Afterward, however, local relations improved and Macedonia's population approached fifty in the early 1950s. Unlike some of the land-trust and subsistence-homestead colonies then popular, Macedonia was economically heavily communal, with common ownership of property and communal cottage industries. The community always struggled for economic survival, but it eventually developed a fairly successful dairy herd and, in 1947, a business that made good wooden children's furniture and toys under the name Community Playthings.[109]

When the Society of Brothers (Bruderhof) decided to open an American community, pioneer members spent several weeks in 1953 and 1954 at Macedonia exploring the possibility of a three-way venture combining the two groups along with the Kingwood Community, a Quaker enclave at Frenchtown, New Jersey. The religious sentiments of many Macedonia residents, never far below the surface, became increasingly explicit with the contact with the evangelical Brothers, and some decided, as did several members of Kingwood, to join the new Bruderhof venture. Even those who decided not to join were deeply influenced by the Christian communists of the German-founded Bruderhof. Macedonia was split right down the middle with the departure of three or four of its six or seven families (exact counts vary from source to source) for the new movement. Its most important industry was also divided; thereafter Community Playthings was run jointly by the two groups, each specializing in certain product lines. Macedonia managed to struggle back from the loss of half its full members, rebounding to near its former peak in membership. Then in 1957 a new round of intense discussions was opened with the Bruderhof, and in September of that year a decision was made to close Macedonia, with the understanding that many members would be joining the Society of Brothers. Fifteen members followed through, moving to the Bruderhof communities in New York and Pennsylvania; the rest scattered. The Macedonia property was sold in the summer of 1958.

Macedonia was important, despite its small numbers, because of its relatively thorough communitarianism, its sincere spiritual searching, and its stalwart pacifism; it was widely admired as a groundbreaker by its fellow members of the Fellowship of Intentional Communities in the 1940s and 1950s.[110]

One of the last communities to be founded in the 1930s was Bryn Gweled, near Philadelphia, a housing cooperative with goals that transcended the mere provision of residences to its members. Georgia and Herbert Bergstrom, Bryn Gweled's principal founders, had been influenced by the School of Living and set out to emulate it. They sought to provide affordable housing in a cooperative setting, to deter real estate speculation, to maintain community control of the land itself, to encourage racial integration, and to provide to residents certain common facilities and activities. As the community's bylaws put it, the purpose of Bryn Gweled was

to establish, maintain, and develop a community for the mutual benefit of all its members, who are seeking stable, productive homes on adequate ground free from land speculation, with the positive advantages of land controlled by the community, permanent provision for recreation and wholesome outdoor life, opportunity for individual freedom and creative initiative, as well as for sharing in the responsibility for and development of community facilities and activities.[111]

The Bergstroms and a group of like-minded cooperators acquired some 240 acres near Southampton, Pennsylvania, just north of Philadelphia, in 1939, and their "Hill of Vision" (the name's Welsh meaning) began to take shape—slowly at first, but then more rapidly with an influx of pacifists after World War II. Families took out ninety-nine-year renewable leases on homesites of about two acres each from the community and built their own homes, leaving eighty acres with a community building—the two hundred-year-old farmhouse that stood on the property—and swimming pool held in common. Much of the eighty common acres remained in woods, giving Bryn Gweled a permanently rural atmosphere. Once the community was fully populated it enjoyed a stable, quiet existence, gradually becoming a relatively prosperous suburb with three hundred or so persons living in some seventy homes. The egalitarian vision remains very much in force, giving the community ongoing racial and religious diversity, and the land continues to be in common ownership. That the sense of cooperation survives is perhaps best illustrated by the fact that members still pitch in frequently to keep up the common property. Bryn Gweled's housing is not free, however; a feature article on the community written in 1991 reported that by then households were assessed a fee of $3,850 per year for upkeep of common facilities, on top of which they had to pay an average of $600 per year for the lot lease—all besides the cost of the house itself.[112] But it was reported in the same year that the last two houses to change hands had sold for less than $145,000 each—about 60 percent of what houses in the surrounding subdivisions were bringing.[113]

Celo, Macedonia, and Bryn Gweled were the first of a new generation of communitarian ventures. In 1940, under the direction of Arthur Morgan, the Fellowship of Intentional Communities was established as a nexus of communication for communities and as an advocacy agency seeking to encourage the formation of new communities throughout the land. A new communal energy was clearly in the air, one that would stimulate the formation and continuation of communities for the two or three decades before the great communal explosion of the 1960s arrived.

5

New Communities in the 1940s and 1950s

A nation mobilized for the largest war in human history would not be likely to expend extensive resources on new social experiments, so it is probably not surprising that the founding of intentional communities reached a low ebb during the early 1940s. A few new communal outposts did struggle into existence, however, in some cases in response to the exigencies of war. Because the pursuit of human compassion and understanding were not top priorities for most Americans, members of the antiwar minority (Quakers, especially), largely voiceless in wartime, found the development of intentional communities to be one of the few ways in which they could pursue their ideals. Furthermore, given the massive public support that the war effort experienced, the few who bucked the current and declined military service were socially isolated and needed mutual support, which in several cases they found in intentional communities.

With the arrival of peace, however, the pursuit of community bloomed anew. The late 1940s and the 1950s saw the initiation of many communal experiments, several of them building on the determination of those who had continued the search for community during the grim war years. Foremost among the postwar community organizers was Arthur Morgan.

The Morgan Legacy

Perhaps the most important contribution to community in the early 1940s was the founding and development of two related organizations, Community Service, Inc., and the Fellowship of Intentional Communities, by Arthur Morgan. The multitalented Morgan, who built distinguished careers both as an engineer and as an innovative educator, became president of Antioch College in Yellow Springs, Ohio, in 1920, and revitalized the institution by introducing a curriculum that joined classroom work with jobs in the local community. His abilities—and also his reputation as something of a utopian dreamer whose outlook had been heavily influenced by Edward Bellamy's *Looking Backward*[1]—caught the eye of Franklin D. Roosevelt, who named him the first chairman of the Tennessee Valley Authority. Morgan used the TVA not only to build dams and provide power but also to promote cottage industries and cooperative enterprises of many kinds and to create planned towns in the spirit of the English garden city movement.[2]

In 1940 Morgan founded Community Service, Inc., to promote family life and small towns—the world's classic small communities—as the best hope for a rational human future. The rapidly urbanizing nation seemed to denigrate small towns as vestiges of the past whose only value was in providing services to farmers; Morgan saw them as places where persons living in an overly urban world could recover mutual respect, personal relationships, and neighborly cooperation.[3] But the promotion of village life had larger cooperative implications, and at any rate Morgan's interests had always included communal settlements as well as small towns and families. He had been the main force, for example, behind the founding of the Celo community in North Carolina in 1936. Morgan soon began holding regular conferences in Yellow Springs on the promotion of small communities, and at the suggestion of his associate, Alfred Andersen, the agenda was soon expanded to include intentional communities.

As intentional communities began to assert their presence in American life more boldly after the difficult years of World War II, they formed the InterCommunity Exchange, an organization that facilitated the exchange of products among various communities. Soon it became apparent that communitarians were interested in visiting with each other, and the Inter-Community Exchange evolved, largely under the direction of Art Wiser, into the Fellowship of Intentional Communities, which sought not only the exchange of products but communication among the communities and between them and the larger world. The FIC, closely tied to Community Service, Inc., helped provide focus and direction for the many pacifist communitarians who were distressed not only at the massive destructiveness of the war itself but also at the ongoing cold war, in which militarism and hostility toward pacifists ran at a high level in the culture. A fair number of Quakers, trying to find congenial surroundings for themselves and the rearing of their children, left the country, most commonly for western Canada; others decided that they would seek refuge in intentional communities of like-minded souls in which the values they cherished could be reinforced. Thus several new communities were founded in the postwar years and joined several existing communities, including Gould Farm, Celo, Koinonia Farm, and the Macedonia Cooperative Community, in the FIC. The Fellowship encompassed a loose confederation of communal styles. Member communities' economic arrangements ranged from fully communal, with members living from a common purse, to land-trust situations in which family finances were largely private, and spiritually the FIC communities ranged from Quaker (probably the most prominent religious presence) to mainline Protestant to avowedly secular.

The Fellowship was a major focal point of communal life in America throughout the 1950s. Toward the end of the decade, however, its largest and most prosperous member, the Bruderhof, withdrew, and the Fellowship did not long survive that defection, its dissolution finally coming in 1961. Al Andersen, the last president of the original FIC, surmised in 1996 that beyond the blow dealt by the defection of the Bruderhof, the FIC was undermined as John F. Kennedy, with his stirring calls to selfless volunteer service, steered American idealists in new directions—into the Peace Corps, for example, rather than into intentional communities.[4]

CSI, however, survived, and at this writing still promotes communal values from its original headquarters in Yellow Springs. Moreover, the FIC came back to life in 1986 when a new generation of communitarians revitalized and expanded it under a slightly different name, the Fellowship for Intentional Community. It has resumed its former role as an organization that helps scattered communities communicate with one another and promotes the cooperative ideal in a culture that seems hopelessly addicted to "me first" attitudes. The new FIC's first major contribution to the promotion of community living was the publication, in 1990, of a directory of contemporary communities. The directory's listing of more than three hundred communities in North America and fifty overseas, along with supporting articles and listings of resources and services, constituted a dramatic announcement that communal living was far from dead in the late twentieth century.[5] But that is getting far beyond the 1940s.

THE COMMUNITIES OF THE FIC

Hidden Springs. The first of the post-1940 FIC communities to be founded may have been Hidden Springs, although the few sources of information on the community disagree about the founding date, placing it as early as 1940 or as late as 1953. A date in the late 1940s seems most likely. Whatever its precise time of origin, this small community, located on 140 acres at Neshanic Station, New Jersey, sought to promote cooperative values as well as the spiritual development of its members. Like many other communities of its day, Hidden Springs embodied a mix of communal and private activities, with common housing, gardening, and worship services, but most meals taken in private family groups. A 1954 visitor reported that twelve members, including one child, were then resident. The equality-minded residents of Hidden Springs developed close relations with Koinonia Farm, Georgia, and in fact discussed trying to turn their community into a replica of the famous Georgia experiment in community and racial integration.[6] As the proponents of integration quickly learned, however, New Jersey had its racists just as surely as Georgia did, and an openly integrated community could expect conflict. Discussion of the prospects of an integrated community in their midst led to considerable opposition from neighbors, and that contributed to the collapse of the community sometime in the late 1950s.[7]

Tanguy Homesteads. Dating becomes firmer with two FIC communities founded in 1945, Tanguy Homesteads and Tuolumne Co-Operative Farms. The former was one of several founded shortly after World War II that had many conscientious objectors among their membership. Tanguy's founders intended it to be a close-knit, structured community with one or more industries to provide an economic base, but it never developed along those lines, instead remaining a relatively loose community of like-minded residents who worked hard at mutual respect and support and made their decisions by consensus.[8] As one who grew up there later reminisced,

One of the things I remember most clearly was how wonderful it was for a kid to be able to roam around anywhere in the community and be welcome in anyone's house and at anyone's table as a member of the same extended family. It gave me a tremendous feeling of security and belonging. Within Tanguy, the world felt like a seamless whole, a world where all places felt like home, instead of the fragmented alienated patchwork that sprawled over the "outside world." It was almost like living on an island that had a strikingly different culture from the mainland.[9]

Tanguy was modeled on its larger neighbor in suburban Philadelphia, Bryn Gweled Homesteads, which had been founded in 1939. Its principal organizer was Dan Wilson, an insurance agent who gradually accumulated a list of persons interested in intentional community during his business travels. Tanguy was situated on about a hundred acres near West Chester, Pennsylvania, giving each family two acres for a homesite and leaving common land that accommodated a community building, fields and woods, and a swimming and ice skating pond. Community work days, holiday festivities, membership meetings, and various mutual support activities have continued over the years and have helped promote the sense of community the founders strove for. The population of Tanguy has long been eclectic; probably the two best-known residents were humor writer Dave Barry and naturalist Euell Gibbons, the latter still remembered for bringing odd wild foods to the weekly community potluck dinners. In the 1990s Tanguy was still providing good and cooperative homes for many families just as it had done for half a century.[10]

Tuolumne Co-operative Farms. This rural community was founded about the same time as Tanguy, in the fall of 1945, but a continent away, along the Tuolumne River near Modesto in the Central Valley of California. Like many other communal enclaves of its day, it had many Quakers among its participants. The four founding families saw their project as providing not only a cooperative home for themselves but also a training and resource center for persons who wanted to learn about intentional community living and, with some experience under their belts, then move on to live the collective life elsewhere. The community, located on 155 acres, was heavily agricultural, with cows, goats, orchards, and field crops. It was more thoroughly communal than some others of its day, with a common purse that distributed money to members on the basis of need (family size was considered the main determinant of need) and some communal taking of meals as well as regular devotional and worship exercises. Membership seems never to have exceeded twenty, and turnover was high, but Tuolumne was reported to be operating successfully at least into the late 1950s.[11]

Skyview Acres. Another community of pacifists, again mainly Quakers, in the postwar era was Skyview Acres, opened in 1948 on 161 thickly wooded acres at Pomona, New York, not far from New York City, and similar in outlook and structure to Bryn Gweled and Tanguy Homesteads. The founders sought close community, racial integration, and semirural life and quickly developed a good assortment of mutual support services and activities ranging from baby-sitting to folk dancing to a buying club. They originally intended to hold all the land in common, but could not secure building loans without having plots deeded to individuals. A projected community building was never built because of disputes among the forty-five members over the degree of financial cooperation the community should mandate, but nevertheless a sense of common purpose fueled Skyview for some years, gradually fading with the passage of time and turnover in residency.[12]

Parishfield. Another small community from the era of Tanguy, Tuolumne, and Skyview was Parishfield, founded in 1948 as a communal training center for Episcopalians who sought to become lay workers in their church. It was sited near Brighton, Michigan, on thirty-eight acres owned by the church. As of the mid-1950s the permanent community consisted of three families who operated the training program; they adhered to community of property as well as a strong spiritual life. At that time new buildings were under construction and the residents envisioned an expanding program, although over time the features of the center that made it an intentional community appear to have dropped away.[13]

Kingwood. Yet another community resembled several of those discussed above and is as thinly documented as most of the others are. Kingwood, a communally operated retreat center founded in 1949 near Frenchtown, New Jersey, was another Quaker-dominated enclave. Economically, Kingwood operated with a common purse, making its living from subsistence farming on its twenty-four acres, the hosting of retreat groups, and apparently some outside job income. In 1953 its membership consisted of seven adults and two children. Later that year, the community closed, however. Like several other similarly oriented communities, Kingwood came into conversation with representatives of the Society of Brothers (Bruderhof), who journeyed to the United States from their Paraguayan base in the early 1950s to lay foundations for an American Bruderhof, and most of the members eventually decided to join the Brothers.[14]

Quest. In 1950, the year after the founding of Kingwood, another small community emerged, Quest, near Royal Oak, Michigan, this time rooted in Methodism rather than the Quakerdom. The five member families (not all always resident) reported to be participating a few years later made some income from a chicken-raising operation, but were largely dependent on outside jobs. They practiced pooling of income, were housed in two duplexes, and governed themselves democratically. Because the record on the group is scanty, one can surmise that its existence was not overly lengthy.[15]

Canterbury. Yet another small community emerged the following year, 1951, this time again in the Quaker mold. These communards certainly had a propitious communal site, occupying land and a building purchased from the Canterbury Shaker Village outside Concord, New Hampshire, then one of the last remaining functioning Shaker sites with only a handful of residents itself. The group's participants met as members of the Macedonia Community in Georgia;[16] from there they moved to Newton, Kansas, where they helped operate Meadowlark Homestead, a home for the elderly and for convalescent mental patients. Finally settling at Canterbury, the three member families managed their own finances, although at least two of the men of the community had a cooperative business, Community Builders, which did remodeling work in the area. The community apparently survived for a few years, but seems to have suffered from an attempt to enter into fuller community of property in 1960. In the middle of that year only two families remained. Scholars working at the Shaker site in the 1980s surmised that it probably did not last much longer than that.[17]

May Valley. The interest in land trust–style housing that was manifested in several places in the East in the 1940s and early 1950s also occasionally showed up in the West, notably in the Seattle suburbs, where a long-lived community emerged, one that eventually spawned a second-generation community from within and that still exists, although with its cooperative features largely gone. The group that founded the May Valley Cooperative Community did so after several years of planning that started in 1949. They were energized in 1953 when they came into contact with representatives of the Bruderhof who were traveling with a slide show to recruit members for the Woodcrest colony, their first American outpost then being built in New York State—so much so, in fact, that one family in the May Valley discussions joined the Bruderhof and moved to Woodcrest. The remaining Washingtonians finally bought thirty-seven mainly wooded acres in the May Creek valley near Renton, Washington, in the 1950s, and began moving there in 1957. Like several other FIC communities, May Valley was deliberately racially integrated and had a wide range of cooperative features, including a food co-op that eventually moved into Seattle and became a major cooperative food store. Because the founding families could not agree on a single pattern of home ownership, two distinct but converging forms were allowed, mutual ownership that respected individual rights and preferences, and private ownership laden with restrictions for the common good.[18]

A major change of direction came in 1973, when May Valley dropped most of its cooperative features and became a homeowners' association. By then the previously rural area had become substantially developed, and many of the residents wanted to abandon May Valley's program of providing cooperative, low-cost housing in favor of cashing in on the run-up in property values in the neighborhood. Some of the veteran cooperators, unhappy with what seemed like the betrayal of their long-standing dream, regrouped and organized a new community-within-the-community known as Teramanto (Esperanto for "loving earth") on part of the land of the larger May Valley community. Most of the Teramanto homes were shared, and housing costs were kept deliberately low—in 1991, $95 per bedroom plus utilities.[19] The vision that had fueled the original May Valley community endured.

The Vale. It would seem only logical that the communal activists who ran Community Service, Inc., would live in community, and in the 1950s a CSI-related community began to take shape. Located eight miles from Yellow Springs, Ohio, where CSI is headquartered, the Vale was unofficially founded and led by Griscom Morgan, son of CSI founder Arthur Morgan, and his wife, Jane Morgan. Several families—never as many as a dozen, many of them composed of committed Quakers involved in pacifist activism—gradually moved onto a forty-acre tract owned by one of them and began developing various cooperative projects. The centerpiece of the community eventually became an elementary school for the Vale's resident children.[20] Never, however, did more structure than that emerge. As the residents declared in a statement circulated in 1959, "we need to start with a framework that requires no more sharing than we are ready for." For their community they sought not "formulated degrees of development for participation, but mutual agreement on what is essential to a functioning community and encouragement in growth in capacity for sharing and mutuality."[21]

St. Francis Acres/Glen Gardner. St. Francis Acres, originally called the Glen Gardner Cooperative Community, was a small community near Glen Gardner, New Jersey, that went beyond communal living to a complete rejection of the very idea of land ownership. David and Betty Dellinger and three other couples purchased twenty acres with a house and outbuildings (soon converted into living quarters) in 1947, at first forming a cooperative that held the land in common but allowed each family to maintain largely private finances and to have private living quarters. David Dellinger and some of the others had long been involved in radical printing and publishing, and a cooperative print shop soon became the focus of the community. Five years after the community's founding, and after some membership turnover, the Glen Gardner community was reorganized, the members pooling their finances and expanding their printing and publishing operation, by then known as the Libertarian Press. Dellinger was the community's leading light throughout its history; as a student at Union Theological Seminary he had refused to register for the World War II draft, and later had honed his social critique at Macedonia Co-operative Community and in a variety of radical political groups. He would soon become a leading critic of American involvement in the war in Vietnam and one of the Chicago Seven who were tried for conspiracy to disrupt the 1968 Democratic National Convention in the 1960s era's most spectacular courtroom drama.

In the 1950s the community, at the suggestion of members Gerry and Denise Landry, changed its name to St. Francis Acres and deeded the land to God, the members proclaiming themselves mere trustees of the property, not its owners. "God, the lord of the universe, is naturally sole owner of 'St. Francis Acres,' with all its appurtenances, resources, equipment, and industrial means of production," they declared; those who lived and worked there were opposed to "drawing rent, interest, and profit, to which they are conscientious objectors."[22]

On a day-to-day basis St. Francis Acres functioned like many other small communities of its era, its members gardening and raising livestock and pooling all financial resources. They continued to operate the Libertarian Press, issuing books and, for a time, the newsletter *Cooperative Living,* the chief organ of the intentional community movement in the 1950s. In 1955 the community counted eighteen members, equally divided between adults and children. Seeking to put the community on a solid base by learning from mistakes made by earlier communities, in 1956 the St. Franciscans announced the founding of the Research Center for Community and Cooperation, inspired by the work of a sociologist of intentional community, Henrik Infield.

St. Francis Acres disbanded in 1968. Perhaps some members had not shown sufficient communal spirit; Ammon Hennacy, the radical Catholic pacifist who spent five months there, wrote that "the trouble is that very few people there are responsible workers, except Dave."[23] The larger problem, however, was outside pressure. In 1967, when David Dellinger was rising to national prominence as an opponent of the war in Vietnam, the community suffered a series of attacks. The print shop, the focus of the community, was vandalized one night; Betty Dellinger's teaching contract in a nearby school was not renewed; someone began to send bombs to David Dellinger in the mail. Early in 1968 the Dellinger family left the area, and the community quietly passed out of existence.[24]

KOINONIA AND THE BRUDERHOF

Two FIC member communities stand out for their exceptional duration and visibility. Koinonia Farm and the Bruderhof became known for their commitment to high ideals and remain widely admired as exemplary intentional communities of the twentieth century.

Koinonia Farm. An experiment in interracial community in the deep South that has survived for half a century, Koinonia unfolded from the life and character of its founder and charismatic leader, Clarence Jordan, a Georgian who held a doctorate in Greek New Testament from a Baptist seminary but preached a gospel little heard in the white South at the time, a gospel of a Jesus who should be followed rather than worshiped and who made extraordinary demands on the lives of the faithful. In 1942 Jordan established Koinonia Farm near Americus, Georgia, as an interracial commune, and also as a center from which modern agricultural techniques could be introduced to inefficient traditional farmers. Koinonia members were given homes and tools; the products they created were marketed cooperatively, and proceeds went into a common fund. Families then drew reasonable living wages from the fund based on their needs, not their productivity. Surplus profit went into a "Fund for Humanity" that helped finance a variety of projects, especially self-help construction projects for displaced farmers.

White southerners were hostile to the project from its inception, or at
least as soon as it became publicly known that at Koinonia, blacks and
whites ate their meals at the same table. Real antagonism developed, however, with the rise of the civil rights movement in the mid-1950s, when the
community became the object of racist violence after Jordan had affronted
local sensibilities in 1956 by supporting the effort of two black students to
enroll at a white state college in Atlanta. Almost overnight an economic
boycott of Koinonia developed, meaning that the farm could not sell its
produce or buy necessary supplies. Petty vandalism erupted: signs for
Koinonia's roadside market were torn down, sugar in the gas tank ruined
the engine of a farm vehicle, garbage was dumped on the land, and other
similar incidents occurred repeatedly. Then, beginning in midsummer, the
violence intensified; the roadside market was bombed twice and completely demolished, hundreds of fruit and pecan trees were chopped
down, fences were cut and livestock let loose, and much of the farm's produce was destroyed. In 1957 there were repeated incidents of shooting at
persons and property. With economic help from sympathetic northerners
and courage within its ranks, however, Koinonia managed to survive its
trials and continue its witness for what it considered the essential message
of the New Testament. Jordan, using his academic skills, translated most
of the New Testament into a vernacular "Cotton Patch" version, reset in
the rural American South; the several volumes of the work circulated
widely.[25]

The community has had ups and downs since Jordan's death in 1969,
but still continues its work today.[26] It is less fully communal economically
than it once was, but workers at the farm continue to put its ideals into
action.

Only recently has Koinonia come to have its widest effect yet on the
larger culture. The community's Fund for Humanity has long worked at
helping the poor build housing, and for many years has provided both
lots and new homes to needy farm families who are not members of
Koinonia. Those who could afford to build houses have been given lots;
those in direr straits have been invited to help Koinonia members build
their homes and then given interest-free twenty-year loans to pay for
them. From that effort has grown Habitat for Humanity under the leadership of Millard Fuller, who many years ago gave away his fortune, joined
Koinonia, and turned to a simple life of service. Habitat now builds and
rehabilitates homes nationwide. The basic principles of Koinonia remain

central to Habitat: work equity is required, the persons involved must have genuine need, and all loans are interest free.[27]

The Bruderhof (Society of Brothers). As a German teenager Eberhard Arnold had a powerful Christian religious experience, and after finishing a Ph.D. in 1909 he became a Christian socialist activist and a leader in the German Youth Movement, a broad-based revolt against entrenched tradition in German religious bodies and other social institutions. Searching for a vital and radical Christianity, he and his wife, Emmy, with a few comrades, rented a farmhouse in Sannerz, Hesse, in 1920, and opened a Christian commune there. The passionate but somewhat unstructured life at Sannerz made it, in Benjamin Zablocki's phrase, "very similar to many [1960s-era] hippie communes."[28] In 1926 the group moved toward stability by purchasing its own farm in the Rhön mountains and calling it the Rhön Bruderhof. There community members began to read the works of the early Anabaptists, and they became enchanted with the history and witness of the communal Hutterites. Only later did they learn that the Hutterites still existed, and in 1930 Arnold spent a year visiting them in the United States and Canada. During that trip the Hutterites received Arnold into membership and ordained him a minister, giving their blessing to his promotion of Hutterite ideals in Germany. From that time on the Bruderhof has consciously followed Hutterite practices in many ways, although it has retained certain distinctive features as well.

The rise of the Nazis in 1933 meant restrictions on community life that the Bruderhof members could not countenance. The community's children and its young men who were subject to a new military draft were taken to a new *hof* in Liechtenstein, the Alm Bruderhof. The community was not safe from the nearby Nazis, however, and early in 1936 a Bruderhof was founded in England. Amid the external crisis the community also suffered an internal blow: Arnold, after unsuccessful surgery, died in November 1935. The community responded heroically, however, and by 1938 all the members were in England, where the group grew rapidly with English converts.[29]

After England's declaration of war on Germany, a program of interning Germans was undertaken, and the Bruderhof decided to emigrate rather than see the group divided. Canada and the United States rejected the Bruderhof's applications for sanctuary; finally, the group was accepted by Paraguay, to which country some 350 of its members traveled in 1941. They purchased a twenty thousand-acre ranch that they named Primavera and on the land developed three separate *hofs,* or colonies. The group grew to about six hundred inhabitants by 1950, but economically it never became stable, remaining dependent for survival on donations from outsiders, especially Americans.

In 1953 a delegation of Bruderhof members was sent to the United States to speak and prospect for land and support there. They were warmly received at several intentional communities, some of whose members joined their ranks. The following year they purchased land near Rifton, New York, on which they founded Woodcrest, the first American Bruderhof. A bit of a golden age ensued: membership expanded rapidly, as did the number of *hofs,* which reached nine (in five countries) in 1956. The movement had been rekindled in England; the three colonies in Paraguay founded a new *hof* in Uruguay; one Hutterite colony, Forest River (North Dakota), changed its affiliation to the Bruderhof; a new colony was started back in Germany.[30] Meanwhile, when half the members of the Macedonia Cooperative Community in Georgia decided to join the Bruderhof, they took a Macedonia industry, Community Playthings, with them. That concern, which developed specialty lines of large, expensive children's toys of the type used in nurseries and day-care centers, eventually became enormously successful and insured the movement's economic prosperity.

The Bruderhof's history has not been one of unbroken harmony and peaceful progress since then. Problems have periodically arisen, most notably from 1959 to 1961, when Heini Arnold, one of Eberhard's sons, asserted political leadership over the movement and in a complicated series of events was involved in tumult that caused more than six hundred of the then fifteen hundred or so members, most of them at Primavera, to resign or be expelled. Arnold's primacy from that point on was clear, and he was subsequently named *Vorsteher* (bishop), the only community member (to that point) since Eberhard Arnold to hold that title.[31] All the South American Bruderhofs, along with Wheathill in England and Sinntal in Germany, were closed by 1962.

Although some of those who left during the crisis eventually returned to the fold, most did not and formed the nucleus of what has become a substantial group of former members, who now have a newsletter and regular reunions. Meanwhile, there were defections for other reasons; for example, some who grew up in the movement left because they found the group to have such a hallowed sense of its own history, such an exalted estimate of its first-generation leaders, that no human being could measure up to the moral standards that the community theoretically embraced.[32]

Others have simply found the life of the community wanting in important ways; one criticism former members have leveled at the Bruderhof (the same one that some Bruderhofers have leveled at the Western Hutterites) is that the group lives according to the letter of its law but not according to the spirit of that law, or, more broadly, the spirit of Christian love.

In the late 1980s such criticism, mainly from former members, became both more vocal and more focused. A loose network of former member critics began to coalesce around a newsletter called *KIT*, for "Keep in Touch." The newsletter mainly consists of open letters written by the Bruderhof's critics, including some formerly of high position in the movement and several descendants of founder Eberhard Arnold, some of whom have been expelled by their relatives in power. *KIT* was started by Ramón Sender Barayon, who joined the community as a novice in its early years at Woodcrest. He soon realized that the life was not for him, but his wife and young daughter stayed on when he departed. In ensuing years he was allowed to see his daughter only once (whether their lack of contact was by her choice or Bruderhof edict is a matter of contention), and was not informed of her marriage or of her becoming twice a mother until long after the fact. When she suddenly died of cancer at age thirty-three, he was not informed of her illness, much less her death, until well after her funeral. Searching out others who felt similarly personally hurt, Sender founded *KIT* and has been a key antagonist of the Bruderhof ever since. Today his newsletter has some two hundred subscribers, an indication that the Bruderhof claim of a life of peace and true unity may not apply in all circumstances.[33]

Neither have relations with the traditional ("Western," in Bruderhof parlance) Hutterites been consistently smooth. In 1955 over half of the members of the Forest River colony in North Dakota decided to switch their affiliation to the Bruderhof; the substantial minority were cast out of their homes and thrust upon other Western colonies. Relations between Forest River and the rest of Hutterism were essentially severed. Although the renegade colony soon returned to the Schmiedeleut Hutterite fold, relations between Bruderhof and Western Hutterites were in a deep freeze for nearly two decades.[34] Finally, in 1974, the hatchet was buried and for almost two decades relations between the Bruderhof and the Western Hutterites (especially the Schmiedeleut) improved mightily. The warming of relations was even marked by several marriages of Bruderhof members and Western Hutterites.

The 1990s, however, saw another breach between East and West, along with serious internal division among the Schmiedeleut Hutterites themselves. Jacob Kleinsasser, the bishop of the Schmiedeleut, was accused by some of his flock of bad business decisions and vindictive acts against certain Hutterites, and the Schmiedeleut colonies and ministers eventually divided into pro- and anti-Kleinsasser factions. The Bruderhof sided with Kleinsasser and tried to support his claim to hold authority over all the Schmiedeleut, and that alliance further alienated him from his detractors, many of whom had never been fond of the Bruderhof connection.[35] In middecade the fractured Schmiedeleut and Bruderhof severed relations, and the leadership of the Bruderhof lashed out at their former comrades, declaring that the Western Hutterites had "little or no spiritual leadership" and that their colonies were seething with misbehavior: "Alcoholism is rampant, even among some community leaders. Premarital sex is widespread, and there are illegitimate children. In other words, the church has lost its salt and has become lukewarm, shallow, and superficial."[36] The Bruderhof, which for several years had heavily emphasized its Hutterian identity, was again on its own.

The Bruderhof was also challenged in the 1990s by problems in its overseas expansion work. A new beachhead in the movement's ancestral Germany was established in 1988 at Michaelshof, near Bonn—and then abandoned six years later. Some neighbors and government officials were hostile to these foreigners (despite the German ethnicity of many of them) whose religion and manner of living were unconventional, and the community's attempt to build suitable facilities on its sixty-acre site were rebuffed.[37] The Bruderhof also expanded into Nigeria with a settlement called Palmgrove, into which the Bruderhof claimed it poured some $2 million. As other denominations have discovered, however, the understanding of a particular version of Christianity, especially one that requires heavy lifestyle commitments from members, may not be the same among a third-world population as it is in the parent church, and despite intermarriages and other measures that sought to fully unify the Nigerians with the American Bruderhofers, the union fell apart amid bitter recriminations.[38]

Despite the controversies, which remain deep at this writing, the Bruderhof story over the past several decades has largely been one of growth and prosperity. The group seems secure as an ongoing example of a vital, working, deeply communal society. Indeed, if size and a robust economy are the hallmarks of success (an assertion many, probably most, communitarians would reject), then by far the most rousing success story among the FIC members was that of the Bruderhof. Ironically, decades before the later controversies arose, the Bruderhof undermined the FIC and several of its member communities; the stability and moral certainty of the Bruderhof drew members from several other FIC communities, weakening them and directly causing at least one (Kingwood) to cease operations. When the Bruderhof finally decided to withdraw from the FIC, the FIC could not withstand the trauma and went into hibernation.

SIMILAR COMMUNITIES NOT MEMBERS OF THE FIC

Several intentional communities were founded in the 1940s and 1950s that had much in common—including, often, pacifism—with other Fellowship of Intentional Communities members but did not choose to join the FIC. In some cases they were in dialogue with FIC communities; in other cases they kept largely to themselves. In the aggregate they contributed substantially to the communal presence in American society in the postwar era.

San Fernando Farm. Among the non-FIC communities spawned during World War II was San Fernando Farm, which was about twenty-five miles north of downtown Los Angeles. It was founded in 1943 by the families of four conscientious objectors who had been in Civilian Public Service camps early in the war and had developed close friendships. Each family earned its own living, but the community members together owned their small parcel of farmland and the homes and other buildings on it in common, and as a community produced beef, milk, eggs, chickens, vegetables, fruits, nuts, and honey. The Quaker-oriented group housed a Friends Meeting that attracted a number of families from the surrounding area. Although the community never grew very large, it was still alive and well, trying to figure out how to cope with rapid urbanization in its immediate vicinity, in the mid-1950s.[39]

Bass Lake Farm. One of the least documented of all the intentional communities founded in the 1940s and 1950s was another refuge for pacifists, but this time one not run by Quakers. Bass Lake Farm, according to the one published account describing it, was founded by a Father Marston, an Episcopal priest, and two associates on eighty acres near Minneapolis in 1941. The cofounders as pacifists refused military service and were assigned to a Civilian Public Service camp. After the war they returned to Bass Lake, and others moved there as well; about ten members were eventually resident, all living in a single cramped building. The community remained shaky, though, because several members, native southerners, had trouble enduring the cold climate, and the lack of farming skills in the group made self-support in an isolated location difficult. Marston died suddenly, and young, in 1946, and the community disbanded.

Koinonia (Maryland). Koinonia Farm in Georgia was not long the only Koinonia among American intentional communities. A similarly named community not related to the original one was opened on New Year's Day, 1951, on a quiet forty-five-acre tract in Greenspring Valley north of Baltimore. Glenn Harding was one of several founders and the first executive director of the center. Originally, Koinonia aimed to train "Christian Ambassadors" to serve human needs overseas, particularly in areas that had been devastated by World War II and through the worldwide missionary literacy programs of Frank Laubach. In the 1960s and early 1970s, with the rise of the Peace Corps and other assistance and development programs, Koinonia's world mission seemed less urgent than before, and Koinonia staffers under newly appointed director David Poist felt compelled to address the 1960s-era cultural upheaval among the young. Thus the focus of the community came to be the operation of seminars and retreats on vital issues of the day—world peace, literacy, race relations, and hunger, for example. Later the programs at Koinonia tended to focus on personal and spiritual growth, creativity, and cooperative living. Preparation for overseas service and insistence on Christian commitment disappeared as major themes. One report likened the atmosphere at Koinonia to that of "a rich private school," although wealth never characterized the community's finances.[40]

Koinonia remained an active intentional community for about thirty-five years, with fifty or so residents typically present. A communal staff of about twenty-five directed activities and classes, and a major emphasis was a residential program in which participants stayed for several months, studying academic and practical subjects and performing physical labor. Staff and other residents shared housing, meals, work, and learning and spiritual growth activities.[41] Gradually, members tended to become more transient and less firmly committed to the community, and that decline in community values plus financial exigency led to the sale of the property to a private family in 1985. Some members remained on the property thereafter, and the scattered body of former members maintained a newsletter for several years, but the residential community essentially ceased to exist after the sale.[42]

The Ma-Na-Har Cooperative Fellowship and the Bhoodan Center of Inquiry. One of the many Quaker-oriented efforts to establish intentional communities in the 1930s through the 1950s resulted in two interrelated organizations that functioned communally. The Bhoodan Center of Inquiry (the Hindi word "bhoodan" was used by Gandhi and others to mean a system of land-sharing in which those with surplus land give it to others who have little or none[43]), organized in 1953, owned eighty acres in the foothills of the Sierra Nevada near Oakhurst, California, and ran seminars and dialogues on intentional community, low-cost building construction, and other topics. As the Center described its goals in 1971,

We are trying to provide an ashram type of situation, where we may seek together for spiritual enlightenment through meditation, practical knowledge through study and experience, integrated human relations through mutual sharing and working together, understanding our part in nature through association with our natural environment, and physical rejuvenation through more natural living.[44]

The Ma-Na-Har Cooperative Fellowship (the name means "harmony of man and nature") was the communal organization of the Bhoodan staff and supporters. Community members could live on the Bhoodan land or they could occupy private homes on nearby tracts. In either event they worked with one another in cooperative gardening, education, food purchasing and preparation, and other such endeavors. The community had an extensive collection of community-owned tools and equipment that included several vehicles ranging from a Volkswagen microbus to a two-ton truck. Within the larger Ma-Na-Har community some families took their sharing further, pooling employment, some housing, and meals.

In 1970 the community reported that it was not only succeeding at its goals but working to buy more land and build more buildings. Eventually, the communal focus seems to have disappeared, however, and by the 1990s the community had vanished.[45]

Other Religious Communities

Several of the member groups of the Fellowship of Intentional Communities were religious in basis; most frequently they were either Quaker or quasi-Quaker in orientation, although other religions were represented as well. Several other religious communities were also founded in and after 1940, however, on a broader variety of ideological and doctrinal bases, ranging in their spiritual foci from evangelical Protestant to Hindu and including a number of idiosyncratic groups led by independent visionaries who claimed to have new solutions to the problems of the universe.

INDEPENDENT CHRISTIAN COMMUNITIES

The Colony. In 1940 Brother John Korenchan, a onetime Catholic who had a defining spiritual experience early in life, led some eighteen followers from the Seattle area into a communal household that settled near Hawkins Bar, California. Supporting itself with an intensive farming operation on its lush sixteen acres and, more recently, with a plumbing and construction company, the celibate group has endured more than half a century with relatively few defections, and experienced a smooth transition of leadership when Korenchan died in 1982.

In the early 1970s, attrition had reduced the Colony's population to four when a new wave of members began to arrive. By middecade the population had climbed back to about a dozen, where it has remained since. Once viewed with suspicion by its neighbors, the communal family has become respected in the larger local community. Agnes Vanderhoof, Korenchan's successor as spiritual leader, has continued to teach the founder's tenets about the Power that can move persons from within and the necessity of a life of the spirit. Colony members reject all human-created forms, doctrines, and ceremonies in favor of living the teachings of Christ in everyday life. At this writing the Colony is one of the longest-lived and apparently most stable intentional communities in the United States.[46]

Shiloh. Another Christian community that has flourished for over half a century has been Shiloh, or Shiloh Farms, founded in Chautauqua County, New York, in 1941. Shiloh's founder, Eugene Crosby Monroe, taught a perfectionist brand of Christianity that rejected social activism in favor of personal spiritual development alone. He also taught that the Holy Spirit could give new revelations to present-day human beings, a principle that came into play when the well-established group suddenly, obeying what it took to be a divine mandate, moved to Sulphur Springs, Arkansas, in 1968. Although nearly half the membership rejected the move and resigned, the movement has recovered and by the late 1970s had more than a hundred residents at its new location in downtown Sulphur

Springs. From a base of a small retail bakery, the community has developed a prosperous industry of wholesale nationwide distribution of health foods and bread products under the Shiloh Farms label, and thereby has achieved a financial stability not many communities founded in the 1940s attained. Shiloh continues to thrive as a charismatic Protestant church whose members live in close community and worship daily.[47] The impact of Shiloh is augmented by many associate members who live on adjacent properties, sometimes work in Shiloh jobs, and share much of the life of the full members.[48]

Church of the Savior. Gordon Cosby was a Baptist preacher who, like many critics of the religious status quo, found most churches lukewarm and sought not only a vital personal faith but also a community that would engage its members in extensive social outreach. In that quest he and a handful of others organized the Church of the Savior in 1946 at Alexandria, Virginia. The following year the church moved its headquarters to a run-down rooming house in Washington, D.C., and then in 1950 to a larger brownstone in the city. In 1953, in a fashion reminiscent of the Catholic Worker, the church bought a 175-acre rural retreat, Dayspring, in Maryland. From the beginning, outreach work has been strong, and community involvement has drawn into the church and its programs a broadly diverse congregation. The church has sponsored neighborhood community centers, a coffeehouse, an art center, housing projects, a School of Christian Living, and any number of mission and service groups. Mission work has involved advocacy of rights for the aging, health care for the homeless, and peace activism, among other things. Undergirding everything is a strong sense of spiritual purpose, with members engaging in daily prayer and Bible study. Small fellowship groups within the larger church keep member involvement personal. Core members continue to live communally; others in the church's larger worshiping community live independently. The twin focus on deep spiritual experience and social service has continued to anchor the church for half a century. As member and author Elizabeth O'Connor has written, "One cannot belong to Christ without belonging to His community, or to the community without belonging to Him in whom it coheres."[49]

Bethany Fellowship. Still another dedicated and energetic community of committed evangelicals is Bethany Fellowship, whose central focus is the support of missionaries to other countries. The Fellowship had its roots in the dissatisfaction that several families felt toward their two local congregations of the Lutheran Free Church in Minneapolis, and when their ideas about ecclesiastical revitalization were ignored by higher-ups, they proceeded to purchase a small church building in 1943. Under founding pastor Theodore A. Hegre the members decided to sell their homes and pool their money to become full-time Christian evangelists. In 1947 they purchased a sixty-acre site in the Minneapolis suburb of Bloomington and moved there, opening a church and a missionary training institute in the process. Although nonmembers of the Fellowship, or commune, are accepted into the Bethany Missionary Church, the Fellowship remains the core of the organization. For decades the church has pursued its missionary goals successfully, training hundreds of missionaries and supporting dozens of them in the field at any given time. Over the years, Bethany's publication program has also become substantial, producing various kinds of literature including manuals for those who would lead more committed Christian lives.[50] As commune, church, educational institution, mission center, and publishing house, Bethany Fellowship has become a notable institution in the world of evangelical Protestantism.[51]

Reba Place Fellowship. In the mid-1950s several Mennonites interested in the renewal of their faith and of their denomination began to seek new models for committed Christian living. These seekers, some at Goshen College in Indiana and some elsewhere, became especially inspired by several living Christian intentional communities (among them the Bruderhof) and, after various experiments with house churches and other grassroots renewal efforts, decided to take the unprecedented and radical step of planting a Christian community not in a rural area, as the Hutterites and Bruderhof had done before them, but in metropolitan Chicago—a place where they could use the traditional Anabaptist vision of righteousness to confront endemic social evil. The Fellowship saw urban settlement patterns in urgent need of transformation:

Our cities are beginning more and more to resemble vast ant heaps, lacking within them the vital smaller communities that alone make a truly human life possible. . . . When possible we want to live within easy walking distance of one another. Scattered as many of us are during the working days across the sprawling network of the city, we want to come home at evening time to one neighborhood where we are readily available to one another in times of need. We want to be able to meet daily if necessary without climbing into our cars and going half a city away. We want our children to grow up experiencing more than the lonely crowd. We want them to know in their daily life the reality of a closely knit circle of families and friends.[52]

Led by John Miller, an Old Testament scholar at Goshen whose relations with his college and with the larger Mennonite establishment were strained for several years by his radical advocacy of communitarianism, the pioneers purchased a house at 727 Reba Place in Evanston in the summer of 1957. In less than a year the house had thirteen residents plus several visitors, and a second house was purchased across the street. Membership and property continued to grow (the organization owned twenty-one buildings with 120 living units in 1987), and Reba Place Fellowship was soon a thriving community of individuals whose commitment to Christian service dominated their lives.[53]

The typical pattern at Reba Place Fellowship has been for members to work at compatible outside jobs (teaching, social work, and providing mental health services, for example) and place their earnings in the community's common purse.[54] Regardless of the outside occupations of members, however, the overriding communal focus is service to persons in need. To that end the community supports and conducts extensive social service programs that have ranged from a halfway house for persons leaving mental hospitals to providing relief to victims of the war in Vietnam to operating a day-care center to helping Central American refugees find safe places to settle. The social witness of the people of Reba Place has been strong in other ways as well; community members have been frontline activists for peace, civil rights, and other social-justice causes.

Reba Place has long had a special affinity for other intentional Christian communities, and at various times has had mutually supportive relationships with Koinonia Farm, the Bruderhof, the Sojourners Community of Washington, D.C., and the unconventional Forest River Hutterite colony in North Dakota. Interest in starting a rural branch of Reba Place led to the founding of what became a separate, rural, intentional community, Plow Creek Fellowship, in 1971.

Most communities experience internal conflicts, and Reba Place has had its share of discord. Differences of opinion over the role of women in a male-dominated church arose in Reba Place just as they did in other churches, and although some attention was given to expanding leadership opportunities for women, the eldership, the highest office in Reba Place, remained an exclusively male domain. A wave of charismatic activity swept the Fellowship in the early 1970s, in part as a result of contact with the charismatic, communal Church of the Redeemer in Houston, with episodes of speaking in tongues, faith healing, and utterance of prophecy. In the end the charismatic presence sparked a new surge of growth, with Reba Place again expanding into new buildings to house its growing numbers.

In 1980 Reba Place began admitting noncommunal members, and with that shift many living in community decided to move away from the communal center as well—an unexpected by-product of the addition of a new category of membership. By the late 1980s only about half the members were fully communal, living in common facilities and with common finances, and the community was moving to a model in which religious activity centered in small, intense fellowship groups. Nevertheless, the high level of commitment continues; Reba Place continues to be a center of strong faith and many social-service programs.[55]

FACING EAST: THE NEW MONASTERIES AND ASHRAMS

Some few Americans began to participate in communal living under the auspices of non-Western religions as early as the opening years of the twentieth century. American interest in religions and spiritual movements other than Judaism and Christianity expanded and widened over the years, eventually branching out to embrace a variety of Asian religions as well as several kinds of independent spirituality, mysticism, and visionary experience not nominally rooted in any of the world's major religious traditions. In the 1940s and 1950s many of those divergent spiritual interests developed communal expressions.

The non-Western spiritual communities ranged widely in structure as well as in spiritual outlook. Several of the stricter of them espoused, in pursuit of spiritual enlightenment, an asceticism that approached the austerity of classic medieval monasticism or of some of the Asian ashrams and monasteries. That interest in asceticism was part of a larger wave of new interest in disciplined monasticism that surfaced in North America and Europe, one embodied by, for example, an unusual French experiment in Protestant-Catholic ecumenical monasticism, the Taizé community in Burgundy in southern France, founded by Roger Schutz in 1940, which, like other monasteries, encouraged hard work and creative arts in a structured atmosphere of spiritual contemplation.[56] In the United States no one was more influential in popularizing rigorous communal spirituality than Thomas Merton, the Cistercian whose eloquent advocacy of contemplation was published in the 1940s and 1950s in a series of widely read books, including his best-selling autobiography *The Seven Storey Mountain*.[57]

The new interest in monasticism affected not only all the major branches of Christianity in the United States—many Protestants as well as Catholics and Eastern Orthodox were caught up in it—but several non-Western traditions as well. It dovetailed well with the work of the Asian spiritual teachers who had been gathering followings of Americans since the 1890s and were more than willing to offer their disciples the disciplined life of a Hindu ashram or Buddhist monastery. Some of these communities that emerged in the 1940s and 1950s endured for many years, although they have been little noticed by the outside world and hence little documented. The International Babaji Yoga Sangam, for example, dates its founding to 1952, under the direction of Yogi S. A. A. Ramaiah; by 1981 it claimed fifty-two separate centers, some of them residential, where followers received instructions in various kinds of yoga, breathing, and meditation techniques.[58] The Aum Temple Desert Sanctuary, founded in 1956 at Newberry Springs, California, defined its purpose thus in 1981: "We are here to have dominion over our carnal natures whereby we make do as Jesus—transmute these physical bodies."[59] Mysticism and spiritual discipline, which many had presumed to be in retreat ever since, perhaps, the Protestant Reformation, were finding a new following.

Trabuco College. One of the new Eastern-inspired communities that has been relatively well documented was Trabuco College ("college" referring not to education but to the *collegium,* community), founded in 1942 by Gerald Heard, a British writer living in Los Angeles. Heard had arrived in southern California in the late 1930s and had soon joined such other literary and film-industry celebrities as Aldous Huxley and Christopher Isherwood in the Vedanta Society of Hollywood under the direction of Swami Prabhavananda.[60] With world war looming, Heard had come to an apocalyptic sense of the direction in which society was heading: "Humanity is failing. We are starving—many of us physically, all of us spiritually—in the midst of plenty. Our shame and our failure are being blatantly advertised, every minute of every day, by the crash of explosives and the flare of burning towns." The rapidly escalating war was, he believed, a symptom of a civilization beset by "diseased egotism and individualism—the fundamental appeal to greed and fear as the two sole compelling motives of man."[61] And the crisis was absolute: "Our choice is to go on to a new state of being or to end."[62] The solution? "It is very old, and narrow, and difficult to find. It is the way of humility and of self-discipline and re-education. It is the way back to God."[63] Thus Heard sought seclusion and the pursuit of contemplation for himself and other like-minded seekers who would be the neo-Brahmins, the spiritual leaders for an age of crisis.

After several years of arguing the case for building "gymnasia for the mind,"[64] Heard was able to secure a substantial amount of money from various donors[65] and purchase a 392-acre ranch in Trabuco Canyon some sixty miles south of Los Angeles. Scurrying to avoid impending wartime shortages of building supplies, Heard found enough materials to build what looked like, as Isherwood characterized it, a small Franciscan monastery in the Apennines—a group of tile-roofed stone buildings with cloisters, a simple, monastic interior, and great views of the ocean, big enough to house fifty residents.[66] Although it was Vedantist in spiritual outlook, the discipline was modeled on Western Benedictine monasticism: there were long periods of silence, living was quite frugal, and meals were simple and vegetarian.[67] Still, it was a monastery occupied by the English, with, as David King Dunaway characterized it, "tea at four, brilliant conversation, fog hanging over green meadows."[68] It also reflected the literary bent of many of its members, possessing an excellent library of mystical literature.

The Trabuco envisioned by Heard in his prospectus was "un-denominational, and its doors are open to both men and women." It would encompass more than intellectual and spiritual development; even by the time of the prospectus, Heard wrote, "A start has been made to prepare the land surrounding the Center so that later a co-operative and 'self-subsisting' economy may be developed which would be the complement of its psychological practice." To that end, "manual and household work" was to be part of the routine for all.[69]

A statement Huxley made concerning his interest in mystical religion about the time of Trabuco's opening conveys something of the spiritual intent of the project:

I have mainly lived in the world of intellectual life and art. But the world of knowing-about-things is unsatisfactory. It's no good knowing about the taste of strawberries out of a book. . . . Beauty is imprisoned, as it were, within the white spaces between the lines of a poem, between the notes of music, in the apertures between groups of sculpture. . . . They throw a net and catch something, though the net is trivial. . . . But one wants to go further. One wants to have a conscious taste of these holes between the strings of the net.[70]

Even though his prospectus set up separate classes of students, masters (teachers), and doctors (missionaries), Heard claimed from the beginning that he sought not to have any resident guru in the classic master-disciple model, but to gather a community that would serve as a clearinghouse for religious experiences and ideas, a community of collegial seekers.[71] Clearly, however, he dominated the community, ending up functioning, as Guinevera Nance has put it, "as a sort of resident guru" despite his desire for an acephalous community.[72] According to one of the few accounts of daily life there, Heard gave two long "seminars" daily. Beyond that, spiritual practice tended to be rigorous and austere, centered on three hours a day of meditation—Heard himself was said to do six—in a windowless room constructed for the purpose. Silence was maintained from sunset until after breakfast. Heard required celibacy of his devotees and even of visitors, a rule that reportedly sent several of his monastic fellows packing.[73] (Celibacy came easily to Heard, who never fully came to grips with his homosexuality and thus tended to avoid sexual involvements in any direction.) The diet was austere and plain; one woman went so far in dietary self-mortification as to eat mud.[74] Residents were to do manual work (gardening, especially, but all the other work associated with the community as well) and seek spiritual engagement. They also had ample time for their own pursuits; Aldous Huxley wrote one of his most important books, *The Perennial Philosophy*, at Trabuco.[75] Heard turned out a fair amount of writing despite his lengthy meditation sessions and lectures, urging his readers to pursue "moral research" to help solve the fundamental "problem of human cohesion" (certainly a crucial need during wartime) and to structure meditation and other spiritual disciplines into their lives.[76]

For several years the community flourished. One participant, writing decades later, characterized it as no less than "a miniature revival of the Transcendentalist spirit of Brook Farm" and even as having been the birthplace of what became known as postmodernism.[77] Problems, however, some of them stemming from human fallibility, were there as well. Heard seems to have been something less than a perfect guru. As Laurence Veysey concluded on the basis of interviews with several former Trabuco residents,

There was an aloof shyness in his make-up, a tendency to retreat into isolation, which suggested that he was fundamentally ill suited to group living. His own emotional conflicts also lay too near the surface, creating a tone of tension. . . . Public quarrels were at a minimum, but the everyday mood was one of mutual isolation and somber indrawing. Life at Trabuco became a form of solitary confinement. One man even retreated to his room, where he spent his time cutting out paper dolls.[78]

Heard eventually announced, in 1947, that it was God's will that Trabuco close. Two years later he gave the property to the Vedanta Society, which had a constituency that could make good use of it. It opened as a more conventional Vedanta institution, called the Ramakrishna Monastery, in September of 1949, with an all-male membership and a rigorous program of hard work, worship, and meditation.[79] Heard remained interested in the idea of founding centers for the development of human potential, however. In 1961, when Michael Murphy and Richard Price began to work toward the founding of what would become the Esalen Institute, perhaps the most renowned personal-growth center of the 1960s, they consulted Heard, among others, and found his input the most enthusiastic and energizing they had encountered.[80] Freewheeling Esalen was hardly a reincarnation of disciplined Trabuco, but as a center for human growth it took up the same standard Heard had raised two decades earlier.

NEW AGE AND INDEPENDENT RELIGIOUS COMMUNITIES

Twentieth-century religious movements, communal or otherwise, have in many cases not been directly connected to the major religious traditions of either East or West, although they may garner and utilize spiritual insights from a wide variety of sources. What are often called New Age religions, for example, are typically marked by a thoroughgoing eclecticism as they draw on spiritual resources that may range from Buddhism to American Indian teachings to belief in the powers of crystals. As has been the case in every age, some modern charismatic leaders have set up their own movements and charted their own independent spiritual directions.

The Emissary Communities. One of the largest and longest-lived of the religious community movements that emerged in the 1940s and 1950s was rooted in the independent spiritual experiences of some thoroughly Western individuals. The Emissaries of Divine Light originated in 1932, when Lloyd Meeker, after an extended period of spiritual seeking, began to attract a following for his innovative thinking about the regeneration of human potential. He met Lord Martin Cecil, a British aristocrat (the seventh Marquess of Exeter, specifically), in 1940, and the two soon began to plan an intentional community based on their common spiritual outlook, a community that finally came to fruition in 1945 with the founding of Sun-

rise Ranch near Loveland, Colorado. Starting with a played-out tract of
dry land at the foot of the Rocky Mountains and fewer than a dozen members, the Emissaries have turned Sunrise into a New Age showplace, with
dozens of buildings, extensive organic farming and gardening operations,
a hydroponic greenhouse, a large domed auditorium for meetings, and
various conference rooms and support facilities.

Martin Cecil since young adulthood had been overseeing his family
cattle ranch in the wild interior of British Columbia. In 1948 another
Emissary community was established on the Cecil holdings at 100 Mile
House, an isolated trading post. That community has, like Sunrise Ranch,
grown to a population in the hundreds and has a goodly variety of buildings and programs. Sunrise and the "Hundred" constitute the heart of the
Emissary movement, but they are supplemented by dozens of centers
throughout the United States and Canada and to some extent in other
countries. The satellite centers vary in size, some consisting of little more
than a family or two, but all of them make distinctive contributions to the
Emissary movement and to their localities. Perhaps the most notable of
the other Emissary communities is Glen Ivy Hot Springs, or "Club Mud,"
a southern California health resort that features natural mineral water hot
pools and red clay mud baths as well as a full range of massage and per-
sonal-grooming services.

The spiritual orientation of the Emissary communities could be characterized as of a New Age variety, focusing on inner enlightenment and personal spiritual growth. The movement stresses "attunement," or the lining
up of bodily and mental energy for the healing and wellness of body and
soul. Attunement Centers, rather like medical or chiropractic clinics but
without any physical contact between patient and healer, are found at
some of the communities. The Emissary communities earn much of their
living from conducting public seminars and courses in their concepts—in
personal growth, spiritual development, and creativity. They also have a
vigorous publishing program, issuing several periodicals and various inspirational books (many by Martin Cecil) as well as audio- and videotapes.[81]

Lemurian communities. For about a century some Americans have been
fascinated by the myth of Lemuria, purportedly a lost Pacific continent
that is said to be going to rise again with potentially disastrous consequences for North America—consequences that may be averted, however,
by those who have access to the special ancient knowledge that Lemurians
have carefully guarded over many centuries, knowledge that can not only

avert the pending disaster but also lead to the creation of a communal heaven on earth for all.[82]

Lemuria eventually became the focus for several religious groups, the first of them founded by Robert D. Stelle as the Lemurian Fellowship in Chicago in 1936. After several moves the group established a communal headquarters near Ramona, California, in 1941. The land eventually came to consist of 260 acres in two separate tracts with a school, a chapel, a library, and other facilities. Much of the cooperative work centers on the Lemurian educational programs, including a correspondence school with a nationwide student body. Fees are charged for correspondence study; the center also has an industry, the Lemurian Crafts, that manufactures and distributes craft works embodying the Lemurian outlook and earning income for the community.[83]

A later offshoot is the Stelle Community, located in a rural part of northern Illinois. In 1963 Richard Kieninger, who had written a book that purported to transmit messages from ancient brotherhoods to contemporary humans,[84] broke with the Lemurian Fellowship and began to develop his own Lemurian group, which purchased property and moved to the Stelle site in 1973. Kieninger warned of impending global disaster, with Stelle residents in their isolated enclave among the few to survive. A falling out among Kieninger and other members led to his departure in 1976 and his initiation of yet another community, the Adelphi Group, at Adelphi, Texas. In 1982 the Stelle community opened its doors to non-believers in the Lemurian message and has since functioned with only loosely cooperative features, although many residents still seek to develop a futuristic ideal city. The original Lemurian Fellowship repudiates both the Stelle and Adelphi Groups.[85]

The Children of Light. One small, little-noticed colony has existed quietly in the Arizona desert since 1963, when a previously mobile community stopped and took root there. The Children of Light had their beginnings in British Columbia in 1949 when Grace Agnes Carlson, who took the spiritual name Elect Gold, had a Pentecostal visionary experience that predicted the imminent coming of the Kingdom of God. With the end of the world at hand, she proclaimed, God called on believers to repent and required the faithful to separate themselves from the hopeless rest of the world. The dozen or so persons who became persuaded of the validity of her vision soon agreed to live their dedication fully, pooling their possessions and living sinless, celibate lives. At first they sequestered themselves in a farmhouse, causing a sensation in their small town of Keremeos, British Columbia. Then, nineteen strong, they left Keremeos and for twelve years traveled as a group throughout North America waiting for God to direct them to a place of safety in which to survive the coming catastrophe and picking up an occasional new member. In 1963 Elect Gold announced that God had directed them to settle at Agua Caliente, Arizona. Eventually, they purchased eighty forlorn acres on which they built various buildings and began to grow trees and vegetables. There, having made the desert bloom, they remain, living simply and quietly while waiting for the certain end of the world. Their faith remains powerful; when local officials tried to evacuate them in the face of a flood on the Gila River in 1993, they refused to leave, relying on divine protection—and survived.[86] In 1995 Elect Gold was bedridden and nearing one hundred years of age; aging and death were taking a toll on the group. The seven survivors, however, were still living out their commitment to their unusual faith.[87]

LATTER DAY SAINT COMMUNITIES

Various offshoots of the Mormon tradition have embraced communal living. One new LDS group is known to have entered into community in the 1940s, and another in the early 1950s.

Glendenning: The Levites/Order of Aaron. Maurice Glendenning, a chiropractor who claimed that he had begun receiving divine revelations soon after joining the Mormon Church in the 1930s, eventually broke with the main body of LDS believers and founded his Aaronic Order, whose members are called Levites, in 1942 in Utah. The initial faithful, who numbered about twenty, followed Glendenning to remote western Utah in 1949 and, after experimenting with forms of communal living in several temporary settings, in 1956 established a communal settlement called EskDale, which is alive and well with a population of about a hundred at this writing. The remote EskDale, deep in the desert, is largely agricultural, with various crops under cultivation as well as a dairy operation. So successful has the movement been under Glendenning's successor, Robert J. Conrad, that small satellite colonies have been started, and other converts now live, noncommunally, in various places around the American West. After forty years of communal life the Order of Aaron appears to be thriving.[88]

Kilgore: Zion's Order. Marl V. Kilgore had been a member of Maurice Glendenning's Levites for about a year when he announced that he had begun receiving divine revelations himself. In 1951 he formed his own religious movement called Zion's Order, and soon thereafter with his followers purchased land near Mansfield, Missouri, where an intentional community was erected for his followers on land that eventually totaled 1,175 acres. Life was austere in the early years there, and the group has never achieved great worldly prosperity, but over time basic amenities have been provided. Since the 1960s the group has conducted extensive missionary work among the Navajo Indians, and Kilgore himself resigned the presidency of his movement (in favor of one of his sons, Nathan) to work in the mission fields; he died in 1989. The community seems to have experienced some decline in numbers in recent years; in 1967 membership at the colony was reported to be ninety, including children, but by 1993 the total had dropped to thirty-two.[89] As with the Levites, the families in Zion's Order are monogamous, not polygamous.[90]

And Others . . .

As has ever been the case, some of the communities founded in the 1940s and 1950s cannot be easily categorized. This survey will close by taking notice of four communities that were widely varying pieces in the kaleidoscope of American communal history.

THE DES MOINES UNIVERSITY OF LAWSONOMY

One of the most unusual of the midcentury experiments in community was the Des Moines University of Lawsonomy, which represented the communal phase of an older movement centered on the distinctive teachings of Alfred W. Lawson. Lawson had been a minor-league (and very briefly major-league) baseball player in the late nineteenth century who turned his attention to the air early in the aviation age. Among other things, he claimed to be the inventor of the airliner, and indeed he did build a relatively large working airplane—one that could carry, with seats in the aisle, twenty-six passengers—as early as 1919.

In the 1920s Lawson turned his attention to physics and economics. In several self-published books he presented nothing less than a revision of the basic laws of the universe. Suction and pressure were the basics of physical motion, he announced, and penetrability—the ability of one substance to penetrate another—was the fundamental law of physics. Crucial to everything was zig-zag-and-swirl, which says that motion does not take place simply between two points, but within a gigantic matrix of suction and pressure currents. Other unfamiliar terms—equaeverpoise, lesether—and redefined familiar ones describe a physical universe ruled by forces that seem to owe little to Newtonian mechanics and are, to say the least, difficult to comprehend readily.[91]

Once he had his physics in place, Lawson turned his genius to economics and soon, early in the depression era, he was pushing for *Direct Credits for Everybody*, as another of his book titles had it, a system in which new money would be issued as interest-free loans to the people.[92] Physics, physiology, economics, philosophy, even religion—Lawson had the world and its inhabitants entirely figured out, and the system as a whole was, of course, called Lawsonomy.[93] Mainly because of his populist Direct Credits scheme, Lawson managed to attract surprising numbers of troops to his banner during the depression, and Lawsonomy took root as an American social movement.

The communal phase of the Lawson phenomenon began when Lawson bought, at the bargain-basement price of $80,000, the fourteen acres and six large buildings of the defunct Des Moines University in 1943. Renamed the Des Moines University of Lawsonomy, the institution was from day one not your average college, despite Lawson's early promise to the citizens of Des Moines that it would be a full-service accredited institution. Although the DMUL had a good potential recruitment base in Lawson's Direct Credits Society, which at one time boasted many thousands of members, enrollment probably never reached a hundred. The curriculum was never remotely like that of any other college, consisting as it did almost entirely of the memorization of Lawson's written works.[94] The students lived in communal isolation, keeping themselves largely removed from the rest of Des Moines and working to achieve self-sufficiency in food by gardening on various lots near the campus. Lyell Henry, Lawson's biographer, characterizes a typical day at DMUL as consisting of, besides classes, individual work on memorizing the Lawsonian corpus and participation in the physical fitness programs of which Lawson was much enamored, "planting, hoeing, harvesting, and canning crops, preparing and serving meals, washing dishes, doing laundry and making up the beds, cleaning and dusting, renovating and maintaining buildings, keeping up the grounds and flower gardens, shoveling coal and hauling ashes, patrolling the property, selling books and advertising space."[95]

Students were told not to bring money or property when they came to the school, because their needs would all be provided, and they would work for the common good. Indeed, the financial equality of the students undoubtedly contributed to communal solidarity. But to outsiders the whole thing was virtually a prison camp. Residents of the neighborhood of the DMUL quickly came to regard the institution as an alien presence, and relations deteriorated rapidly, culminating in an evening of violence against the school in October 1944, and subsequently in a decree from Lawson that no one not authorized by him, including public officials, could set foot on campus.

The DMUL lasted a decade, despite declining enrollments that saw the student body shrink to twenty or so, finally collapsing in the wake of a fraud that Lawson perpetrated on the U.S. government. In the aftermath of World War II a federal agency disposed of excess wartime machine tools by selling them to colleges—for use within the purchasing institution only—for 5 percent or less of market value. The DMUL managed to get some of the largesse, buying more than $200,000 worth of machines for $4,400. But Lawsonian officials turned around and sold the machines for a profit of about $150,000. Senate hearings in 1952 unraveled the chicanery, and soon thereafter came the end of the Des Moines University of Lawsonomy.[96] The property was sold in 1954. Lawson died two weeks later at age eighty-five. Within a year the campus had been razed to make way for a shopping center.[97]

QUARRY HILL

Artists' colonies experienced a heyday about the turn of the twentieth century with the establishment of a dozen or so colonies during the era of the arts and crafts movement. Other enclaves of artists have been founded subsequently, and one of the most enduring of them has been Quarry Hill. Irving Fiske, a playwright, and his wife, Barbara Hall Fiske, a painter, were married in 1946 and purchased an old farm near Rochester, Vermont, on which to live. They immediately began inviting friends to visit and, if they liked, to move in. New residents erected new houses, and a community slowly developed. Although being an artist was never a specific prerequisite for residency there, Quarry Hill has had something of a bohemian artistic character from the beginning. Philosophically, the community has long had a strong focus on child rearing and has been an outspoken center of opposition to violence against children, including corporal punishment, through its operation of a children's advocacy group known as Free the Kids!

The surge of countercultural communalism in the 1960s and early 1970s attracted waves of young rebels to Quarry Hill, which had long resembled a hippie commune. Many moved in, building various handmade homes to live in and a community center that housed Quarry Hill's private school. The population eventually peaked at about a hundred, and probably would have kept rising had not zoning and land-use issues stopped the influx. The community continues its life today much as it has for half a century, a center of independent, peaceful, free souls with a wide variety of jobs and avocations, residing in a jumble of modest self-built homes and living a loose-knit cooperative life together.[98]

MELBOURNE VILLAGE

The work of Ralph Borsodi was most prominent in the 1930s, when his School of Living and various subsistence homesteads projects received a fair amount of attention as alternatives to the nation's deteriorating industrial cities and to the hardships of the depression. The last major project to be undertaken under Borsodi's inspiration and, to some degree, personal direction was Melbourne Village, an enclave near the city of Melbourne, Florida, that was founded in 1947.

Three women were collectively the motive force behind Melbourne Village. Virginia Wood, Elizabeth Nutting, and Margaret Hutchinson, all of Dayton, Ohio, where they had worked with Borsodi's Liberty Homesteads project, established the American Homesteading Foundation in 1946. After due consultation with Borsodi and Arthur Morgan, whose advocacy of small communities remained strong, land was purchased and the general outlines of the project were adopted: the first eighty acres would be given over to fifty homesteads of a half acre to one acre each, with forty acres designated for community use. Melbourne Village would have a cooperative store, producers' cooperatives, community recreation facilities, and other institutions to promote the common life. The emphasis on cooperation raised some suspicion in Melbourne, as similar schemes had and would elsewhere, that something akin to communism was being undertaken in the new land development, but the organizers of the project deflected those fears and by 1948 the village was well established and growing steadily. A report in the summer of 1949 counted twenty-one homes and cottages, and small-scale businesses, including a craft works cooperative, were soon present as well. Ralph Borsodi's influence on the project was underscored with the founding of a School of Living to provide practical educational programs for homesteaders. Indeed, Borsodi himself moved to Melbourne Village in 1950.

Borsodi's grandest venture was the establishment in 1956, after years of

preliminaries, of Melbourne University, a graduate school that would focus on a single course in "praxiological philosophy"—the study of human
thought and action, dedicated to the solving of real-life problems.[99] As
impressive as Borsodi's books were, however, he was never good at dealing with people, and personality clashes and financial problems kept the
university from amounting to much. Some seminars and short courses
were held, but Borsodi resigned as chancellor and eventually the skeleton
university merged with the Florida Institute of Technology.

The 1950s saw the steady growth of the enclave, but problems grew as
well. Disagreements over the direction village development and life were
taking—this within a context of rapid growth of the whole south Florida
area, which made the ideal of a bucolic hamlet hard to maintain—became
endemic. Some of the cooperative features of village life, such as the co-op
store, were discontinued. Real estate speculators began making predatory
investments in the village. Melbourne Village today retains some of its
distinctive character, but its original purpose as a village of cooperative
homesteaders was never fully realized.[100]

WKFL FOUNTAIN OF THE WORLD

Several communitarian experiments have ended in one kind of disaster
or another. One of them was the WKFL Fountain of the World. The *Book
of Mormon* and other Latter Day Saint literature had an early impact on
founder Francis H. Pencovic, who took the name Krishna Venta. An admirer of Mormon founder Joseph Smith, Venta had numerous sexual encounters with his female followers, depicting them as polygamous marital
liaisons, and the organization of his movement was inspired by that of the
Mormon Church, featuring a prophetic president and a council of twelve
apostles. However, he stood far enough from the Latter Day Saint tradition that it seems most logical to categorize his group as independent, not
sectarian LDS.

Krishna Venta turned up in Los Angeles in the late 1940s, claiming to
have originally been from the Himalayas and to have been miraculously
transported to the United States in 1932. (He was born in 1911 in San
Francisco and before founding the WKFL movement had been a petty
criminal and mental patient.[101]) He was, he claimed, one in a long line of
saviors who had attempted to rescue humanity from its errors but had
never heretofore succeeded. Giving the process another try, Krishna Venta
called on his followers to live communally, giving up all their possessions

to the group in the interest of total unity. They were to practice the virtues of wisdom, knowledge, faith, and love, whence came the movement's titular acronym. The group survived mainly by seeking donations—of money, food, clothing, building materials, and other necessities—from the public.[102] Krishna Venta was said to be a spellbinding lecturer, often captivating a crowd for many hours.

For some years the group lived quietly in Box Canyon off the San Fernando Valley in southern California, and in the mid-1950s even spawned a satellite center at Homer, Alaska, where adherents are still remembered as the "Barefooters" for their practice of going barefooted most of the time. The California believers were probably best known to the general public as firefighters who, in the biblical robes that were their standard attire, turned up to help construct firebreaks and provide other assistance at conflagrations in their vicinity. Occasional publicity stunts also brought attention to Venta and his followers, as when, in 1955, he had his followers raise him on a large cross in a mock crucifixion ceremony on a hilltop. He soon claimed many thousands of followers in California and Alaska, although a count in the low hundreds seems more judicious.[103]

Krishna Venta's spectacular and tragic end came in December 1958, when two disaffected male members bombed him, seven followers, and the central colony building into oblivion. They charged that Venta had been having sex systematically with female members of the movement, including their wives and various underage girls. His death did not end the movement, however; his wife, Ruth, managed to keep many of the faithful together, and they quietly survived into the 1980s, ever loyal to the teachings of their departed prophet.[104] A small resurgence is reported to have taken place in the late 1960s when communally oriented hippies visited in some numbers. It may be that the group narrowly averted disaster in the process, because one group of visitors, a former member reports, was none other than the Charles Manson family. Manson and his followers camped out on WKFL property and interacted with members for some three months before moving on to the nearby Spann Movie Ranch and then to their agenda of brutal mass murder.[105]

6

1960 *and Beyond*

The communities of the first six decades of the twentieth century set the stage for an amazing future, but the residents of St. Francis Acres, or the depression-era settlements, or the early FIC communities could hardly have anticipated what lay just over the horizon. The thousands upon thousands of communes of the hippies that erupted in the 1960s and 1970s would introduce the concept of common endeavor to a whole new generation.

The new wave of communes began to take shape as early as 1962. That was the year of the founding of Gorda Mountain at Gorda, California, a pioneering settlement that operated as "LATWIDN"—Land Access to Which Is Denied No One. As many as two hundred short- and long-term residents would take advantage of Amelia Newell's offer to let anyone live on the land she legally owned but regarded as belonging to all.[1]

Not long after Newell had thrown her doors open, an intentional community with a Hindu focus—then quite novel for non-Asian Americans—opened at Virginia City, Nevada. The master, Subramuniya, an American who had gone to Ceylon for spiritual training, was interested in new and inclusive spiritual patterns and thus helped inaugurate the fascination with non-Western religions that came to characterize so many of the 1960s-era communes.[2]

While Subramuniya was helping young Americans explore Eastern ways, John Presmont, who took the name Brother Jud, was experimenting with new lifestyles that would take institutional form as the Kerista commune in San Francisco. Kerista's hallmark was "polyfidelity," a form of free love in which members of the commune or one of its subgroups would sleep with members of the group of the opposite sex on a systematic rotating basis. Kerista and Gorda Mountain were also among the first communes to be fairly open about the use of marijuana and more potent mind-expanding substances.[3] It may be in Kerista that the eventual hippie trinity of sex, drugs, and rock and roll first came together in a communal setting.

Yet another communal innovation came in 1963 with the opening of Tolstoy Farm in eastern Washington state on land provided by the family of Huw "Piper" Williams. Williams was a veteran of pacifist activism and sought to create a community that would embody the ideals of Gandhi and Tolstoy and be open to all, devoid of regulations, and committed to poverty and simplicity.[4] Tolstoy prefigured the peace commitment as well as the anything-goes atmosphere that characterized so many communes active during the Vietnam War. And in Drop City, founded near Trinidad, Colorado, in 1965, these themes came together more concretely than ever before when a handful of bohemian artists founded an open community with virtually no material resources but plenty of robust spirit and built spectacularly original dome homes out of scrounged materials.[5] The hippie communal era had commenced.

But that gets ahead of the story. The post-1960 groups will have the successor to this volume all to themselves.

What remains to be said, however, is that what happened after 1960 was clearly related to earlier communitarianism, contrary to what some have argued.[6] The hippie portion of the sixties-era communal scene was largely ahistorical in the sense that most of its participants knew little about the communal past into whose line they were stepping, but the early founders, those who pointed the way to the new communal genre, had a wide variety of connections to earlier communitarianism and collectivity in diverse venues. The founders of Morning Star Ranch and Drop City, two pathbreaking early communes, had personal and familial exposure to such diverse influences as the Oneida Community, the Bruderhof, the Communist Party, and the long tradition of communal sharing among bohemian artists. The past was resurrected repeatedly as the thousands of new communes sprang up: when Lou Gottlieb of Morning Star, for example, deeded his property to God, he was reenacting what had been done a decade or two earlier at the Glen Gardner community in New Jersey and nearly a century before that at Celestia in Pennsylvania. Pioneering new and open sexual relationships had been undertaken at the Oneida Community and elsewhere in the 1850s and before.

Communitarianism after 1960 certainly took off in directions all its own. But the seeds of the remarkable wave of communal living that would capture the imagination of a generation were assuredly sown in the American communal past.

Notes
Selected Bibliography
Index

Notes

ACKNOWLEDGMENTS

1. Timothy Miller, "Artists' Colonies as Communal Societies in the Arts and Crafts Era," *Communal Societies* 16 (1996): 43–70.

2. Elly Wynia, *The Church of God and Saints of Christ: The Rise of Black Jews* (New York: Garland Publishing, 1994).

INTRODUCTION: THE PERSISTENCE OF COMMUNITY

1. Everett Webber, *Escape to Utopia: The Communal Movement in America* (New York: Hastings House, 1959), 419.

2. Arthur Bestor, *Backwoods Utopias: The Sectarian Origins and the Owenite Phase of Communitarian Socialism in America—1663–1829* (Philadelphia: Univ. of Pennsylvania Press, 2d ed., 1970), 252. This part of Bestor's book was originally published as "Patent-Office Models of the Good Society: Some Relationships Between Social Reform and Westward Expansion," *American Historical Review* 58 (Apr. 1953): 505–26.

3. Robert Fogarty, *All Things New: American Communes and Utopian Movements 1865–1914* (Chicago: Univ. of Chicago Press, 1990).

4. The balance of this book will easily demonstrate that the number of intentional communities operating in the United States in the first six decades of the twentieth century was well into the hundreds. Various lists of communities, moreover, provided by various authors contain entries I could not verify independently, but which if correct would send the total still higher.

5. Some historians have seen communes before the twentieth century as deeply withdrawn from the larger society. For a recent argument to the contrary see Lyman Tower Sargent, "Dreams and Other Products of Nineteenth-Century Communities," *Communities Directory: A Guide to Cooperative Living* (Langley, Wash.: Fellowship for Intentional Community, 1995), 165–71.

6. Some have argued that communal living is an episodic phenomenon tied to economic conditions in the larger society or other social variables. See, for example, Michael Barkun, "Communal Societies as Cyclical Phenomena," *Communal Societies* 4 (1984): 35–48; Brian J. L. Berry, *America's Utopian Experiments: Communal Havens from Long-Wave Crises* (Hanover, N.H.: Univ. Press of New England, 1992). Although my purpose here is not to refute the specific arguments those scholars have made, the present volume as whole demonstrates that though the life of the intentional community movement has not been without its ups and downs, it does have a continuity that should not be overlooked.

7. For an example of a situation during the McCarthy era in which an intentional community was repeatedly scrutinized by its neighbors for signs of communism, see Richard C. Crepeau, *Melbourne Village: The First Twenty-five Years (1946–1971)*

(Orlando: Univ. of Central Florida Press, 1988), 26–28, 85–87, 112. Red-baiting even extended to the floor of Congress; see the discussion of the government-sponsored subsistence homestead communities later in this volume for a description of the congressional attack on the communities as outposts of communism.

8. On this theme see Jesse Pitts, "The Counter Culture: Tranquilizer or Revolutionary Ideology?" *Dissent* 18:3 (Apr. 1971): 216–29.

9. Albert Bates and Allen Butcher, "Options for Incorporation of Intentional Communities," in *The 1990/91 Directory of Intentional Communities* (Evansville, Ind., and Stelle, Ill.: Fellowship for Intentional Community and Communities Publications Cooperative, 1990), 98–99.

10. Some community-minded persons have spent years trying to gather members and get a project rolling, all without much success. That phenomenon of well-intentioned futility has long been with us; witness the case of Alcander Longley a century ago, who repeatedly announced the establishment of new communities but never had much luck at attracting others to share his vision and apparently did not last very long himself at the one or two communities led by others that he had joined earlier in life. His case is discussed in a later chapter. Recent issues of what is now called the *Communities Directory* have listed many communities as "forming," meaning that they have not yet reached a membership of five or more. Some such communities have been listed repeatedly in this candidate status, indicating that vision and reality do not always line up but that some visionaries are loath to desist from pursuing their communal dreams.

11. See Rosabeth Moss Kanter, *Commitment and Community: Communes and Utopias in Sociological Perspective* (Cambridge, Mass.: Harvard Univ. Press, 1972), 241–44, for a discussion of such definitions.

12. Daniel B. Greenberg, "Growing Up in Community: Children and Education within Contemporary U.S. Intentional Communities" (Ph.D. diss., Univ. of Minnesota, 1993). Dr. Greenberg has graciously made his lists of intentional communities available to me.

13. The principal source on Spragg's community is contained within a novel: Louis Bromfield, *The Strange Case of Miss Annie Spragg* (New York: Frederick A. Stokes Co., 1928), 46–65. Several historians have taken the story as factual, and some claim to have corroborated it with separate, confirming testimony—which, however, is never cited explicitly. (See, for example, Vance Randolph, "God Works in Illinois," *Americans Who Thought They Were Gods: Colorful Messiahs and Little Christs* [Girard, Kans.: Haldeman-Julius Publications, 1943], 7–8, wherein we are assured that the author has secured oral confirmations of Bromfield's story from "many elderly people in Illinois.") Perhaps the best answer is that proposed by Bromfield critic David Anderson, who regards the work as fictional but based on one or more groups of Perfectionists near Bromfield's hometown of Mansfield, Ohio. (See David D. Anderson, *Louis Bromfield* [New Haven, Conn.: College and Univ. Press, 1964]: 57.) In Bromfield's tale, Spragg located his New Jerusalem in Illinois and there built a temple into which he retreated and in the darkness of which he apparently had sexual relations with a goodly procession of willing consecrated virgins.

1. THE CONTINUING TRADITION

1. The definitive history of the Shakers is Stephen Stein, *The Shaker Experience in America: A History of the United Society of Believers* (New Haven, Conn.: Yale Univ. Press, 1992). On the rift between the Canterbury and Sabbathday Lake communities,

see 384–94. For additional references to the Shaker tradition see the major bibliography of the movement, Mary L. Richmond, *Shaker Literature: A Bibliography* (Hancock, Mass.: Shaker Community, Inc., 1977); two volumes.

2. Bertha M. H. Shambaugh, *Amana: The Community of True Inspiration* (n.p.: State Historical Society of Iowa, 1988 reprint; first published in 1908), 21–77.

3. Diane L. Barthel, *Amana: From Pietist Sect to American Community* (Lincoln: Univ. of Nebraska Press, 1984), 67–74. Barthel's data and analysis come largely from Jonathan G. Andelson, "Communalism and Change in the Amana Society, 1855–1932" (Ph.D. diss., Univ. of Michigan, 1974).

4. For Duss's own, self-serving version of the events of his rule see John S. Duss, *The Harmonists: A Personal History* (Ambridge, Pa.: Harmonie Associates reprint, 1970; originally published in 1943). The definitive history of the Harmony Society has been compiled in several volumes by Karl J. R. Arndt. See especially Arndt, *George Rapp's Harmony Society, 1785–1847* (Philadelphia: Univ. of Pennsylvania Press, 1965) and Arndt, *George Rapp's Successors and Material Heirs, 1847–1916* (Rutherford, N.J.: Fairleigh Dickinson Univ. Press, 1971).

5. Little scholarship seems to have followed the postbreakup life of the original Oneidans and their descendants at the Mansion House. Perhaps the best source for ongoing information is the *Oneida Community Journal*, published by the Oneida Community Mansion House, the nonprofit corporation that now owns the building and grounds and directs historic preservation activities even as the living community continues to inhabit the premises. For a history, see Maren Lockwood Carden, *Oneida: Utopian Community to Modern Corporation* (Baltimore: Johns Hopkins Univ. Press, 1969). A more recent history is Spencer Klaw, *Without Sin: The Life and Death of the Oneida Community* (New York: Penguin, 1993).

6. A survey taken in 1983 found that 138 Schmiedeleut, 89 Lehrerleut, and 128 Dariusleut colonies had been founded. A few in each *leut* had become extinct. See "List of Hutterite Colonies, 1983," compiled by Prof. Lawrence Anderson, Mankato (Minn.) State Univ., Center for Communal Studies archive, Univ. of Southern Indiana, Evansville.

7. John A. Hostetler, *Hutterite Society* (Baltimore: Johns Hopkins Univ. Press, 1974), 273.

8. Ernest S. Wooster, *Communities of the Past and Present* (Newllano, La.: Llano Colonist, 1924), 64.

9. For the basic contours of the social gospel movement, see, among many other works, C. Howard Hopkins, *The Rise of the Social Gospel in American Protestantism, 1865–1915* (New Haven, Conn.: Yale Univ. Press, 1940); Ronald C. White Jr. and C. Howard Hopkins, *The Social Gospel: Religion and Reform in Changing America* (Philadelphia: Temple Univ. Press, 1976).

10. Quoted in Ralph Albertson, "The Christian Commonwealth in Georgia," *Georgia Historical Quarterly* 29 (June 1945): 128.

11. Frances Davis, *A Fearful Innocence* (Kent, Ohio: Kent State Univ. Press, 1981), 17.

12. A useful personal history of the colony is provided by Albertson in the article cited above. For a scholarly account see James Dombrowski, *The Early Days of Christian Socialism in America* (New York: Columbia Univ. Press, 1936), chap. 12.

13. Wilbur F. Copeland, "The Straight Edge after Eleven Years," *Independent* 69 (Nov. 3, 1910): 981.

14. William A. Hinds, *American Communities and Co-Operative Colonies* (Chicago: Kerr, 3d ed., 1908), 548.

15. Ibid.

16. Wilbur F. Copeland, "Straight Edge Industrial Settlement," in William D. P. Bliss, ed., *The New Encyclopedia of Social Reform* (New York: Funk and Wagnalls, 1908), 1164.

17. Robert S. Fogarty, "Straight Edge Industrial Settlement," in *Dictionary of American Communal and Utopian History* (Westport, Conn.: Greenwood, 1980), 167.

18. Otohiko Okugawa, "Annotated List of Communal and Utopian Societies, 1787–1919." Published as an appendix to Robert Fogarty, *Dictionary of American Communal and Utopian History,* 225–26.

19. Booth had long supported rural colonization in England and the United States. See William Booth, *In Darkest England and the Way Out* (Chicago: Charles H. Sergel, 1890), for his views on the matter. For the programmatic outlook of his son-in-law, the chief promoter of colonies in the United States, see Frederick Booth-Tucker, *Back to the Land! Or the Ten-Acre Farms of the Salvation Army* (n.p.: Salvation Army, 1898).

20. Albert Shaw, "A Successful Farm Colony in the Irrigation Country," *American Review of Reviews* 26 (Nov. 1902): 561.

21. The standard monograph on the Salvation Army colonies is Clark C. Spence, *The Salvation Army Farm Colonies* (Tucson: Univ. of Arizona Press, 1985). This sketch has been largely based on that work. Spence includes in his volume a substantial bibliographic essay detailing other primary and secondary materials on the colonies.

22. Willard was located near Andrews, North Carolina, and operated in 1895 and 1896. The principal founder was William C. Damon, who later became active in the Christian Commonwealth Colony. Several short sketches of Willard survive; see, for example, "Willard Colony," *Appleton's Annual Cyclopedia,* 3d ser., 1896 (New York: D. Appleton, 1897), vol. 1:535–36.

23. Roscoe Sheller, *Courage and Water: A Story of Yakima Valley's Sunnyside* (Portland, Oreg.: Binfords and Mort, 1952), 23–27.

24. Frederick A. Bushee, "Communistic Societies in the United States," *Political Science Quarterly* 20 (1905): 664.

25. William Lawrence Smith, "Urban Communitarianism in the 1980's: Seven Religious Communes in Chicago" (Ph.D. diss., Notre Dame Univ., 1984), 126–40. I thank Dr. Smith for lending me a copy of his dissertation that was otherwise unavailable to me.

26. Alexander Kent, "Cooperative Communities in the United States," *Bulletin of the Department of Labor* 6 (July 1901): 634.

27. Okugawa, "Annotated List of Communal and Utopian Societies," 219.

28. The Shiloh story is told in detail in Shirley Nelson, *Fair Clear and Terrible: The Story of Shiloh, Maine* (Latham, N.Y.: British American Publishing, 1989), and in William Charles Hiss, "Shiloh: Frank W. Sandford and the Kingdom, 1893–1948" (Ph.D. diss., Tufts Univ., 1978). Several articles tell pieces of the story; for the tragic sea voyage, for example, see Arnold L. White, "The Tragic Voyage of the Shiloh Schooner 'Coronet,'" *Down East* (May 1974): 54–57, 72–76.

29. Sally Kitch, *Chaste Liberation: Celibacy and Female Cultural Status* (Urbana: Univ. of Illinois Press, 1989), 102.

30. George P. Garrison, "A Woman's Community in Texas," *Charities Review* 3 (Nov. 1893): 33.

31. Margarita Spalding Gerry, "The Woman's Commonwealth of Washington," *Ainslee's Magazine* 10 (Sept. 1902): 138–39.

32. Kitch, *Chaste Liberation,* 12–13, 153.

33. The principal scholarly study of the Bryn Athyn community is Mary Ann Meyers, *A New World Jerusalem: The Swedenborgian Experience in Community Construction* (Westport, Conn.: Greenwood Press, 1983).

34. Gertrude Wishnick Dubrovsky, *This Land Was Theirs: Jewish Farmers in the Garden State* (Tuscaloosa: Univ. of Alabama Press, 1992), 19.

35. For survey histories of the New Jersey colonies see Joseph Brandes, *Immigrants to Freedom* (Philadelphia: Univ. of Pennsylvania Press, 1971), and Ellen Eisenberg, *Jewish Agricultural Colonies in New Jersey, 1882–1920* (Syracuse: Syracuse Univ. Press, 1995).

36. Uri D. Herscher, *Jewish Agricultural Utopias in America, 1880–1910* (Detroit: Wayne State Univ. Press, 1981), 61–70.

37. For a comprehensive history of Point Loma see Emmett A. Greenwalt, *The Point Loma Community in California: 1897–1942: A Theosophical Experiment* (Berkeley: Univ. of California Press, 1955). A revised edition is entitled *California Utopia: Point Loma: 1897–1942* (San Diego: Point Loma Publications, 1978).

38. For a sympathetic history of the development of Krotona at Hollywood see Joseph E. Ross, *Krotona of Old Hollywood* (Montecito, Calif.: El Montecito Oaks Press, 1989), vol. 1. For the larger story of Krotona (in the form of a novel) see Jane Levington Comfort, writing under the pseudonym Jane Annixter, *From These Beginnings* (New York: Dutton, 1937).

39. The Temple of the People has published its own voluminous works, but little outside material on the group is available. For short accounts see William Alfred Hinds, "Temple Home Association," *American Communities and Co-operative Colonies,* 577–80; J. Gordon Melton, "Temple of the People," *Encyclopedia of American Religions* (Detroit: Gale Research, 4th ed., 1994), 781–82.

40. For a book-length account of Wilson and his followers see John Oliphant, *Brother Twelve: The Incredible Story of Canada's False Prophet and His Doomed Cult of Gold, Sex, and Black Magic* (Toronto: McClelland and Stewart, 1991). For an article-length scholarly account see James A. Santucci, "The Aquarian Foundation," *Communal Societies* 9 (1989): 39–61.

41. Biodynamic farming is a type of organic agriculture developed within the Anthroposophical movement. Perhaps the most accessible of the many works on the Camphill movement is Cornelius Pietzner, ed., *A Candle on the Hill: Images of Camphill Life* (Edinburgh, Scotland, and Hudson, N.Y.: Floris Books and Anthroposophic Press, 1990).

42. Pasquale Marranzino, "Denver Mystic Is Constructing Atomic Armageddon Refuge," *Rocky Mountain News* (Denver), Aug. 30, 1946, p. 22; Michael Mehle, "Mountain Village Fights Cult Image, Mysterious Past," *Rocky Mountain News,* Oct. 14, 1990, p. 13. For a popular overview of the Brotherhood see Walter Kafton-Minkel, *Subterranean Worlds: 100,000 Years of Dragons, Dwarfs, the Dead, Lost Races and UFOs from Inside the Earth* (Port Townsend, Wash.: Loompanics Unlimited, 1989), 154–60.

43. On the Koreshan Unity see R. Lyn Rainard, "Conflict Inside the Earth: The Koreshan Unity in Lee County," *Tampa Bay History* 3 (1981): 5–16; Rainard, "'In the Name of Humanity': The Koreshan Unity," M.A. thesis, Univ. of South Florida, 1974.

44. Documentation of the Harmonial Vegetarian Society is thin; for a brief account see Alvin Seamster, "Harmonial Vegetarian Society," *Benton County Pioneer* (Siloam Springs, Ark.: Benton County Historical Society, 1962), vol. 8: 12–14.

45. For a recent account of life at Lily Dale see Frank Bruni, "A Booming Little

Ghost Town," *New York Times,* Aug. 25, 1997, p. A13. For a somewhat anecdotal account of Cassadaga's history and contemporary life see Robert Harrold, *Cassadaga: An Inside Look at the South's Oldest Psychic Community With True Experiences of People Who Have Been There* (Miami: Banyan Books, 1979).

46. M. J. Votruba, "The Preston Story," 1971. Manuscript at the Institute for the Study of American Religion.

47. Only brief accounts of the colony have been published. See Fern Colman, "Vegetarian Health Seekers of Orange County," in Quill Pen Club, ed., *Rawhide and Orange Blossoms* (Santa Ana, Calif.: Pioneer Press, 1967), 227–31.

48. *Oahspe: A New Bible in the Word of Jehovih and His Angel Embassadors* (Los Angeles: Kosmon Press, 1942; originally published in 1882).

49. See, for example, Wing Anderson, *Prophetic Years, 1947–1953* (Los Angeles: Kosmon Press, 1946); Anderson, *Seven Years That Change the World, 1941–1948* (n.p.: Educational Book Co., 1940).

50. Probably the best summary history of the whole Oahspe-Shalam saga is Jim Dennon, *The Oahspe Story* (Seaside, Oreg.: author, 1965). For a standard historical sketch, see Julia Keleher, "The Land of Shalam: Utopia in New Mexico," *New Mexico Historical Review* 19 (Apr. 1944): 123–34. Keleher's history has been hotly contested by a colony veteran, however, who takes strong exception to what the author says are Keleher's "wild statements and prevarications." See Jane Howland (writing under the pseudonym "Jone Howlind"), "Shalam: Facts Versus Fiction," *New Mexico Historical Review* 20 (Oct. 1945): 281–309.

51. Two major histories of the Spirit Fruit Society were published nearly simultaneously in the 1980s: H. Roger Grant, *Spirit Fruit: A Gentle Utopia* (DeKalb: Northern Illinois Univ. Press, 1988), and James L. Murphy, *The Reluctant Radicals: Jacob L. Beilhart and the Spirit Fruit Society* (Lanham, Md.: Univ. Press of America, 1989).

52. Butler published extensively on his philosophy; see, for example, Hiram Erastus Butler, *Solar Biology* (Boston: Esoteric Publishing Co., 1887). Secondary works, however, have been extremely meager. One of the more substantial journalistic accounts, based on an interview with a relatively new member of the community, is Charles Hillinger, "Sex Is a No-No in This Fraternity," *Los Angeles Times,* Aug. 13, 1980, pp. 3, 23. For a brief historical sketch see J. Gordon Melton, "Esoteric Fraternity," *Encyclopedia of American Religions,* 4th ed., 646–47.

53. A useful scholarly work on the community is David Steven Cohen, "The 'Angel Dancers': The Folklore of Religious Communitarianism," *New Jersey History* 95 (spring 1977): 5–20 (the concluding quotation is found on p. 20). Other brief accounts of the Lord's Farm are provided in several of the standard surveys of American communal life; see, for example, Ernest S. Wooster, *Communities of the Past and Present,* 66–70.

54. See Bolton Hall, *A Little Land and a Living* (New York: Arcadia Press, 1908). A good secondary work on Hall and Free Acres is Martin A. Bierbaum, "Bolton Hall's Free Acres Experiment: The Single Tax and Anarchism in New Jersey," *Communal Societies* 6 (1986): 61–83.

55. Fairhope and the single-tax movement received much publicity early in the twentieth century. George's basic work on his theories is *Progress and Poverty* (New York: J. W. Lovell, 1879). The most complete secondary work on Fairhope is Paul E. Alyea and Blanche Alyea, *Fairhope 1894–1954* (Tuscaloosa: Univ. of Alabama Press, 1956). Charles White Huntington edited at least thirteen volumes of *Enclaves of Economic Rent* (Harvard, Mass.: Fiske Warren) beginning in 1921, reproducing basic

documents of the enclaves as well as histories of each of them, including foreign enclaves.

56. The definitive work on the Washington colonies is Charles P. LeWarne, *Utopias on Puget Sound, 1885–1915* (Seattle: Univ. of Washington Press, 1975). For an even more detailed account, see LeWarne's dissertation upon which his book is based: Charles P. LeWarne, "Communitarian Experiments in Western Washington, 1885–1915" (Ph.D. diss., Univ. of Washington, 1969). The sketches in this chapter are heavily based on LeWarne's work.

57. On the rationale for the two-acre-plot land division, see E. E. Slosson, "An Experiment in Anarchy," *Independent* 55 (Apr. 2, 1903): 779–85.

58. For a discussion of the role of the paper in attracting new residents and a description of some who joined the colony, see J. W. Gaskine, "The Anarchists at Home, Washington," *Independent* 68:3204 (Apr. 28, 1910): 918–21.

59. For a discussion of the Home periodicals and some of the more notable controversies within and about the colony, see Murray Morgan, *The Last Wilderness* (Seattle: Univ. of Washington Press, 1955), 101–21.

60. The most complete history of Home is found in LeWarne, *Utopias on Puget Sound*, 168–226.

61. That Equality's founders admired Bellamy's works is clear enough. Some Bellamyites, however, argued that Equality and other "Bellamy Colonies" did not accurately reflect the master's thought. See Paul Tyner, "Under the Rose: 'Bellamy Colonies,'" *Arena* 21 (Apr. 1899): 528–29.

62. The name of the Brotherhood of the Co-operative Commonwealth was taken from a manifesto by Laurence Gronlund that embodied the first important exposition of Marxism in the United States and that inspired a wide range of community-minded socialists in the late nineteenth century. See Gronlund, *The Co-operative Commonwealth* (Boston: Lee and Shepard, 1884).

63. For a contemporary account of the Debs-endorsed colonization plan, see Ray S. Baker, "The Debs Cooperative Commonwealth," *The Outlook* 56:10 (July 3, 1897): 538–40. For a scholarly evaluation of the plan, see Bernard J. Brommel, "Debs's Co-operative Commonwealth Plan for Workers," *Labor History* 12 (fall 1971): 560–69.

64. On the appeal of Equality to American radicals, see Carlos A. Schwantes, *Radical Heritage: Labor, Socialism, and Reform in Washington and British Columbia, 1885–1917* (Seattle: Univ. of Washington Press, 1979), 88–90.

65. For sketches of some of the socialists who frequented Equality see Charles P. LeWarne, "Some Socialists from Equality Colony," paper presented at the annual conference of the Communal Studies Association, 1992.

66. Theodor Hertzka, *Freiland: Ein Soziales Zukunftsbild* (Leipzig: Duncker and Humblot, 1890). English translation: *Freeland: A Social Anticipation* (London: Chatto and Windus, 1891; New York: Appleton, 1891). For a discussion of the impact of Hertzka's novel, especially in Europe, see Joyce Oramel Hertzler, *A History of Utopian Thought* (New York: Macmillan, 1923), 236–44.

67. LeWarne, *Utopias on Puget Sound*, chap. 3.

68. "Social Democracy of America: Declaration of Principles and Constitutions of National, State, and Local Organizations, Adopted at Chicago in June, 1897," *Coming Nation* (July 24, 1897): 8.

69. Willard, before he left the colony, provided a sketch of its founding and early development. See Cyrus Field Willard, "As It Is To-day," *Industrial Freedom* (Nov. 12, 1898): supp., p. 2.

70. For an account of the shift toward private enterprise, along with a general historical account of the colony and the Co-operative Brotherhood, see Hinds, *American Communities and Co-operative Colonies,* 3d ed., 536–43.

71. LeWarne, *Utopias on Puget Sound,* chap. 5.

72. Today the name of the island is spelled "Whidbey," but earlier documents often use "Whidby."

73. LeWarne, *Utopias on Puget Sound,* chap. 4.

74. Elliott Shore, "Talkin' Socialism: Julius A. Wayland, Fred D. Warren, and Radical Publishing, 1890–1914" (Ph.D. diss. Bryn Mawr College, 1984); quoted by John Graham, *Yours for the Revolution: The Appeal to Reason, 1895–1922* (Lincoln: Univ. of Nebraska Press, 1990), 5.

75. Sharon E. Neet, "J. A. Wayland, Founding Editor and Publisher of the Appeal to Reason," *Little Balkans Review* 4:1 (1983): 49.

76. W. Fitzhugh Brundage, *A Socialist Utopia in the New South: The Ruskin Colonies in Tennessee and Georgia, 1894–1901* (Urbana: Univ. of Illinois Press, 1996), 42.

77. See, for example, Eltweed Pomeroy, "A Sketch of the Socialist Colony in Tennessee," *American Fabian* 3:4 (Apr. 1897): 1–3; Harold J. Shepstone, "A Modern Utopia," *Wide World Magazine* 3:15 (June 1899): 261–68.

78. For a highly cynical eyewitness account of Ruskin's internal conflicts and the eventual dissolution of the colony, see Isaac Broome, *The Last Days of the Ruskin Co-operative Association* (Chicago: Charles H. Kerr, 1902).

79. Very little is known about the Duke colony or its original members. See Brundage, *A Socialist Utopia in the New South,* 146.

80. Robert E. Corlew, "A Socialist Colony Comes and Goes," *History of Dickson County, Tennessee* (Nashville: Tennessee Historical Commission and Dickson County Historical Society, 1956), 152.

81. The standard history of the Ruskin Colony is Brundage, *A Socialist Utopia in the New South.* For a shorter account see John Egerton, "Ruskin: Julius Wayland and 'The Cooperative Commonwealth,'" *Visions of Utopia: Nashoba, Rugby, Ruskin, and the "New Communities" in Tennessee's Past* (Knoxville: Univ. of Tennessee Press, 1977), chap. 4. Wayland's life and role in the colony are examined in Howard H. Quint, "Julius A. Wayland, Pioneer Socialist Propagandist," *Mississippi Valley Historical Review* 35 (Mar. 1949): 585–606.

82. "Ruskin, Florida: A Brief Guide to Its History" (Ruskin, Florida: Ruskin Chamber of Commerce pamphlet, n.d. [ca. 1990s]).

83. Ralph Albertson, "A Survey of Mutualistic Communities in America," *Iowa Journal of History and Politics* 34:4 (Oct. 1936): 420.

84. "The Niksur Magazine Page" appeared in several issues of the weekly *Literary Light* in early 1899; it describes efforts to site the colony and outlines the philosophy behind it. Two such pages are in the W. A. Hinds Collection of the Oneida Community Papers at the library at Syracuse Univ. A one-paragraph summary of what little is known about the colony can be found in Okugawa, "Annotated List of Communal and Utopian Societies," 225.

85. Okugawa, "Annotated List of Communal and Utopian Societies," 225; Brundage, *A Socialist Utopia in the New South,* 161.

86. H. Roger Grant, "Portrait of a Workers' Utopia: The Labor Exchange and the Freedom, Kan., Colony," *Kansas Historical Quarterly* 43 (spring 1977): 64. Grant's article is the most complete account of Freedom Colony and the basis for most of this sketch.

87. Wayne Delavan, "Freedom Colony, A Kansas Brook Farm," *Kansas Magazine* (1949): 53.

88. An early contemporary account of the community is C. E. Julihu, "Pinon—A New Brook Farm of the West," *National Magazine* 11 (Oct. 1899): 29–34. For more recent evaluations see Duane D. Mercer, "The Colorado Co-operative Company, 1894–1904," *Colorado Magazine* 44 (fall 1967): 293–306, and Ellen Z. Peterson, *The Spell of the Tabeguache* (Denver: Sage Books, 1957).

89. Several survey works provide brief information on the Home Employment colony. The most complete history is H. Roger Grant, "The New Communitarianism: William H. Bennett and the Home Employment Co-operative Company, 1894–1905," *Bulletin of the Missouri Historical Society* 33 (Oct. 1976): 18–26.

90. Kaweah Cooperative Colony was founded by Burnette G. Haskell and others in 1885 and developed rapidly on homesteaded tracts in the foothills of the Sierra Nevada. In 1890, however, Congress created Sequoia National Park, seizing the colonists' land without compensation and thus abruptly bringing Kaweah to an end. See Robert V. Hine, "Kaweah Co-operative Commonwealth," in *California's Utopian Colonies* (Berkeley: Univ. of California Press, 1983; originally published in 1953), 78–100.

91. Hine, *California's Utopian Colonies,* 142–44.

92. Albertson, "A Survey of Mutualistic Communities in America," 394.

93. Bushee, "Communistic Societies in the United States," 664.

94. Okugawa, "Annotated List of Communal and Utopian Societies," 224.

2. ART COLONIES

1. An excellent brief history of the major communal art colonies is Karal Ann Marling, "The Art Colonial Movement," the introduction to *Woodstock: An American Art Colony, 1902–1977* (exhibition catalog, Vassar College Art Gallery, 1977), n.p.

2. The estimate of a dozen was made by David Shi, *The Simple Life: Plain Living and High Thinking in American Culture* (New York: Oxford Univ. Press, 1985), 190.

3. For a sketch of the history of Barbizon and other European artists' colonies see Michael Jacobs, *The Good and Simple Life: Artist Colonies in Europe and America* (Oxford: Phaidon, 1985).

4. Eileen Boris, *Art and Labor: Ruskin, Morris, and the Craftsman Ideal in America* (Philadelphia: Temple Univ. Press, 1986), 156.

5. For a brief historical sketch of the rise of the arts and crafts movement in England and the United States, see Mabel Tuke Priestman, "History of the Arts and Crafts Movement in America," *House Beautiful* 20 (Oct. and Nov. 1906): 15–16 (Oct.) and 14–16 (Nov.).

6. Quoted by Eileen Boris, "'Dreams of Brotherhood and Beauty': The Social Ideas of the Arts and Crafts Movement," in *The Art That Is Life: The Arts and Crafts Movement in America, 1875–1920,* ed. Wendy Kaplan (Boston: Museum of Fine Arts, 1987), 208.

7. Gustav Stickley, "The Use and Abuse of Machinery, and Its Relation to the Arts and Crafts," *The Craftsman* 11:2 (Nov. 1906): 202–7.

8. A. F. Sanborn, "The Scope and Drift of the American Arts and Crafts Movement," *The Forum* 40 (Sept. 1908): 259.

9. The suggestion that Shaw may have introduced Hubbard to Morris is provided by Felix Shay, *Elbert Hubbard of East Aurora* (New York: William H. Wise, 1926), 176.

10. Dard Hunter, who designed many of the books, was ambivalent about their

artistry. He wrote in his autobiography, "Even though the books produced at the Roycroft Shop were bizarre and lacked taste and refinement, they were, nevertheless, a step in the right direction. These books were better made than most of the work done in this country at the time." See Dard Hunter, *My Life with Paper: An Autobiography* (New York: Knopf, 1958), 43.

11. Leslie Greene Bowman, *American Arts and Crafts: Virtue in Design* (Los Angeles: Los Angeles County Museum of Art, 1990), 41–42.

12. Quoted in Shay, *Elbert Hubbard of East Aurora*, 201.

13. A typical epigram: "To civilize mankind: Make marriage difficult and divorce easy." Quoted by Shay, *Elbert Hubbard of East Aurora*, 491.

14. Freeman Champney, *Art and Glory: The Story of Elbert Hubbard* (New York: Crown, 1968), 92. Felix Shay remarks casually that one issue about 1914 had a press run of 225,000; but Shay's adulation of Hubbard is uncritical, and no dispassionate witness vouches for any figure in that range. See Shay, *Elbert Hubbard of East Aurora*, 547.

15. Boris, *Art and Labor*, 147. The reference is to one of Ruskin's most popular works; see John Ruskin, *Fors Clavigera: Letters to the Workmen and Labourers of Great Britain* (New York: J. Wiley and Sons, 1880).

16. On Dard Hunter, see Dard Hunter II, *The Life Work of Dard Hunter* (Chillicothe, Ohio: Mountain Press, 1981).

17. See, for example, [Elbert Hubbard], *The Book of the Roycrofters* (East Aurora, N.Y.: Roycrofters, 1907); Hubbard, *The Roycroft Shop: A History* (East Aurora, N.Y.: Roycrofters, 1908), 6.

18. See, for example, W. D. P. Bliss, *The New Encyclopedia of Social Reform* (New York: Funk and Wagnalls, 1908), 586.

19. Champney, *Art and Glory*, 64.

20. Ibid., 80.

21. Coy L. Ludwig, *The Arts and Crafts Movement in New York State, 1890s–1920s* (Hamilton, N.Y.: Gallery Association of New York State, 1983), 36.

22. On Leclaire see Kim McQuaid, "The Businessman as Reformer: Nelson O. Nelson and Late Nineteenth Century Social Movements in America," *American Journal of Economics and Sociology* 33:4 (Oct. 1974): 423–35; McQuaid, "The Businessman as Social Innovator: Nelson O. Nelson as Promoter of Garden Cities and the Consumer Cooperative Movement," *American Journal of Economics and Sociology* 34:4 (Oct. 1975): 411–22.

23. Even Hubbard's critics generally acknowledge his benevolence as an employer. See, for example, Bowman, *American Arts and Crafts*, 39–41.

24. Boris, *Art and Labor*, 147–48.

25. The figure comes from Albert Lane, *Elbert Hubbard and His Work* (Worcester, Mass.: Blanchard Press, 1901), as quoted by Boris, *Art and Labor*, 148.

26. Kirsten Hoving Keen, *American Art Pottery 1875–1930* (Wilmington: Delaware Art Museum, 1978), 55; Hunter, *My Life with Paper*, 31.

27. Ludwig, *Arts and Crafts Movement in New York State*, 29.

28. See an advertisement headed "Congress of Socialism," *The Fra* 3:3 (June 1909): xxi. In the same issue of the magazine another full-page advertisement (p. xii) lists five summer conferences at Roycroft, including ones on New Thought and women's suffrage as well as the one on socialism, and advises "Wise Advertisers" that "Such Folks lend class to your following. Win them today and they are with you for all time."

29. Boris, *Art and Labor*, 146.

30. Quoted by Shay, *Elbert Hubbard of East Aurora*, 328.

31. Hubbard, *The Roycroft Shop: A History*, 24.

32. For a critique of the supposed communitarianism of the Roycrofters, see Frederick Lewis Allen, "Elbert Hubbard," *Scribner's Magazine* 104 (Sept. 1938): 12–14, 49–51. See Also Robert L. Beisner, "'Commune' in East Aurora," *American Heritage* 22:2 (Feb. 1971): 72–77, 106–9.

33. Shay, *Elbert Hubbard of East Aurora*, 122.

34. Frank Luther Mott, *A History of American Magazines, 1885–1905* (Cambridge, Mass.: Belknap/Harvard Univ. Press, 1957), v. 4, p. 644.

35. *Philistine* 10 (Apr. 1903): 134; *Philistine* 37 (Oct. 1913): 133–34; quoted by Mott, *A History of American Magazines*, v. 4, pp. 643–44.

36. Upton Sinclair, *The Brass Check* (Pasadena: author, 1931), 314–17. Sinclair's complaint was essentially a recapitulation of an anonymous article published several years earlier. See "Elbert Hubbard's Price," *Harper's Weekly* 60 (Jan. 30, 1915): 112.

37. Elbert Hubbard, "A Message to Garcia." The piece was first published without a heading in the March 1899 issue of the *Philistine*. Fairly soon, orders for that issue increased sharply, and then reprints of the essay alone proliferated. See the *National Union Catalog* for an extensive listing of the various editions of the "Message." For details about the proliferation of editions and the content of the essay, see Champney, *Art and Glory*, 86–92.

38. Charles A. Sandburg, "Subjugation of Elbert Hubbard," *To-Morrow* 1 (Oct. 1905): 32.

39. J. Wade Caruthers, "Elbert Hubbard: A Case of Reinterpretation," *Connecticut Review* 1 (Oct. 1967): 67–77.

40. To cite just one example, in a single book of essays Hubbard denounced anti-Catholic prejudice, praised unfettered liberty of thought, and provided a light utopian fantasy, among other things. See Elbert Hubbard, *As It Seems to Me: Being Some Philistine Essays Concerning Several Things* (East Aurora: Roycroft Shop, 1898).

41. Robert Koch, "Elbert Hubbard's Roycrofters as Artist-Craftsmen," *Winterthur Portfolio III* (1967): 82.

42. Wayne Andrews, *Architecture, Ambition, and Americans* (New York: Harper and Brothers, 1955), 248–49.

43. A widely told, but probably apocryphal, tale has it that after the torpedo hit the ship, Hubbard commented to his wife, "Think of it, Alice—tomorrow the headlines will say 'Elbert Hubbard killed on the Lusitania!'" See Lionel Lambourne, *Utopian Craftsmen: The Arts and Crafts Movement from the Cotswolds to Chicago* (Salt Lake City: Peregrine Smith, 1980), 156–57.

44. Shi, *The Simple Life*, 183.

45. Eleanore Price Mather, "The Arts and Crafts Community," in *A History of Rose Valley*, ed. Peter Ham, Eleanore Price Mather, Judy Walton, and Patricia Ward (Delaware County, Pa.: Borough of Rose Valley, 1973), 11.

46. For information on the earlier period in Rose Valley and photographs of the ruins before their restoration, see Mabel Tuke Priestman, "Rose Valley, A Community of Disciples of Ruskin and Morris," *House and Garden* 10:4 (Oct. 1906): 159–65.

47. Twenty-five thousand dollars in stock was authorized, but much of it did not find buyers, leaving a lingering financial problem in the community. See William Ayres, "'A Poor Sort of Heaven; a Good Sort of Earth': A Chronology of the Arts and Crafts Community," in *A Poor Sort of Heaven, A Good Sort of Earth: The Rose Valley Arts and Crafts Experiment*, ed. William Ayres (Chadds Ford, Pa.: Brandywine River Museum, 1983), 18.

48. George E. Thomas, "Rose Valley Architecture: Where Art Served Life," in Ayres, *A Poor Sort of Heaven*, 29.

49. Hawley McLanahan, quoted in David Karsner, *Horace Traubel: His Life and Work* (New York: Egmont Arens, 1919), 80.

50. George E. Thomas, "William L. Price (1861–1916): Builder of Men and Buildings" (Ph.D. diss. Univ. of Pennsylvania, 1975), 305.

51. Albert Parry, *Garrets and Pretenders: A History of Bohemianism in America* (New York: Dover, 1960; originally published in 1933), 156–57.

52. Horace Traubel, *With Walt Whitman in Camden*. Traubel published three volumes before his death, but could not find a publisher for the fourth, which he had completed, or the others, which needed minor editing. At this writing, six volumes have been published, with more forthcoming. Vol. 1: Boston: Small, Maynard and Co., 1906. Vol. 2: New York: Appleton and Co., 1908. Vol. 3: New York: Mitchell Kennerley, 1914. Vols. 4–6: Carbondale: Univ. of Southern Illinois Press, 1959, 1964, 1982.

53. Horace Traubel, "Rose Valley in General," *The Artsman* 1 (Oct. 1903): 23–26.

54. Elizabeth Cumming and Wendy Kaplan, *The Arts and Crafts Movement* (New York: Thames and Hudson, 1991), 172. See William Morris, *News from Nowhere* (London: Longmans, Green, and Co., 1891).

55. For a detailed discussion of the social life of the community, see Ann Barton Brown, "'Joy Is Not Joy That Is Not Shared'—Life in Rose Valley," in Ayres, *A Poor Sort of Heaven*, 81–93.

56. Thomas, "William L. Price," 312.

57. Estimates of Rose Valley's population have been as high as a hundred (see Priestman, "Rose Valley," 163), but a few more than fifty seems closer to the actual count. See Daniel Richard Stoddard, "Horace Traubel: A Critical Biography" (Ph.D. diss. Univ. of Pennsylvania, 1970), p. 227.

58. Priestman, "Rose Valley," 165.

59. William Smallwood Ayres, "A Poor Sort of Heaven; A Good Sort of Earth; The Rose Valley Arts and Crafts Experiment (1901–1910)" (M.A. thesis. Univ. of Delaware, 1982), pp. 11, 51.

60. Ayres, "A Poor Sort of Heaven," 39–40.

61. Karsner, *Horace Traubel*, 83.

62. Information on New Clairvaux is relatively limited. Most secondary accounts are based on Pressey's papers, in the archives at Harvard University, and on the community's periodical, *Country Time and Tide*. For brief accounts see T. J. Jackson Lears, *No Place of Grace: Antimodernism and the Transformation of American Culture, 1880–1920* (New York: Pantheon, 1981), 335; Boris, *Art and Labor*, 158–60; Max West, "The Revival of Handicrafts in America," *U.S. Bureau of Labor Bulletin* 9:55 (Nov. 1904): 1614–15.

63. Boris, *Art and Labor*, 166.

64. Karal Ann Marling, "The Byrdcliffe Colony of the Arts and Crafts," *Woodstock: An American Art Colony*, n.p.

65. William Claiborne, "A Utopian Art Colony in the Face of Reality," *Washington Post*, Mar. 16, 1976, p. B3.

66. Quoted in Anita M. Smith, *Woodstock: History and Hearsay* (Saugerties, N.Y.: Catskill Mountains Publishing Corp., 1959), 43.

67. Ralph Radcliffe Whitehead, "A Plea for Manual Work," *Handicraft* (June 1903): 72.

68. Quoted in Smith, *Woodstock*, 41. Punctuation as in original.

69. Brown, a sometime member of the Stanford University faculty, was also a skilled mountaineer. A peak in the Sierra Nevada has been named for him. See Clinton Adams, "We Knew That," *Sierra* (Sept.–Oct. 1992): 14.

70. Poultney Bigelow, "The Byrdcliffe Colony of Arts and Crafts," *American Homes and Gardens* 6:10 (Oct. 1909): 393, 389.

71. The most complete account of the planning, building, and life of Byrdcliffe seems to be Alf Evers, *Woodstock: History of an American Town* (Woodstock: Overlook Press, 1987), 398–449. This recounting of the story draws heavily from Evers's work.

72. Robert Edwards, "Byrdcliffe: Life by Design," in *The Byrdcliffe Arts and Crafts Colony: Life by Design* (Wilmington: Delaware Art Museum, 1984), 7.

73. Claiborne, "A Utopian Art Colony in the Face of Reality," B3.

74. Whitehead, "A Plea for Manual Work," 70–71.

75. Bolton Brown, Whitehead's close associate in the project, used the phrase "happy-go-lucky Bohemia" to describe Whitehead's ideal. Brown preferred a more disciplined structure for the colony. See Bolton Brown, "Early Days at Woodstock," *Woodstock Historical Society Publications* 13 (Aug.–Sept. 1937): 3–14. The phrase "benevolent despotism" was used to describe Byrdcliffe by Bigelow in "The Byrdcliffe Colony of Arts and Crafts," 393.

76. Evers, *Woodstock,* 422.

77. Carl Eric Lindin, "The Woodstock Landscape," in *Publications of the Woodstock Historical Society* 7 (July 1932): 18; quoted in Alf Evers, *The Catskills: From Wilderness to Woodstock* (Garden City, N.Y.: Doubleday, 1972), 622.

78. Claiborne, "A Utopian Art Colony in the Face of Reality," B3.

79. Bowman, *American Arts and Crafts,* 34.

80. Claiborne, "A Utopian Art Colony in the Face of Reality," B1, B3. (Quote is from B3.)

81. A. F. Sanborn, "The Scope and Drift of the American Arts and Crafts Movement," *The Forum* 40 (Sept. 1908): 259.

82. Karal Ann Marling, "Heavens on Earth," *Woodstock: An American Art Colony,* n.p.

83. Several historical sketches of Byrdcliffe note that other artists in town sometimes spoke derisively of the pioneer enclave and, occasionally, of artwork produced there. See, for example, Jacobs, *The Good and Simple Life,* 170–71.

84. Smith, *Woodstock,* 43.

85. Jane Perkins Claney, "White Pines Pottery; the Continuing Arts and Crafts Experiment," in *The Byrdcliffe Arts and Crafts Colony: Life by Design,* 17.

86. Jane Whitehead had resisted moving to Byrdcliffe permanently in its early days, reportedly put off by her husband's womanizing, and stayed on at the couple's elegant former home in Santa Barbara. Eventually, though, they both lived at the colony in apparent harmony. See Edwards, "Byrdcliffe: Life by Design," 8.

87. Claiborne, "A Utopian Art Colony in the Face of Reality," B3.

88. According to one historian, Fritz Vanderloo helped White finance the purchase of land for the Maverick, but left the area shortly afterward. See Henry Morton Robinson, "The Maverick," *Publications of the Woodstock Historical Society* 11 (Aug.–Sept. 1933): 3–11.

89. The "rural Hull House" characterization is quoted by Evers, *Woodstock,* 454, from White's manuscript autobiography.

90. For the history of the Maverick Press and further information on the writings of Hervey White, see "An Unrecorded Private Press," *The Book Collector's Packet* 2 (June–July 1933): 21–25.

91. Smith, *Woodstock,* 55–56.

92. Much of this information comes from Evers, *The Catskills,* 628–38 and pass., and from Evers, *Woodstock,* 450–59 and 468–82.

93. Quoted by Evers, *The Catskills,* 655.

94. Smith, *Woodstock,* 66.

95. For the Cooney colony, see Evers, *Woodstock,* 600–602.

96. The principal source on Beaux Arts Village is Norman J. Johnston, "A Far Western Arts and Crafts Village," *Journal of the Society of Architectural Historians* 35 (Mar. 1976): 51–54. See also Walter L. Creese, *The Search for Environment: The Garden City: Before and After* (New Haven: Yale Univ. Press, 1966), 138–39.

97. Rollo Walter Brown, "Mrs. MacDowell and Her Colony," *Atlantic* 184:1 (July 1949): 42–46.

98. "Rustic Studios for Creative Folk," *Literary Digest* 124:2 (July 10, 1937): 24.

99. Herbert Kubly, "The Care and Feeding of Artists," *Horizon* 5:4 (Mar. 1963): 26–33.

100. L. E. Brown-Landone, "A New Idea in Art," *Harper's Weekly* 55:2862 (Oct. 28, 1911): 15.

101. For an account of his conversion from skeptic to enthusiast, see Edwin Arlington Robinson, "The Peterborough Idea," *North American Review* 204:730 (Sept. 1916): 448–54.

102. Theodore Pratt, "Place of Dreams Untold," *New York Times Magazine,* Mar. 24, 1957, pp. 19–22.

103. Marling, "Heavens on Earth," n.p.

104. "Yaddo and Substance," *Time* 32 (Sept. 5, 1938): 50.

105. "Life Visits Yaddo," *Life* 21 (July 15, 1946): 110–13.

106. Hanna Astrup Larsen, "The Craft Work on the Hills of Fairies," *Craftsman* 30 (Sept. 1916): 634–37.

107. Ludwig, *Arts and Crafts Movement in New York State,* 47, 48.

108. Advertisement for "Briar Cliff Furniture," *House Beautiful* 18 (Aug. 1905): 27. The advertisement featured chairs for $6.50 and $7.50, and stools for $4.00.

109. Stickley and his associates published several articles about Craftsman Farms in Stickley's journal, *The Craftsman.* See, for example, Gustav Stickley, "A Message from Craftsman Farms," *The Craftsman* 21:1 (Oct. 1911): 112–13; Raymond Riordan, "A Visit to Craftsman Farms: The Impression It Made and the Result—The Gustav Stickley School for Citizenship," *The Craftsman* 23:2 (Nov. 1912): 151–64.

110. The most complete account of Black Mountain College is in Martin Duberman, *Black Mountain: An Experiment in Community* (Garden City, N.Y.: Doubleday/Anchor, 1973).

111. Oliver Evans, "The Pad in Brooklyn Heights," *The Nation* 199 (July 13, 1964): 15.

112. Humphrey Carpenter, *W. H. Auden: A Biography* (London: George Allen and Unwin, 1981), 304. Carpenter is quoting James Stern.

113. See, besides the works cited just above, Oliver Evans, *The Ballad of Carson McCullers: A Biography* (New York: Coward-McCann, 1965), 82–87.

114. "Quarry Hill," *Communities: Journal of Cooperation* 79 (winter 1993): 25.

115. Timothy Miller, "Drop City: Historical Notes on the Pioneer Hippie Commune," *Syzygy: Journal of Alternative Religion and Culture* 1:1 (winter 1992): 23–38.

3. NEW COMMUNES, 1900–1920

1. On the early history of Pentecostalism, including the activities at Bethel Bible College, see James R. Goff Jr., "Charles F. Parham and His Role in the Development of the Pentecostal Movement: A Reevaluation," *Kansas History* 7:3 (autumn 1984): 226–37; Robert Mapes Anderson, *Vision of the Disinherited: The Making of American Pentecostalism* (New York: Oxford Univ. Press, 1979), chap. 3.

2. The figure on Zion City's acreage is provided by Monica Kusch, "Zion, Illinois: An Attempt at a Theocentric City" (Ph.D. diss. Univ. of California at Los Angeles, 1954), 273.

3. For a review of press coverage of the New York debacle, including several acerbic cartoons from New York newspapers, see "Dowie and His Troubles in New York," *Literary Digest* 27 (Oct. 31, 1903): 572.

4. For a description of Voliva's flat-earth theory, see Walter Davenport, "They Call Me a Flathead," *Collier's* 79 (May 14, 1927): 30–31.

5. Zion City has been the subject of many articles, books, theses, and dissertations. The leading scholarly work is Philip L. Cook, *Zion City, Illinois: Twentieth Century Utopia* (Syracuse: Syracuse Univ. Press, 1996).

6. One former colonist was still there in 1944. See Margaret Marshall, "Solitary Settler at Hunter's Bay: 'Grandpa' Wilson Is Last Remaining Resident of Lopez Island Religious Colony," *Seattle Times,* Dec. 4, 1944, magazine sec., p. 11.

7. The foremost historian of Lopez Island, as of other intentional communities in the Pacific Northwest, is Charles P. LeWarne. The most complete of his several recountings of the colony's history is "'And Be Ye Separate': The Lopez Island Colony of Thomas Gourley," *Communal Societies* 1 (1981): 19–35.

8. Edwin Smyrl, "Burning Bush," *Southwestern Historical Quarterly* 50 (Jan. 1947): 335–43. Smyrl's account is based on interviews and local records; because one Ed Smyrl is on his list of interviewees, it would appear that he or his father or both were members. This account is based on Smyrl's article.

9. The Metropolitan Church Association, however, survives. Its periodical *The Burning Bush* was recently still in publication at Lake Geneva, Wis.

10. Gordon Lindsay, *The Gordon Lindsay Story* (Dallas: Christ for the Nations, 1992), 16.

11. The most complete account of Pisgah Grande, and a heavily illustrated one, is in Paul Kagan, *New World Utopias: A Photographic History of the Search for Community* (New York: Penguin, 1975), 138–57.

12. For a sketch of the Bethel facilities see Richard Harris, "A Reporter at Large: I'd Like to Talk to You for a Minute," *New Yorker* 32 (June 16, 1956): 72–105.

13. For an overview of the farm see Nadine Brozan, "Jehovah's Witnesses: A Mini Conglomerate That's Self-Sustaining," *New York Times,* Jan. 2, 1973, p. 40.

14. For an overview of the millennial excitement centered in upstate New York in the first half of the nineteenth century, see Whitney R. Cross, *The Burned-Over District: The Social and Intellectual History of Enthusiastic Religion in Western New York, 1800–1850* (New York: Harper and Row, 1965; originally published in 1950). On the Adventist movement specifically, see Ronald L. Numbers and Jonathan M. Butler, eds., *The Disappointed: Millerism and Millenarianism in the Nineteenth Century* (Bloomington: Indiana Univ. Press, 1987). This edited volume contains essays on phases of Adventist history and biography and the relationship of the movement to other religious movements and currents in the larger society.

15. Barbara Gruzzuti Harrison, *Visions of Glory: A History and a Memory of Jehovah's Witnesses* (New York: Simon and Schuster, 1978), 130.

16. For a good but somewhat skeptical account of life at Bethel, see M. James Penton, *Apocalypse Delayed: The Story of Jehovah's Witnesses* (Toronto: Univ. of Toronto Press, 1985), 221–27. The author is a former high-ranking Witness who was disfellowshipped from the organization for his earlier writings about it.

17. A large literature records the history of the more prominent Jewish farm colonies, especially the New Jersey colonies, but historical material on the post-1900 colonies, which tended to be smaller and more obscurely located than their predecessors, is scarce. The best overall source is Richard E. Singer's comprehensive study of Jewish communitarianism, *The American Jew in Agriculture, Past History and Present Condition* (prize essay, 1941, manuscript at the American Jewish Archives). Two vols. Also on microfilm.

18. Ibid., 343–44.

19. Ibid., 336–37.

20. The only substantial article on the colony, and therefore the account on which this sketch is based, is Louis J. Swichkow, "The Jewish Colony of Arpin, Wisconsin," *American Jewish Historical Quarterly* 54 (1964–65): 82–91.

21. The principal historical survey of the colony, and the one on which this sketch is based, is Arnold Shankman, "Happyville, the Forgotten Colony," *American Jewish Archives* 30 (Apr. 1978): 3–19.

22. Singer, *The American Jew in Agriculture*, 522–27.

23. Ibid., 240–41. Singer laments the paucity of information about the colony.

24. Federal Writers' Project, *Massachusetts, a Guide to Its Places and People* (Boston: Houghton Mifflin, 1937), 600.

25. Norton B. Stern, "Orangevale and Porterville, California, Jewish Farm Colonies," *Western States Jewish Historical Quarterly* 10 (Jan. 1978): 159–67.

26. Jacob Maze of the Western Office of the Jewish Agricultural Society in Los Angeles was quoted as having said in 1959, "The farms were successful but in the course of years the children moved to town and new settlers did not come." Thus some ongoing presence seems to have existed for perhaps a generation. See Stern, "Orangevale and Porterville," 160.

27. Singer, *The American Jew in Agriculture*, 543–44.

28. See, for example, Charles J. Freund, "The Significance of the Jewish Farm Colony," *Improvement Era* 16 (Jan. 1913): 248–53.

29. Robert A. Goldberg, "Zion in Utah," *Jews of the American West*, ed. Moses Rischin and John Livingston (Detroit: Wayne State Univ. Press, 1991), 74.

30. The most comprehensive history of Clarion is Robert A. Goldberg, *Back to the Soil: The Jewish Farmers of Clarion, Utah, and Their World* (Salt Lake City: Univ. of Utah Press, 1986). Goldberg situates the colony within the larger Jewish colonization movement and provides extensive bibliographical references.

31. Rose L. McKee, *"Brother Will" and the Founding of Gould Farm* (Great Barrington, Mass.: William J. Gould Associates, 1963), 75.

32. Alfred Andersen, a former president of the Fellowship of Intentional Communities, recalled in 1996 that the largest group of patient-residents at Gould Farm consisted of alcoholics who were drying out, and the second-largest group was composed of sex offenders. Standard literature on the community, however, emphasizes the broad scope of Gould Farm's therapeutic efforts and downplays any emphasis on those two groups of patients. (Alfred Andersen, interviewed by Timothy Miller, Eugene, Oreg., July 12, 1996.)

33. Probably the most complete independent report on Gould Farm is Henrik Infield, "Gould Farm: A Therapeutic Cooperative Community," in his *American Intentional Communities* (Glen Gardner, N.J.: Glen Gardner Community Press, 1955), 73–109.

34. "Gould Farm," *Directory of Intentional Communities* (Evansville, Ind., and Rutledge, Mo.: Fellowship for Intentional Community and Communities Publications Cooperative, 1992), 189.

35. On the Southcott movement in Britain see James K. Hopkins, *A Woman to Deliver Her People* (Austin: Univ. of Texas Press, 1982). Hopkins covers the British movement in detail but does not deal with Southcott's American successors.

36. On the activities of Jezreel, Mills, and others in the United States and Britain, see G. R. Balleine, *Past Finding Out: The Tragic Story of Joanna Southcott and Her Successors* (New York: Macmillan, 1956).

37. The Southcott tradition's connections to the House of David are detailed in Robert S. Fogarty, *The Righteous Remnant: The House of David* (Kent, Ohio: Kent State Univ. Press, 1981). Fogarty's book was the first major study of the movement, although it has since been supplanted in part by the work of Clare Adkin, cited below, which focuses on the work in Benton Harbor and on the spectacular events of Purnell's disappearance, trial, and death from 1922 to 1927, and developments in the movement thereafter.

38. Clare Adkin, *Brother Benjamin: A History of the Israelite House of David* (Berrien Springs, Mich.: Andrews Univ. Press, 1990), 23.

39. R. James Taylor, *Mary's City of David* (Benton Harbor, Mich.: Mary's City of David, 1996), 80, 130.

40. Adkin, *Brother Benjamin*, 81.

41. For a detailed accounting of the settlement between Mary Purnell and Dewhirst, see Adkin, *Brother Benjamin*, 210–11.

42. For an illustrated history of Holy City see Betty Lewis, *Holy City: Riker's Roadside Attraction in the Santa Cruz Mountains* (Santa Cruz: Otter B Books, 1992). See also Paul Kagan, *New World Utopias: A Photographic History of the Search for Community* (New York: Penguin, 1975), 102–17.

43. Father Divine, when asked about his origins, liked to answer in terms of having "combusted" in New York City and the like. Several scholars have investigated his earthly origins; the most convincing case has been compiled by Jill Watts, who determined that he was born in Rockville, Maryland, in 1879 as George Baker. See Jill Watts, *God, Harlem, U.S.A.: The Father Divine Story* (Berkeley: Univ. of California Press, 1992), 5.

44. Father Divine was married twice (his first wife died in 1937), but it was understood in the celibate movement that the union was symbolic of unity, not conjugal.

45. For a history see Robert Weisbrot, *Father Divine and the Struggle for Racial Equality* (Urbana: Univ. of Illinois Press, 1983); Watts, *God, Harlem, U.S.A.*

46. Rosemary Armao and Greg Schneider, "'Black Jews' Step Out of the Shadows," *Virginian-Pilot* (Norfolk), Apr. 1, 1988, pp. 1, 6–7.

47. The standard history of the Church of God and Saints of Christ is Elly Wynia, *The Church of God and Saints of Christ: The Rise of Black Jews* (New York: Garland Publishing, 1994). This sketch is based on Wynia's work except as otherwise attributed.

48. Ira De A. Reid, "Let Us Prey!" *Opportunity: A Journal of Negro Life* 4 (Sept. 1926): 274–78.

49. "Negro Elder Held in $50,000 Bail," *New York Times,* Apr. 16, 1926, p. 12.

50. "'Black Messiah' Gets 18 Months," *New York Times,* May 20, 1926, p. 27.

51. On these early and limited attempts at communitarianism, see Mario S. De-Pillis, "The Development of Mormon Communitarianism, 1826–1846" (Ph.D. diss. Yale Univ., 1960); Lyndon W. Cook, *Joseph Smith and the Law of Consecration* (Provo, Utah: Grandin Book Co., 1985).

52. The Latter Day Saints conducted various experiments in cooperation and community from their early days in Kirtland, Ohio, onward; some of them are discussed elsewhere in this volume. Some communal sharing is mandated by passages in Mormon special scriptures (see, for example, Mosiah, chap. 4, in the Book of Mormon, and secs. 42 and 82 of the Doctrine and Covenants). Several histories of LDS communitarianism have been written; the most comprehensive is Leonard J. Arrington, Feramorz Y. Fox, and Dean L. May, *Building the City of God: Community and Cooperation among the Mormons* (Salt Lake City: Deseret Book Co., 1976).

53. Several useful historical surveys of Orderville have been published. See, for example, Andrew Jenson, "Orderville: An Experiment in a Communistic System, Called the 'United Order,'" *Utah Genealogical and Historical Magazine* (July 1916): 128–41; Mark A. Pendleton, "Orderville United Order of Zion," *Utah Historical Quarterly* 7 (Oct. 1939): 141–59; Emma Carroll Seegmiller, "Personal Memories of the United Order," *Utah Historical Quarterly* 7 (Oct. 1939): 159–200.

54. On Strang and his movement see Milo M. Quaife, *The Kingdom of St. James: A Narrative of the Mormons* (New Haven: Yale Univ. Press, 1930); Roger Van Noord, *King of Beaver Island: The Life and Assassination of James Jesse Strang* (Urbana: Univ. of Illinois Press, 1988).

55. On the Cutlerite movement see Daisy Whiting Fletcher, *Alpheus Cutler and the Church of Jesus Christ* (Independence, Mo.: author, 1970); Biloine W. Young, "Minnesota Mormons: The Cutlerites," *Courage* (Lamoni, Iowa) 3; reprinted in *Restoration* 2 (July 1983): 1, 5–12.

56. On the post-Mormon phase of Rigdon's movement see Thomas J. Gregory, "Sidney Rigdon: Post Nauvoo," *Brigham Young University Studies* 21 (winter 1981): 51–67. For Brewster's movement see Steven L. Shields, "Church of Christ (James Colin Brewster)," *Divergent Paths of the Restoration: A History of the Latter Day Saint Movement* (Bountiful, Utah: author, 3d ed., 1982), 55–56. Additional references to each of these movements can be found in my *American Communes, 1860–1960: A Bibliography* (New York: Garland, 1990), 364–420.

57. Ephraim Peterson, *An Ideal City for Ideal People* (Independence, Mo.: author, 1905).

58. Steven L. Shields, "United Order of Equality," *The Latter Day Saint Churches: An Annotated Bibliography* (New York: Garland, 1987), 140–41.

59. "Religious Colonies," *Comanche County History* (Coldwater, Kans.: Comanche County Historical Society, 1981), 164.

60. Shields, *Divergent Paths of the Restoration,* 118–20.

61. A brief sketch of the colony can be found in Shields, *Divergent Paths of the Restoration,* 117–18; for a full account see Carlton Culmsee, *A Modern Moses at West Tintic* (Logan: Utah State Univ. Press, 1967).

62. Sister Christine [Greenstidel], in Swami Chidatmananda, *Reminiscences of Swami Vivekananda* (Calcutta: Advaita Ashrama, 1964), 176–77; quoted in Laurence Veysey, *The Communal Experience* (Chicago: Univ. of Chicago Press, 1973), 220.

63. Dorothy F. Mercer, *The Vedanta in California;* quoted in Swami Gambhi-

rananda, *History of the Ramakrishna Math and Mission* (Calcutta: Advaita Ashrama, 1957), 181.

64. Carl T. Jackson, "The Swami in America: A History of the Ramakrishna Movement in the United States, 1893–1960" (Ph.D. diss. Univ. of California at Los Angeles, 1964), 298–303. Additional details are provided in Gambhirananda, *History of the Ramakrishna Math and Mission,* 180–81, 247–48.

65. Veysey, *The Communal Experience,* 222–23.

66. Ibid., 245. Veysey provides the most complete account of Paramananda's communal work; see pp. 224–46. See also Jackson, "The Swami in America," 461–65. A few details about Paramananda's work and the history of the Massachusetts and California centers can be found in "Nature's Sanctuary," a brief pamphlet distributed by the movement (Cohasset, Mass.: Vedanta Centre, n.d.).

67. Veysey, *The Communal Experience,* 266–70.

68. Carl Jackson lists four communal sites among the southern California Vedanta establishments: the monastery at the headquarters in Hollywood, the nearby Sarada Convent, the Ramakrishna Monastery at Trabuco, and another Sarada Convent near Santa Barbara. See Carl T. Jackson, *Vedanta for the West: The Ramakrishna Movement in the United States* (Bloomington: Indiana Univ. Press, 1994), 123.

69. Swami Swahananda, "Vedanta Convents in the West," *Monasticism: Ideal and Traditions* (Mylapore Madras, India: Sri Ramakrishna Math, 1991), 257–76.

70. G. L. Price, "North Michigan's Jane Addams," *Detroit Saturday Night* 16 (Dec. 16, 1911).

71. See, for example, G. L. Price, "The Angel of the Roundheads," *World's Work* 26 (July 1913): 349–52.

72. K. Marianne Wargelin Brown, "Maggie Walz: Entrepreneur and Temperance Crusader," in *Women Who Dared: The History of Finnish American Women,* ed. Carl Ross and K. Marianne Wargelin Brown (St. Paul: Immigration History Research Center, Univ. of Minnesota, 1986), 151–57.

73. For a detailed portrait of the Molokans in Russia, see Frederick C. Conybeare, *Russian Dissenters* (New York: Russell and Russell, 1962; originally published in 1921), 289–330. Conybeare depicts Molokan life and thought in some detail and provides information on the "communists," a subsect practicing community of goods.

74. For a detailed and illustrated depiction of the colony after it had become well established, see Oscar Schmieder, "The Russian Colony of Guadalupe Valley," *University of California Publications in Geography* 2 (1928): 409–34.

75. For a historical sketch of the Guadalupe Valley colony, see John K. Berokoff, *Molokans in America* (Los Angeles: Stockton-Doty, 1969), 40–43.

76. Willard B. Moore, "Communal Experiments as Resolution of Sectarian Identity Crises," *International Review of Modern Sociology* 6 (spring 1976): 91–92. Moore provides a good overview of Molokan efforts at colony building.

77. Berokoff, *Molokans in America,* 55–58. For an account of wartime conflicts between the Arizona Molokans and the government over conscription, together with some basic information on the colony, see William Haas Moore, "Prisoners in the Promised Land," *Journal of Arizona History* 14 (winter 1973): 281–302.

78. Marianne L. Mooijweer, "A Socialist Eden in North Carolina? Frederik van Eeden and his American Dreams," *European Contributions to American Studies* 20 (Amsterdam: VU Univ. Press, 1991), 282–305.

79. The principal source on the Bohemian colony, and the one on which this sketch is based, is Ernest I. Miller, "The Bohemian Cooperative Farming Company,"

Some Tennessee Utopias (Monograph No. 1, Special Studies in Sociology) (Knoxville: Department of Sociology, Univ. of Tennessee, 1942), 62–72.

80. On Harriman's rhetorical skills in promoting the colony, see Paul Greenstein, Nigey Lennon, and Lionel Rolfe, *Bread and Hyacinths: The Rise and Fall of Utopian Los Angeles* (Los Angeles: California Classics Books, 1992), 90–91.

81. Ernest Wooster, *Communities of the Past and Present* (Newllano, La.: *Llano Colonist*, 1924), 132–33.

82. Paul K. Conkin, *Two Paths to Utopia: The Hutterites and the Llano Colony* (Lincoln: Univ. of Nebraska Press, 1964), 109.

83. For reproductions of many of the plans and diagrams, see Dolores Hayden, *Seven American Utopias: The Architecture of Communitarian Socialism, 1790–1975* (Cambridge, Mass.: MIT Press, 1976), chap. 10, "Feminism and Eclecticism."

84. Ernest S. Wooster, "Bread and Hyacinths: How the Socialist Llano Colony Bungled Business and Succeeded in Enriching Its Social Life," *Sunset*, Aug. 1924, pp. 23, 59. Wooster was a longtime member of the colony.

85. Paul Greenstein, Nigey Lennon, and Lionel Rolfe speculate that Otis may have sent undercover agitators to Llano, noting that he "had often employed such agents to infiltrate labor unions and union job sites." See Greenstein et al., *Bread and Hyacinths,* 108.

86. James K. Morris, "Outpost of the Cooperative Commonwealth: The History of the Llano Del Rio Colony in Gila, New Mexico, 1932–1935," *New Mexico Historical Review* 56 (Apr. 1981): 177–95.

87. Commonwealth College is examined in more detail in the following chapter.

88. The definitive study of the Nevada Colony is Wilbur S. Shepperson, *Retreat to Nevada: A Socialist Colony of World War I* (Reno: Univ. of Nevada Press, 1966). Shepperson provides a helpful context for his history, setting the colony enterprise into the larger framework of communitarian experiments and American socialism generally in the early twentieth century.

89. Wooster, *Communities of the Past and Present,* 133.

90. Geraldson, quoted in Wooster, *Communities of the Past and Present,* 136.

91. Robert V. Hine, *California's Utopian Colonies* (San Marino, Calif.: Huntington Library, 1953), 153.

92. The title of the magazine varied slightly; it was originally called *Mother Earth: Monthly Magazine Devoted to Social Science and Literature;* later it was called *Mother Earth Bulletin,* under which title it is often found in library catalogs.

93. For Cohen's own account of the history and goals of the community, see Joseph J. Cohen, *In Quest of Heaven: The Story of the Sunrise Co-operative Community* (New York: Sunrise History Publishing Committee, 1957; repr., Philadelphia: Porcupine Press, 1975), 25–26.

94. For an outline of the Ferms' educational philosophy see Alexis Ferm, "Report of the Stelton Modern School," *Freedom* (New York) n.s., v. 2 (Feb. 1934): 6–7.

95. The most complete account of Ferrer is found in Veysey, *The Communal Experience,* 77–177, the source of most of this retelling. For a more concise history and analysis see Terry M. Perlin, "Anarchism in New Jersey: The Ferrer Colony in Stelton," *New Jersey History* 89 (fall 1971): 133–48.

96. John William Lloyd, *The Natural Man: A Romance of the Golden Age* (Newark, N.J.: Benedict Prieth, 1902); Lloyd, *The Dwellers in the Vale Sunrise: How They Got Together and Lived Happy Ever After* (Westwood, Mass.: Ariel Press, 1904). See the National Union Catalog for a listing of Lloyd's other books.

97. Leonard D. Abbott, "J. William Lloyd and His Message," *Mother Earth* 3 (Dec. 1908): 367. This article provides what seems to be the best surviving summary of Lloyd's thought.

98. James L. Murphy, *The Reluctant Radicals: Jacob L. Beilhart and the Spirit Fruit Society* (Lanham, Md.: Univ. Press of America, 1989), 212.

99. Henry F. Bedford, *Socialism and the Workers in Massachusetts, 1886–1912* (Amherst: Univ. of Massachusetts Press, 1966), 179.

100. Quoted by Eileen Boris, *Art and Labor: Ruskin, Morris, and the Craftsman Ideal in America* (Philadelphia: Temple Univ. Press, 1986), 161; the refrain was published in nearly every issue of the *Ariel*.

101. Alice Spencer Geddes, "A Living from an Acre," *Technical World* (July 1912): 574–77.

102. Ralph Albertson, "A Survey of Mutualistic Communities in America," *Iowa Journal of History and Politics* 34 (Oct. 1936): 421.

103. Boris, *Art and Labor*, 162.

104. Robert Fogarty, *All Things New: American Communes and Utopian Movements, 1860–1914* (Chicago: Univ. of Chicago Press, 1990), 219.

105. Boris, *Art and Labor*, 162.

106. Topolobampo colony was an American venture founded in Sinaloa, Mexico, in 1886 by Albert Kimsey Owen, who envisioned it as a great Pacific port and an anchor of a new railroad on which goods would be carried for shipment to Asia. Christian B. Hoffman, a prosperous miller at Enterprise, Kansas, joined the project in 1887 and soon was raising money for the colony and encouraging families to move there. On Topolobampo see Ray Reynolds, *Cat'spaw Utopia* (El Cajon, Calif.: author, 1972); on Hoffman see Patricia Michaelis, "C. B. Hoffman, Kansas Socialist," *Kansas Historical Quarterly* 41:2 (summer 1975): 166–82.

107. Otohiko Okugawa, "Annotated List of Communal and Utopian Societies, 1787–1919," published as an appendix to Robert Fogarty, *Dictionary of American Communal and Utopian History* (Westport, Conn.: Greenwood, 1980), 230.

108. Hine, *California's Utopian Colonies*, 148–49.

109. Boris, *Art and Labor*, 162.

110. Bolton Hall, *A Little Land and a Living* (New York: Arcadia Press, 1908).

111. See, for example, Olga Brennecke, "One Acre and Happiness, as Demonstrated by the Littlelanders of San Ysidro Valley," *The Craftsman* 22:5 (Aug. 1912): 556–58.

112. Richard F. Pourade, *Gold in the Sun: The History of San Diego* (San Diego: Union-Tribune Publishing Co., 1965), 111.

113. Henry Chu, "Instead of Utopia, It Left a Lot of Lots to Be Desired," *Los Angeles Times,* Jan. 8, 1996, pp. B1, B6.

114. Lawrence B. Lee, "The Little Landers Colony of San Ysidro," *Journal of San Diego History* 21 (1975): 26–51.

115. On Mead's vision for the California colony program, see Elwood Mead, "Farm Settlements on a New Plan," *American Review of Reviews* 59 (Mar. 1919): 270–77.

116. Albert Shaw, "California's Farm Colonies," *American Review of Reviews* 64 (Oct. 1921): 397–404.

117. Paul K. Conkin, "The Vision of Elwood Mead," *Agricultural History* 34 (Apr. 1960): 88–97. A version of this article also appears in the larger setting of a study of New Deal rural community projects in the 1930s in Conkin's *Tomorrow a New World:*

The New Deal Community Program (Ithaca, N.Y.: Cornell Univ. Press, 1959), 43–48.

118. With the great expansion of the movement, the student co-ops attracted their first extensive press coverage during the 1930s. For references to several typical articles see Mae T. Sperber, *Search for Utopia: A Study of Twentieth Century Communes in America* (Middleboro, Mass.: The Country Press, 1976), 404.

119. Deborah Altus, "Student Housing Cooperatives: Communitarianism among American Youth," *Communal Societies* (forthcoming).

120. Some sources provide Creffield's given names as Edmund Franz; sometimes his middle (or first) name, by which he was principally known, is spelled "Edmond."

121. Dick Pintarich and J. Kingston Pierce, "The Strange Saga of Oregon's Other Guru," *The Oregonian* (Portland), Jan. 7, 1986, pp. C1–C2.

122. For details of Esther Mitchell's killing of her brother and a brief reprise of earlier events, see "Officials Fear Suicide of Demented Women in Seattle Prison," *Eugene Daily Guard,* July 13, 1906, p. 1.

123. No substantial scholarly article on Creffield has apparently been published. For popular accounts see Dick Pintarich, "The Gospel According to Edmond Creffield," *Oregon Magazine* (Mar. 1983): 44–46; Stewart H. Holbrook, "Oregon's Secret Love Cult," *American Mercury* 40 (Feb. 1937): 167–74; Richard Mathison, "Franz Creffield: Naked Reformer," *Faiths, Cults, and Sects of America* (Indianapolis: Bobbs-Merrill, 1960), 301–5. The longest and most detailed of all the popular recountings of the Creffield saga is Maurice Beam, "Crazy after Women," *Cults of America* (New York: MacFadden-Bartell, 1964), 35–58, but like the others it provides no documentation.

124. Many and serious were the accusations against Lewis for fraud and other financial misbehavior. For some details about the charges, see Sidney Morse, *The Siege of University City: The Dreyfus Case of America* (St. Louis: Univ. City Publishing, 1912). This 772-page polemic by a close associate is a vehement defense of Lewis's innocence in the face of persecution.

125. Edward G. Lewis, "A University That Is a School, a City, and a Nation," *The World To-day* 19 (Aug. 1910): 823.

126. The pottery works is well recorded as an important part of American art history. See, for example, Paul Evans, "University City Pottery," *Art Pottery of the United States* (New York: Feingold and Lewis, 1987), 286–91.

127. The principal historical account of Lewis and the American Woman's Republic is Pauline Meyer, *Keep Your Face to the Sunshine: A Lost Chapter in the History of Woman Suffrage* (Edwardsville, Ill.: Alcott Press, 1980). On Lewis's goals for the Republic, see *Brief Prospectus of the American Woman's Republic* (Univ. City, St. Louis, Missouri: n.p., [1912?]).

128. Gilman wrote extensively about her vision of domestic reform. A series of articles that directly inspired Sinclair to initiate the Helicon experiment appeared in *The Independent* in 1904. The most concrete of them was Charlotte Perkins Gilman, "The Beauty of a Block," *Independent* 57 (July 14, 1904): 67–72, which proposes a unified plan for community living on New York City blocks, complete with diagrams and illustrations of new community-oriented apartment floor plans.

129. For an account of Helicon Hall that details Gilman's objection to this use of her ideas, see Lawrence Kaplan, "Utopia During the Progressive Era: The Helicon Home Colony, 1906–1907," *American Studies* 25 (fall 1984): 59–73.

130. Upton Sinclair, "The Home Colony," *Independent* 60 (June 14, 1906): 1401–8. Reprinted in pamphlet form as "The Home Colony: A Prospectus" (New York: Jungle Publishing Co., 1906).

131. Estimates of the number of members resident at any one time vary, and the steady flow of guests also made precise counting difficult. Typically forty to fifty adults and ten children were probably resident at any given time. Sinclair gives varying counts in his several historical sketches of the colony. See, for example, Sinclair, *American Outpost: A Book of Reminiscences* (Pasadena: author, 1932), 182, where he counts forty adult residents. The count of ten children is provided by Floyd Dell in *Upton Sinclair: A Study in Social Protest* (New York: Albert and Charles Boni, 1930), 121–24.

132. Sinclair, *American Outpost*, 182. According to Sinclair's biographer, Sinclair did sue one newspaper for libel "for scandalous lies concerning the Helicon Home Colony; a retraction and apology were printed, but the American public continued to believe the worst." See Dell, *Upton Sinclair*, 124.

133. Sinclair, *American Outpost*, 188–89.

134. The most complete study of the Helicon Home Colony is Margaret Ann Brown, "Not Your Usual Boardinghouse Types: Upton Sinclair's Helicon Home Colony, 1906–1907" (Ph.D. diss. George Washington Univ., 1993). Brown's finely detailed work includes a comprehensive bibliography and photographs of the property.

135. Upton Sinclair, *The Brass Check: A Study of American Journalism* (Pasadena: author, [1920]), 67.

136. W. D. P. Bliss, "Altruist Community," *New Encyclopedia of Social Reform* (New York: Funk and Wagnalls, 1908), 29.

137. "Articles of Agreement of the Friendship Community," broadside in the Oneida Community Papers, Syracuse Univ. Library.

138. See, among other works, Alcander Longley, *Communism, the Right Way, and the Best Way, for All to Live. An Essay on the Principles, Organization, and Practical Details of Liberal Communism. Also Containing a Complete System of Simple Phonography or Rapid Writing. With Several Communist Songs, Printed in a New System of Phonetic Figure Music* (St. Louis: n.p., 1880); Longley, *What Is Communism? A Narrative of the Relief Community* (St. Louis: Altruist Community, 1890; repr., New York: AMS Press, 1976).

139. H. Roger Grant, "Missouri's Utopian Communities," *Missouri Historical Review* 66 (Oct. 1971): 43.

140. Grant, "Missouri's Utopian Communities," 43. For more biographical information on Longley see Hal D. Sears, "Alcander Longley, Missouri Communist: A History of Reunion Community and a Study of the Constitutions of Reunion and Friendship," *Bulletin of the Missouri Historical Society* 25 (Jan. 1969): 123–37.

141. The only major source on the Farm is Frances Davis, *A Fearful Innocence* (Kent, Ohio: Kent State Univ. Press, 1981). Davis grew up on the Farm; the book is not so much a history as a personal essay and memoir.

142. Certainly the Farm represents a borderline situation in communal history; it was privately owned and not really dedicated to a central ideal. But a large group lived there for many years and shared, at least to some extent, the expenses as well as the real estate. Arthur Schlesinger Jr. found the situation sufficiently communal to label it a "twentieth-century reenactment of Fruitlands or Brook Farm." See Schlesinger, "Foreword," in Davis, *A Fearful Innocence*, ix–xii.

143. Some limited manuscript material and a few clippings relating to the Gibbs colony are in the Oneida Community Papers at the Syracuse Univ. Library.

144. "Bureau of Group Organization," *To-Morrow* magazine. The feature appeared in most issues between Apr. 1907 and July 1908.

4. THE QUIET TWENTIES AND THE ROARING THIRTIES

1. Isaac Broome, *The Last Days of the Ruskin Co-operative Association* (Chicago: Charles H. Kerr, 1902), 23, 89. Broome reproduces a drawing of the envisioned college building opposite p. 60.

2. The most comprehensive scholarly account of Commonwealth College is William H. Cobb, "Commonwealth College: A History" (M.A. thesis. Univ. of Arkansas, 1960). Cobb also published several articles on the college in the *Arkansas Historical Quarterly;* see, for example, Cobb, "Commonwealth College Comes to Arkansas, 1923–1925," *Arkansas Historical Quarterly* 23 (summer 1964): 99–122; "From Utopian Isolation to Radical Activism: Commonwealth College," *Arkansas Historical Quarterly* 32 (summer 1973): 132–47.

3. *Commonwealth, Newllano, Louisiana: A School of, for, and by Hand and Brain Workers Devoted to the Development of Personality and the Creation of a Technique for Co-operative Life* (Newllano: Llano Colony Press, n.d. [ca. 1923]); pamphlet in the communal library of Yad Tabenkin, Ramat Efal, Israel.

4. The move from Newllano to the rural Mena campus inevitably involved several twists and turns. See Cobb, "Commonwealth College Comes to Arkansas," 99–122.

5. Henry Black, "Library Service on No Budget at All," *Library Journal* 59 (Oct. 1, 1934): 746–47; Mark Sandler, "The Workers Must Read: The Commonwealth College Library, 1925–1940," *Journal of Library History, Philosophy, and Comparative Librarianship* 20 (winter 1985): 46–69. Black was a librarian at Commonwealth.

6. Cobb, "From Utopian Isolation to Radical Activism," 137. Cobb says that forty to forty-five students were enrolled in a typical term.

7. Raymond and Charlotte Koch, *Educational Commune: The Story of Commonwealth College* (New York: Schocken, 1972), 72. The Kochs' book is the most substantial account of the college by persons involved in it and the source of some of the information in this sketch.

8. On the crucial conflicts in the mid-1930s see William H. Cobb, "The State Legislature and the 'Reds': Arkansas's General Assembly v. Commonwealth College, 1935–1937," *Arkansas Historical Quarterly* 45 (1986): 3–18.

9. For an account of the financial chaos that attended the opening of Black Mountain, see Theodore Dreier, "Early Close Calls," *Black Mountain College: Sprouted Seeds—An Anthology of Personal Accounts,* ed. Mervin Lane (Knoxville: Univ. of Tennessee Press, 1990), 24–32.

10. Martin Duberman, *Black Mountain: An Experiment in Community* (Garden City, N.Y.: Doubleday/Anchor, 1973), 21.

11. Eric Russell Bentley, "Report from the Academy: The Experimental College," *Partisan Review* 12 (summer 1945): 424.

12. For a history of the college that focuses on the achievements of its participants in the arts, see Mary Emma Harris, *The Arts at Black Mountain College* (Cambridge, Mass.: MIT Press, 1987).

13. Fielding Dawson, *The Black Mountain Book* (Rocky Mount: N.C. Wesleyan College Press, 2d ed., 1991), 7.

14. F. A. Foster, *Black Mountain College* (Montreat, N.C.: author, 1987), 4. This booklet is sold by the Black Mountain Chamber of Commerce.

15. Francine du Plessix Gray, "Black Mountain: The Breaking (Making) of a Writer," in *Adam and Eve in the City* (New York: Simon and Schuster, 1987), 323–34.

16. A statement of the no-grades, graduation-by-examination system is provided

in a reproduction of a college transcript in Lane, *Black Mountain College: Sprouted Seeds,* 65.

17. Dawson, *Black Mountain Book,* 205.

18. Mildred Harding, "My Black Mountain," *Yale Literary Magazine* 151:1 [1984]: 76–89.

19. Most of this information is from Duberman, *Black Mountain.*

20. Janet Lee, "'Sisterhood of the Smiling Countenance and the Merry Laugh': Unsettling the Sentimental in a New York Women's Commune, 1921–24," *Frontiers: A Journal of Women Studies* 17:1 (1996): 1–29.

21. Michael Barkun, "Communal Societies as Cyclical Phenomena," *Communal Societies* 4 (1984): 35–48.

22. For Borsodi's reservations about the single tax applied to small-acreage homesteads, see Borsodi, "Land Tenure," *American Review* 7 (Oct. 1936): 556–63.

23. *I'll Take My Stand: The South and the Agrarian Tradition, by Twelve Southerners* (New York: Harper and Brothers, 1930).

24. On the Catholic wing of the movement generally, see Edward S. Shapiro, "Catholic Agrarian Thought and the New Deal," *Catholic Historical Review* 65 (Oct. 1979): 583–99. For an authorized view of the National Catholic Rural Life Conference, see Raymond Philip Witte, *Twenty-five Years of Crusading: A History of the National Catholic Rural Life Conference* (Des Moines: National Catholic Rural Life Conference, 1948).

25. Herbert Agar and Allen Tate, *Who Owns America? A New Declaration of Independence* (Boston: Houghton Mifflin, 1936).

26. On Agar see William E. Leverette Jr. and David E. Shi, "Herbert Agar and *Free America:* A Jeffersonian Alternative to the New Deal," *Journal of American Studies* 16 (Aug. 1982): 189–206. The journal *Free America* apparently borrowed its title from a book of that name by the single-taxer Bolton Hall. See Hall, *Free America; Short Chapters Showing How Liberty Brings Prosperity* (Chicago: L. S. Dickey, 1904).

27. For an overview of the larger decentralist movement, see Edward S. Shapiro, "Decentralist Intellectuals and the New Deal," *Journal of American History* 58:4 (Mar. 1972): 938–57.

28. Ralph Borsodi, *This Ugly Civilization* (New York: Simon and Schuster, 1929; repr., New York: Porcupine Press, 1975).

29. Ralph Borsodi, *Flight from the City* (New York: Harper and Row, 1933; repr., New York: Harper and Row, 1972), 9.

30. Jacob H. Dorn, "Subsistence Homesteading in Dayton, Ohio, 1933–1935," *Ohio History* 78 (1969): 77. See also Borsodi, "Dayton, Ohio, Makes Social History," *Nation* 136 (Apr. 19, 1933): 447–48.

31. For an overview of the conflicts among Borsodi, the residents, and the government, see "Homesteading Comes a-Cropper," *Architectural Forum* 61 (Aug. 1934): 142–44.

32. The most complete account of the Dayton project and its problems is Dorn, "Subsistence Homesteading."

33. Ralph Borsodi, "Wanted: A School of Living," *Progressive Education* 12 (Jan. 1935): 21.

34. Ibid., 22–23.

35. John Chamberlain, "Blueprints for a New Society," *New Republic* 102:1 (Jan. 1, 1940): 13–16.

36. George Weller, "Design for Living," *Fortune* 18 (Oct. 1938): 12, 18.

37. See George Weller, "Decentralized City Homesteads," *Commonweal* 28 (July 22, 1938): 341–44.

38. Robert Bird, "Homestead Trouble," *Commonweal* 32 (May 17, 1940): 70–71.

39. William E. Leverette Jr. and David E. Shi, "Agrarianism for Commuters," *South Atlantic Quarterly* 79 (spring 1980): 216.

40. David Shi, *The Simple Life: Plain Living and High Thinking in American Culture* (New York: Oxford Univ. Press, 1985), 245.

41. Mildred Loomis, *Alternative Americas* (New York: Universe Books, 1982), 60.

42. Ibid., 75–76.

43. Paul K. Conkin compiled a list of ninety-nine such depression-era government-initiated communities with cooperative or collective features. Other historians of the FSA list various others. In 1942 Joseph Eaton and Saul Katz, for example, published a list of twenty-seven FSA "Cooperative Corporation Farms" that only partly overlaps Conkin's list. Another Eaton list, published in 1950, was different yet. See Conkin, *Tomorrow a New World: The New Deal Community Program* (Ithaca, N.Y.: Cornell Univ. Press, 1959), 332–37; Joseph W. Eaton and Saul M. Katz, *Research Guide on Cooperative Group Farming* (New York: H. W. Wilson Co., 1942), 56; Joseph W. Eaton, "The FSA Cooperative Farms," *Cooperative Group Living*, ed. Henrik F. Infield and Joseph B. Maier (New York: Henry Koosis and Co., 1950), 12.

44. Conkin, *Tomorrow a New World*, 48–58.

45. Ibid., 108–10.

46. M. L. Wilson, "A New Land-Use Program: The Place of Subsistence Homesteads," *Journal of Land and Public Utility Economics* 10:1 (Feb. 1934): 1–12.

47. Joseph G. Knapp, *The Advance of American Cooperative Enterprise: 1920–1945* (Danville, Ill.: Interstate Printers and Publishers, 1973), 298–99.

48. One purpose of the homestead colonies was to reduce poor farmers' dependence on agriculture by developing an industrial job base for them; Tugwell doubted that industries would be drawn to the colonies, and thus the basic rationale for the program was suspect. See Michael V. Namorato, *Rexford G. Tugwell: A Biography* (New York: Praeger, 1988), 110–16.

49. Conkin, *Tomorrow a New World*, 169–70.

50. Russell Lord, *The Care of the Earth* (New York: Thomas Nelson, 1963), 353.

51. Conkin, *Tomorrow a New World*, 330.

52. Joseph W. Eaton, "FSA Cooperative Farms," *Cooperative Group Living*, 5–12. Many works on New Deal policies and projects besides those cited in the preceding endnotes deal to some extent with the Farm Security Administration settlements. One detailed history of the FSA is Sidney Baldwin, *Poverty and Politics: The Rise and Decline of the Farm Security Administration* (Chapel Hill: Univ. of North Carolina Press, 1968). Donald Holley's *Uncle Sam's Farmers: The New Deal Communities in the Lower Mississippi Valley* (Champaign: Univ. of Illinois Press, 1975) deals with New Deal resettlement communities in Arkansas, Louisiana, and Mississippi.

53. Norvelt, located to the northeast of Penn-Craft, near Greensburg, Pennsylvania, was built between 1934 and 1937 and, like Penn-Craft, survives as a neighborhood of privately owned homes today.

54. The most extensive account of the Penn-Craft project is contained in Alison K. Hoagland and Margaret M. Mulrooney, *Norvelt and Penn-Craft, Pennsylvania: Subsistence-Homestead Communities of the 1930s* (Washington, D.C.: Historic American Buildings Survey/Historic American Engineering Record, America's Industrial Heritage Project, National Park Service, 1991). For a more succinct sketch see Henrik In-

field, "Penn-Craft Community," *Utopia and Experiment: Essays in the Sociology of Cooperation* (New York: F. A. Praeger, 1955), 66–70.

55. The most complete history of Delta and Providence is Jerry W. Dallas, "The Delta and Providence Farms: A Mississippi Experiment in Cooperative Farming and Racial Cooperation, 1936–1956," *Mississippi Quarterly* 40:3 (summer 1987): 283–308. For conditions that led to the founding of the farms, and the early history of Delta, see Sherwood Eddy, *A Door of Opportunity, or an American Adventure in Cooperation with Sharecroppers* (New York: Association Press, [1937]).

56. J. Kaaz Doyle, "Digging Out of the Depression: San Antonio's Diga Colony, 1932–1933," *Locus* 4 (spring 1992): 133–51.

57. Robert J. Hendricks, *Bethel and Aurora: An Experiment in Communism as Practical Christianity* (New York: Press of the Pioneers, 1933), 266–71. Hendricks relies for information on the community's mimeographed *Bulletin* and on a series of three articles appearing in early 1933 in the *Eugene Register-Guard*. There seems to be little other information on the community.

58. The most complete account of Saline Valley Farms is Z. Clark Dickinson and Joseph W. Eaton, "Saline Valley Farms," *Cooperative Group Living*, 22–35.

59. Albertson, "A Survey of Mutualistic Communities in America," 421. The principal account of the colony was published when it was three years old and reportedly thriving. See Ernest S. Wooster, *Communities of the Past and Present* (Newllano, La.: Llano Colonist, 1924), 140–42.

60. Morris Lippman, interviewed by Timothy Miller, Santa Clara, Calif., Mar. 21, 1996. Lippman was one of the young commune members who sought a separate operation; feelings about the issue ran so high, he reported, that when the proposal was rejected they had no choice but to leave.

61. The most substantial history of Sunrise is Joseph J. Cohen, *In Quest of Heaven: The Story of the Sunrise Co-operative Farm Community* (New York: Sunrise History Publishing Committee, 1957). Despite Cohen's deep involvement in his subject, his coverage is generally comprehensive and fair. For accounts by outside scholars, see Francis Shor, "A Utopian Project in a Communal Experiment of the 1930's: The Sunrise Colony in Historical and Comparative Perspective," *Communal Societies* 7 (1987): 82–94; Christina M. Lemieux, "The Sunrise Cooperative Farm Community: A Collectivist Utopian Experiment," *Communal Societies* 10 (1990): 39–67.

62. Albertson, "Survey of Mutualistic Communities in America," *Iowa Journal of History and Politics* 34 (Oct. 1936): 18–19. See also "Jews Here to Open Community Farm," *New York Times*, Nov. 29, 1933, p. 17. Albertson provides 1930 as a founding date, but contemporary press accounts place the founding three years later.

63. The Catholic Worker's history is far better known, and much more reliably documented, than that of most of the groups covered in this book, and for that reason its story is recounted here only in its broadest outlines. For history in greater depth see, among many other works, Mel Piehl, *Breaking Bread: The Catholic Worker and the Origin of Catholic Radicalism in America* (Philadelphia: Temple Univ. Press, 1982). Invaluable also is Dorothy Day's *The Long Loneliness: An Autobiography* (New York: Harper and Row, 1952), among her many writings.

64. F. L. Burke, "Back to the Soil," *Catholic Worker* 1:10 (Apr. 1934): 2.

65. James F. Montague, "History of Farming Commune," *Catholic Worker* 6:10 (May 1939): 2, 5, 8.

66. Rosalie Riegle Troester, *Voices from the Catholic Worker* (Philadelphia: Temple Univ. Press, 1993), 249.

67. J. Gordon Melton, *The Encyclopedia of American Religions* (Detroit: Gale Re-

search, 4th ed., 1993), 652. Brief entries in various editions of this work appear to constitute the main secondary sources on the People of the Living God.

68. A good Davidian history through the Florence Houteff era, published before the siege and fire at Mt. Carmel in 1993, is Bill Pitts, "The Mount Carmel Davidians: Adventist Reformers, 1935–1959," *Syzygy: Journal of Alternative Religion and Culture* 2 (1993): 39–54. For a brief post-siege historical synopsis see Pitts, "The Davidian Tradition," *From the Ashes: Making Sense of Waco,* ed. James R. Lewis (Lanham, Md.: Rowman and Littlefield, 1994), 33–39; for a longer version, see Pitts, "Davidians and Branch Davidians: 1929–1987," *Armageddon in Waco: Critical Perspectives on the Branch Davidian Conflict,* ed. Stuart A. Wright (Chicago: Univ. of Chicago Press, 1995), 20–42.

69. Much of this post-1959 Davidian history is based on James D. Tabor and Eugene V. Gallagher, *Why Waco? Cults and the Battle for Religious Freedom in America* (Berkeley: Univ. of California Press, 1995).

70. Tabor and Gallagher, *Why Waco?,* 64–67.

71. For a critical but comprehensive account of the raid, siege, and fire, see Albert K. Bates, "What Really Happened at Waco? 'Cult' or Set-up?" *Communities: Journal of Cooperative Living* no. 88 (fall 1995): 50–60.

72. Melton, *Encyclopedia of American Religions,* 754–55.

73. The standard work on the Short Creek fundamentalists is Martha Sonntag Bradley, *Kidnapped from That Land: The Government Raids on the Short Creek Polygamists* (Salt Lake City: Univ. of Utah Press, 1993).

74. D. Michael Quinn, "Plural Marriage and Mormon Fundamentalism," *Fundamentalisms and Society: Reclaiming the Sciences, the Family, and Education,* ed. Martin E. Marty and R. Scott Appleby (Chicago: Univ. of Chicago Press, 1993; vol. 2 of *The Fundamentalism Project*), 246.

75. Quinn, "Plural Marriage and Mormon Fundamentalism," 246–47.

76. Maureen Zent, "Polygamy War: Polygamists Battle Each Other over Real Estate in Southern Utah," *Private Eye Weekly* (Salt Lake City), Jan. 9, 1997, pp. 8–10.

77. One good source for tracking the scattered United Order groups is Steven L. Shields, *Divergent Paths of the Restoration* (Bountiful, Utah: Restoration Research, 3d ed., 1982). Information on various LeBaronite churches is on pp. 142–43, 159–63, and 189–90. The most complete account, with detailed biographical information on the various members of the family, is an insider work: Verlan M. LeBaron, *The LeBaron Story* (Lubbock, Tex.: Keels and Co., 1981).

78. See Shields, *Divergent Paths of the Restoration,* 175–76.

79. J. Gordon Melton, *Encyclopedic Handbook of Cults in America* (New York: Garland Publishing, 1992), 52–53; Quinn, "Plural Marriage and Mormon Fundamentalism," 250–51.

80. Probably the most complete outside article on the group was an Associated Press feature that ran in several newspapers in late 1992 and early 1993. See David Briggs, "Are They Serving God, or a Sect; Opinions Differ in Iowa," *Wichita Eagle,* Jan. 23, 1993, p. 10C. One thesis has been written about the group: Leland Searles, "Returning to Babylon: Processes of Social Change and Characteristics of Former Participants in a New Religious Movement" (M.A. thesis. Iowa State Univ., 1993).

81. Dwight Goddard, "Where Christ Meets Buddha," *The Forum* 72 (Dec. 1924): 781–86.

82. Goddard translated a number of classic Buddhist works into English and in publishing them put Buddhism before the American reading public. His most

prominent book was an anthology, *The Buddhist Bible: The Favorite Scriptures of the Zen Sect* (Thetford, Vt.: n.p., 1932; rev. ed., New York: E. P. Dutton, 1938).

83. Dwight Goddard, *Followers of Buddha: An American Brotherhood* (Santa Barbara: J. F. Rowny Press, 1934), v.

84. Ibid., vi.

85. For basic biographical information on Goddard see David Starry, "Dwight Goddard—the Yankee Buddhist," *Zen Notes* 27 (July 1980): n.p. See also Rick Fields, *How the Swans Came to the Lake* (Boulder, Colo.: Shambhala, 1981), 184–86.

86. Richard Mathison, *Faiths, Cults, and Sects of America: From Atheism to Zen* (Indianapolis: Bobbs-Merrill, 1960), 317–23. Mathison appears to provide the only extant account of the Briggsites. His book is not documented, but his other chapters capable of independent verification are consistently reliable, and so his account is summarized for inclusion here.

87. The principal early source on Heaven City is Ernest S. Wooster, "Heaven Everywhere," *Communities of the Past and Present*, 143.

88. Michael Zahn, "Heaven City: Time Locks 'Love' Religion into Past," *Milwaukee Journal*, Aug. 13, 1979, part 2, pp. 1, 5.

89. Much of this information comes from Zahn, "Heaven City," and a sequel article by Zahn, "Heaven City Dies with Founder," *Milwaukee Journal*, Aug. 14, 1979, part 2, pp. 1, 3. For a brief account based in large part on these articles, see J. Gordon Melton, "Heaven City," *Encyclopedia of American Religions* 4th ed. supp. (Detroit: Gale, 1994), 59.

90. The standard monograph on Mankind United is H. T. Dohrman, *California Cult: The Story of "Mankind United"* (Boston: Beacon, 1958).

91. Ramón Sender, "Golden Rule," *The Modern Utopian* 3 (Sept.–Oct. 1968): 20.

92. Reproduced in a flyer announcing the fall 1995 board meeting of the Fellowship for Intentional Community, which took place at the church campus.

93. See J. Gordon Melton, "Thelemic Magick in America," *Alternatives to American Mainline Churches*, ed. Joseph H. Fichter (New York: Rose of Sharon Press/Unification Theological Seminary, 1983), 67–87.

94. Clayton R. Koppes, *JPL and the American Space Program* (New Haven: Yale Univ. Press, 1982), 3.

95. Frank J. Malina, "On the GALCIT Rocket Research Project, 1936–1938," in F. C. Durant and G. S. James, eds., *First Steps Toward Space: Proceedings of the First and Second History Symposia of the International Academy of Astronautics* (Washington, D.C.: Smithsonian Institution Press, 1974), 114.

96. Alexander Mitchell, "Revealed for the First Time . . . The Odd Beginning of Ron Hubbard's Career," *Sunday Times* (London), Oct. 5, 1969, p. 11.

97. "Scientology: New Light on Crowley," *Sunday Times* (London), Dec. 28, 1969.

98. Roy Wallis has quoted Hubbard as claiming to have worked out basic Scientological principles at about the time he was associated with Parsons: "I got a nurse, wrapped a towel around my head and became a swami, and by 1947 achieved 'clearing.'" See Roy Wallis, *The Road to Total Freedom: A Sociological Analysis of Scientology* (New York: Columbia Univ. Press, 1977), 22.

99. *Intentional Communities: 1959 Yearbook of the Fellowship of Intentional Communities* (Yellow Springs, Ohio: Fellowship of Intentional Communities, 1959), 28.

100. George Leon Hicks, "Ideology and Change in an American Utopian Community" (Ph.D. diss. Univ. of Illinois, 1969), 25.

101. George L. Hicks, "Utopian Communities and Social Networks," *Aware of Utopia,* ed. David W. Plath (Urbana: Univ. of Illinois Press, 1971), 140.

102. Lynn Murray Willeford, "Celo, North Carolina: A Community for Individualists," *New Age Journal,* May/June 1993, 72–73.

103. "Celo Community," *The 1990/91 Directory of Intentional Communities: A Guide to Cooperative Living* (Evansville, Ind., and Stelle, Ill.: Fellowship for Intentional Community and Communities Publications Cooperative), 176.

104. Hicks, "Utopian Communities and Social Networks," 142.

105. Ibid., 142–43.

106. Basic information on Celo can be found in *The Intentional Communities: 1959 Handbook of the Fellowship of Intentional Communities,* 28–30. The most complete study is Hicks, "Ideology and Change in an American Utopian Community."

107. Statement of principles, reproduced in W. Edward Orser, *Searching for a Viable Alternative: The Macedonia Cooperative Community, 1937–1958* (New York: Burt Franklin and Co., 1981), 44.

108. David Newton, quoted in ibid., 171.

109. For information on the origin and development of the toy business, see Benjamin Zablocki, *The Joyful Community* (Chicago: Univ. of Chicago Press, 1971), 94, 130–38.

110. The standard work on Macedonia is Orser, *Searching for a Viable Alternative.* For a briefer account see Henrik Infield, "Macedonia in Georgia, U.S.A.," *Utopia and Experiment: Essays in the Sociology of Cooperation* (New York: Praeger, 1955), 226–31.

111. *Articles of Incorporation and By-Laws, Bryn Gweled Homesteads,* pamphlet, 1989 ed.

112. Allison Bass, "Welcome Home," *Boston Globe Magazine,* Aug. 11, 1991, pp. 16–29.

113. Cynthia Mayer, "Tie That Binds Two Communities Is a Belief in the Common Good," *Philadelphia Inquirer,* Mar. 16, 1991, p. 10-A. For brief sketches of the community other than the two cited here and just above, see Wendell B. Kramer, "Criteria for the Intentional Community" (Ph.D. diss. New York Univ., 1955), pp. 74–76, and Mildred J. Loomis, "Small Community: Bryn Gweled," in *Alternative Americas,* 118–21.

5. NEW COMMUNITIES IN THE 1940S AND 1950S

1. Edward Bellamy, *Looking Backward, 2000–1887* (New York: New American Library, 1960; originally published in 1888).

2. David Shi, *The Simple Life: Plain Living and High Thinking in American Culture* (New York: Oxford Univ. Press, 1985), 235–36.

3. Jane Morgan, "History of Community Service," *Community Service Newsletter* 36:4 (July/Aug. 1988): 4–5.

4. Alfred Andersen, interviewed by Timothy Miller, Eugene, Oreg., July 12, 1996.

5. *The 1990/91 Directory of Intentional Communities: A Guide to Cooperative Living* (Evansville, Ind., and Stelle, Ill.: Fellowship for Intentional Community and Communities Publications Cooperative, 1990). A revised edition of the *Directory* was published in 1995: *Communities Directory* (Langley, Wash.: Fellowship for Intentional Community).

6. On the relations between Hidden Springs and Koinonia Farm, see Dallas Lee, *The Cotton Patch Evidence* (New York: Harper and Row, 1971), 164–66.

7. Information on Hidden Springs is sketchy. The most substantial account ap-

pears to be Wendell B. Kramer, "Criteria for the Intentional Community" (Ph.D. diss. New York Univ., 1955), 92–93.

8. For a discussion of the group process used at Tanguy Homesteads, see Kramer, "Criteria for the Intentional Community," 77–78.

9. Dick Andersen, "Where All Places Felt Like Home," *Communities: Journal of Cooperative Living* no. 84 (fall 1994): 39.

10. Brief accounts of Tanguy Homesteads can be found in *Intentional Communities: 1959 Yearbook of the Fellowship of Intentional Communities,* 27–28, and Kramer, "Criteria for the Intentional Community," 77–78. See also Mayer, "Tie That Binds Two Communities Is a Belief in the Common Good." The community's own self-description was available in 1996 in a pamphlet entitled "Tanguy Homesteads: A Neighborhood Community Since 1945."

11. No very substantial account of Tuolumne Farms seems to exist. Among several short accounts the most useful are Robert V. Hine, *California's Utopian Colonies* (New Haven, Conn.: Yale Univ. Press, 1966; originally published in 1953), 157–59, and Kramer, "Criteria for the Intentional Community," 71–74.

12. For a statement of Skyview's goals and one member's sense that the community failed to achieve them very fully, see James S. Best, *Another Way of Life: Experiencing Intentional Community* (Wallingford, Pa.: Pendle Hill Pamphlet 218, 1978), 7–8. For a more general brief sketch see Kramer, "Criteria for the Intentional Community," 79–81. See also James S. Best, "Skyview Acres," *WIN* magazine 4:1 (Jan. 1, 1969): 9–10.

13. Kramer, "Criteria for the Intentional Community," 95.

14. The most substantial piece of information on Kingwood, apparently, is slightly more than a page of material in Kramer, "Criteria for the Intentional Community," 93–95. This sketch is adapted from Kramer's depiction.

15. Ibid., 96.

16. "Report of the Saturday Evening Session, Fellowship of Intentional Communities Conference, September 18–20, 1959, Tanguy Homesteads, Pa." Manuscript in the files of Alfred Andersen.

17. Kramer, "Criteria for the Intentional Community," 88–89. A statement of the group's history and ideals is in "The Canterbury Group," *Newsletter of the Fellowship of Intentional Communities,* Aug. 1, 1960, pp. 4–6. That article, written by community members, says that the communitarians arrived in Canterbury from Newton in 1959, but because Kramer's dissertation, completed in 1955, places them at Canterbury, the 1960 article's chronology must be erroneous.

18. John Affolter, "May Valley Co-op, 1957–," *Communities* no. 6 (Dec.–Jan. 1974): 14–17.

19. "Teramanto Community," community broadside, ca. 1991.

20. Kramer, "Criteria for the Intentional Community," 97–98.

21. "The Vale," *The Intentional Communities: 1959 Yearbook of the Fellowship of Intentional Communities,* 20.

22. "Terms of Trusteeship and Non-Ownership for the Workers' Community of the Universal Citizens at St. Francis Acres, Glen Gardner, New Jersey, U.S.A.," *Cooperative Living* 8:1 (spring–summer 1957): 2.

23. Ammon Hennacy, *The Book of Ammon* (n.p.: author, 1965), 374.

24. No single comprehensive account of St. Francis Acres seems to exist. Several references to various stages in its life can be found in David Dellinger's autobiography, however. See David Dellinger, *From Yale to Jail: The Life Story of a Moral Dissenter* (New York: Pantheon, 1993), 145–51, 176–79.

25. Something of the flavor of the Cotton Patch version is conveyed in the title of one of the original pamphlet versions of Jordan's translations: *Letters to the Georgia Convention (Galatians) and to the Alabaster African Church, Smithville, Alabama (Philippians) in the Koinonia "Cotton Patch" Version* (Americus, Ga.: Koinonia Farm, 1964).

26. For a general history of Koinonia Farm see Lee, *The Cotton Patch Evidence*.

27. For a history of Habitat, including information on how it grew from origins in the Koinonia community, see Millard Fuller, *No More Shacks! The Daring Vision of Habitat for Humanity* (Waco, Tex.: Word Books, 1986).

28. Benjamin Zablocki, *The Joyful Community* (Chicago: Univ. of Chicago Press, 1980), 73.

29. A recent historical survey is Iaacov Oved, *The Witness of the Brothers: A History of the Bruderhof* (New Brunswick, N.J.: Transaction, 1996). Another comprehensive work is Zablocki, *The Joyful Community;* for the early years of the movement, see chap. 2. A good insider account of the early years through the aftermath of Eberhard Arnold's death is Emmy Arnold, *Torches Together: The Beginning and Early Years of the Bruderhof Communities* (Rifton, N.Y.: Plough, 1964).

30. In 1956 there were two colonies in England, two (including Forest River) in the United States, three in Paraguay, and embryonic ones in Germany and Uruguay. See Zablocki, *The Joyful Community*, 95.

31. Several former members have written of the crisis in the early 1960s, typically arguing that the community, which previously had been fairly broad-minded, turned authoritarian and narrow in outlook. See, for example, Francis Hall, "Pitfalls of Intentional Community," *Christian Century* 80 (Aug. 14, 1963): 1000–1002; Robert N. Peck, "An Ex-Member's View of the Bruderhof Communities from 1948–1961," *Utopian Studies I,* ed. Gorman Beauchamp, Kenneth Roemer, and Nicholas D. Smith (Lanham, Md.: Univ. Press of America, 1987), 111–22.

32. On not measuring up to the standards set by the heroic founding generation, see Philip Hazelton, "Trailing the Founders: On Being a Second-Generation Bruder," *This Magazine Is about Schools* 4 (spring and summer issues, 1970): 11–41, 54–78.

33. For a summary of the *KIT* controversy, see Timothy Miller, "Stress and Conflict in an International Religious Movement: The Case of the Bruderhof," *KIT Newsletter* 5:7 (July 1993): 9–10. For Sender's account of his situation and the founding of *KIT,* see Ramón Sender Barayon, "The Heart Will Find a Way: Creating a Network of Reunion," *Communities: Journal of Cooperative Living* no. 88 (fall 1995): 61–64. A rejoinder from Bruderhof members Doug and Ruby Moody appears as a sidebar to that article.

34. Fragments of the Forest River story are provided in a number of places. For a Bruderhof version of it see Merrill Mow, *Torches Rekindled: The Bruderhof's Struggle for Renewal* (Rifton, N.Y.: Plough, 1989).

35. For a summary of the Hutterite controversy surrounding Jacob Kleinsasser, see Brian Preston, "Jacob's Ladder," *Saturday Night* (Apr. 1992): 77.

36. J. Christoph Arnold, "An Open Letter from the Bruderhof," *The Plough* no. 41 (winter 1995): 3.

37. Ulrike Posche, "Driven Away for the Second Time," *CALL: "Communes at Large" Letter* no. 7 (winter 1995–96): 22. Trans. from the German news magazine *Stern.*

38. The severing of relations between Nigerians and American Bruderhofers was tracked in the *KIT* newsletter. A summary of the Bruderhof's grievances and the response of Inno Idiong, a Nigerian leader, to them was provided in "Inno Idiong for Palmgrove," *KIT* 7:12 (Dec. 1995): 4.

39. Kramer, "Criteria for the Intentional Community," 78–79. Kramer's dissertation is an invaluable resource for many of the small and little-documented communities active in the postwar years.

40. "Koinonia, Baltimore," *Alternatives!* no. 3 (summer 1972): 44.

41. Glenn Harding, "Background and Historical Notes on Koinonia Foundation," manuscript, 1977; a copy is at the Institute for the Study of American Religion in Santa Barbara. See also Clifford J. Green, "Ambiguities of Community: A Koinonia Experience," *Utopias: The American Experience,* ed. Gairdner B. Moment and Otto F. Kraushaar (Metuchen, N.J.: Scarecrow Press, 1980), 179–93. Information on the community as it operates today is mainly available through Koinonia periodical and promotional publications.

42. Information on the latter years of Koinonia was provided by former member Paul E. Schoen, Nov. 1996.

43. For a brief review of Bhoodan, both as a concept and as a specific twentieth-century social program, see A. J. Muste, "Not So Long Ago," *Liberation* 3:7 (Sept. 1958), 19.

44. "Bhoodan Center," *Alternatives Newsmagazine,* 1971, p. 11.

45. Bhoodan/Ma-Na-Har is another little documented community. The principal source is the community's publication, the *Manahar Cooperative Fellowship Handbook* (Oakhurst, Calif.: Bhoodan Center, 1970).

46. Marcia Meier, "Bible Comes to Life at the Colony," Redding (Calif.) *Record Searchight,* Feb. 25, 1984; Melton, *Encyclopedia of American Religions,* 645–46.

47. Barbara Mathieu, "The Shiloh Farms Community: A Case of Complementarity in Sex-Role Dualism," *Sex Roles in Contemporary American Communes,* ed. Jon Wagner (Bloomington: Indiana Univ. Press, 1982), 155–71.

48. "About . . . The Community of Shiloh," promotional brochure, n.d. (ca. 1996).

49. Elizabeth O'Connor, *Call to Commitment: The Story of the Church of the Saviour, Washington, D.C.* (New York: Harper and Row, 1963), 40. Information for this sketch is taken from this and other works by O'Connor and from Melton, *Encyclopedia of American Religions,* 645.

50. See, for example, Winkie Pratney, *A Handbook for Followers of Jesus* (Minneapolis: Bethany Fellowship, 1977).

51. Donald G. Bloesch, *Centers of Christian Renewal* (Philadelphia: United Church Press, 1964), 128–42.

52. *The Way of Love,* Reba House pamphlet, n.d., p. 3. Excerpts from an earlier pamphlet expressing similar sentiments can be found in George R. Fitzgerald, *Communes: Their Goals, Hopes, Problems* (New York: Paulist Press, 1971), 14.

53. David and Neta Jackson, *Glimpses of Glory: Thirty Years of Community: The Story of Reba Place Fellowship* (Elgin, Ill.: Brethren Press, 1987), 91–92.

54. On employment patterns in the community's early years, see Marguerite Bouvard, *The Intentional Community Movement* (Port Washington, N.Y.: Kennikat Press, 1975), 73–74.

55. The most complete study of Reba Place is probably W. Russell Harris III, "Urban Place Fellowship: An Example of a Communitarian Social Structure" (Ph.D. diss. Michigan State Univ., 1973). Longtime community member Dave Jackson has written extensively about the community; his most substantial account, coauthored with his wife, Neta Jackson, is *Glimpses of Glory.*

56. On the spiritual discipline of Taizé see Roger Schutz, *The Rule of Taizé* (Taizé: Les Presses de Taizé, 1961).

57. Thomas Merton, *The Seven Storey Mountain* (New York: Harcourt, Brace, 1948).

58. Michele and Kevin of The Teachers, eds., *World Directory of Alternative Communities* (Bangor, Wales: The Teachers, 1981), 175.

59. Ibid., 174–75.

60. Heard remained somewhat eclectic in his spirituality, and certainly kept lines of communication with the Christian majority open, writing on Christian as well as non-Christian themes and publishing in such periodicals as the *Christian Century.* See Gerald Heard, *The Creed of Christ: An Interpretation of the Lord's Prayer* (New York: Harper and Brothers, 1940); Heard, *The Code of Christ: An Interpretation of the Beatitudes* (New York: Harper and Brothers, 1941).

61. Gerald Heard, "The Significance of the New Pacifism," *The New Pacifism,* ed. Gerald Heard (London: Allenson, 1936), 17.

62. Gerald Heard, *The Third Morality* (London: Cassell and Co., 1937), 314.

63. "Trabuco" (prospectus), manuscript, (Aldous) Huxley Collection, Univ. of California at Los Angeles library system.

64. Walter Truett Anderson, *The Upstart Spring: Esalen and the American Awakening* (Reading, Mass.: Addison-Wesley, 1983), 12.

65. The source of the money used to build Trabuco is unclear. Laurence Veysey says that a large legacy was the financial cornerstone, but provides no details. The Vedanta Society's history of its work in southern California suggests that living donors were the main contributors. See Laurence Veysey, *The Communal Experience: Anarchist and Mystical Communities in Twentieth-Century America* (Chicago: Univ. of Chicago Press, 1973), 271; *Vedanta in Southern California: An Illustrated Guide to the Vedanta Society* (Hollywood: Vedanta Press, 1956), 49.

66. Christopher Isherwood, *My Guru and His Disciple* (New York: Penguin, 1980), 96.

67. *Vedanta in Southern California,* 49.

68. David King Dunaway, *Huxley in Hollywood* (New York: Harper and Row, 1989), 172.

69. "Trabuco" (prospectus), 1942.

70. Quoted in Christopher Isherwood, "Christopher Isherwood," in Julian Huxley, ed., *Aldous Huxley 1894–1963: A Memorial Volume* (New York: Harper and Row, 1965), 158.

71. Isherwood, *My Guru and His Disciple,* 96.

72. Guinevera A. Nance, *Aldous Huxley* (New York: Continuum, 1988), 14.

73. Anne Fremantle, "Heard Melodies," *Commonweal* 43:15 (Jan. 25, 1946): 385. The name of the community is consistently misspelled "Tzabuco" in this article.

74. Veysey, *Communal Experience,* 271.

75. Aldous Huxley, *The Perennial Philosophy* (New York: Harper and Brothers, 1945).

76. See, for example, Gerald Heard, "The Need for Moral Research," *Christian Century* 62:33 (Aug. 15, 1945): 929–31; Heard, "The Practice of the Presence," *Christian Century* 59:17 (Apr. 29, 1942): 558–59.

77. John E. Whiteford Boyle, *Of the Same Root: Heaven, Earth, and I* (Washington, D.C.: Academy of Independent Scholars/Foreign Services Research Institute, 1990), inside front cover.

78. Veysey, *Communal Experience,* 272.

79. For a description of life in this later phase of Trabuco, see *Vedanta in Southern California,* 51–54.

80. Anderson, *Upstart Spring,* 12–13.

81. Despite the size and longevity of the Emissary communities, no standard work on their history and outlook has yet been published. One of the better brief overviews of the movement was written by a member, Dave Thatcher, "100 Mile Lodge—Emissaries of Divine Light," *Communities* no. 36 (Jan.–Feb. 1979): 39–41. See also Michael S. Cummings, "Democratic Procedure and Community in Utopia," *Alternative Futures* 3 (fall 1980): 35–57.

82. For an exposition of Lemurian ideas see *Lemuria the Magnificent* (n.p.: Lemurian Fellowship, 1937).

83. *Into the Sun* (Ramona, Calif.: Lemurian Fellowship, 1973).

84. Richard Kieninger (writing under the name Eklal Kueshana), *The Ultimate Frontier* (Chicago: Stelle Group, 1963).

85. Charles Betterton and Linda Guinn, "Stelle: Dawn of a New Age City," *Communities: Journal of Cooperation* no. 63 (summer 1984): 9–13.

86. Tony Perry, "Members of 'Children of Light' Say God Will Provide for Them," *Los Angeles Times,* Feb. 28, 1993.

87. Most information about the Children of Light seems to have appeared only in the popular press. At this writing the most recent article was Michelle Boorstein, "'Children of Light's' Aging Survivors Keep the Faith," *Los Angeles Times,* Dec. 10, 1995, p. A49.

88. The major monograph on the Aaronic Order/Levites is Hans A. Baer, *Recreating Utopia in the Desert: A Sectarian Challenge to Modern Mormonism* (Albany: State Univ. of New York Press, 1988). For a brief historical note from the movement itself, see Robert J. Conrad, "Eskdale Community: A Contemporary Commune Intentionally Sited in a Remote, Desert Area," *CALL: "Communes at Large" Letter* no. 6 (summer 1994): 26–27 and no. 7 (winter 1995/96): 23.

89. The report of ninety members is in William A. Hilles, "Of Razor Blades and Beards," *Modern Utopian* 2 (Sept.–Oct. 1967): 2. The count of thirty-two members in 1993 is in a listing in the *Communities Directory* (1995), 208.

90. Besides the two articles cited just above, material on Zion's Order is in Shields, *Divergent Paths of the Restoration,* 155–58.

91. Among the books in which Lawson outlined his cosmology and physics were *Creation* (Philadelphia: Arnold and Co., 1931) and *Manlife* (Detroit: Cosmopower, 1923).

92. Alfred W. Lawson, *Direct Credits for Everybody* (Detroit: Humanity Publishing Co., 1931).

93. Lawson's magnum opus in which he outlined his scheme of things was *Lawsonomy* (Detroit: Humanity Publishing Company, 1935–39); three volumes, individually titled *Lawsonomy, Mentality,* and *Almighty.* Religion was separately covered in *Lawsonian Religion* (Detroit: Humanity Benefactor Foundation, 1949).

94. "Zigzag and Swirl," *Time,* Mar. 24, 1952, p. 49.

95. Lyell D. Henry Jr., *Zig-Zag-and-Swirl: Alfred W. Lawson's Quest for Greatness* (Iowa City: Univ. of Iowa Press, 1991), 233.

96. The controversy over the DMUL's acquisition and sale of machine tools was well covered by the popular press. See William M. Blair, "Big Profit Denied on Surplus Sales," *New York Times,* Mar. 6, 1952, p. 12, plus follow-up articles on Mar. 7 (p. 29), Mar. 8 (p. 7), Mar. 9 (p. 95), and Mar. 20 (p. 21).

97. The definitive account of the Des Moines Univ. of Lawsonomy is in Henry, *Zig-Zag-and-Swirl.* Information not otherwise attributed has been taken from that work.

98. Isabella Fiske McFarlin, Marion R. Nelson, and Allen Sherman, "Free the Kids! and Quarry Hill Community," *Journal of Psychohistory* 21 (summer 1993): 21–27. Additional information was acquired through communications with Quarry Hill residents.

99. For a sympathetic description of Borsodi's vision for Melbourne Univ., see Mildred J. Loomis, "Melbourne University," in her *Alternative Americas* (New York: Universe Books, 1982), 60–61. Loomis also describes related academic work Borsodi undertook in India.

100. The standard account of Melbourne Village is Richard C. Crepeau, *Melbourne Village: The First Twenty-five Years (1946–1971)* (Orlando: Univ. of Central Florida Press, 1988). Information not otherwise credited here is based on Crepeau's work. For a shorter historical sketch, see George L. Hicks, "Ideology and Change in an American Utopian Community" (Ph.D. diss. Univ. of Illinois, 1969), 260–63.

101. James R. Lewis, "Venta, Krishna," *Religious Leaders of America* (Detroit: Gale, 1991), 487–88.

102. Asaiah Bates, former WKFL member, interviewed by Deborah Altus, Sept. 12, 1996.

103. Bates interview. Bates estimated that the membership peaked at 140.

104. Several sources provide an overview of the history of Krishna Venta and his movement. The more substantial ones, perhaps not surprisingly, tend toward sensationalism. See, for example, Richard Mathison, *Faiths, Cults, and Sects of America* (Indianapolis: Bobbs-Merrill, 1960), 212–19; Maurice Beam, *Cults of America* (New York: Macfadden, 1964), 76–90. The survival of the movement until the 1980s is noted by Melton, *Encyclopedia of American Religions,* 654.

105. Melton, *Encyclopedia of American Religions,* 654.

6. 1960 AND BEYOND

1. Ramón Sender, "LATWIDN—Mother Newell's Mountain," *Modern Utopian* 2:6 (July–Aug. 1968): 8–9.

2. Erling Skorpen, "Nevada Communities: The Himalayan Academy," *Modern Utopian* 3:3 (summer 1969): 4, 8, 25–26.

3. An article that captures the flavor of the early Kerista is Robert Anton Wilson, "The Religion of Kerista and Its 69 Positions," *Fact* 2:4 (July–Aug. 1965): 23–29.

4. Richard Fairfield, *Communes USA: A Personal Tour* (Baltimore: Penguin, 1972), 284–90.

5. See my "Drop City: Historical Notes on the Pioneer Hippie Commune," *Syzygy: Journal of Alternative Religion and Culture* 1:1 (winter 1992): 23–38.

6. Several scholars have made such arguments. Bennett M. Berger, a sociologist who studied communes for several decades, for example, argued that the hippie communes may have been part of the centuries-old tradition of countercultures, but found them flatly not historically continuous with earlier American communes. See Bennett M. Berger, "Utopia and Its Environment," *Society* 25:2 (Jan./Feb. 1988): 37–41.

Selected Bibliography

This bibliography represents only a few of the works cited in the foregoing pages. It attempts to list the important survey works on American communitarianism between 1900 and 1960 as well as the most useful books and articles on the major communes covered in this volume. For many more citations see the endnotes.

Adkin, Clare. *Brother Benjamin: A History of the Israelite House of David.* Berrien Springs, Mich.: Andrews Univ. Press, 1990.

Albertson, Ralph. "The Christian Commonwealth in Georgia." *Georgia Historical Quarterly* 29 (June 1945): 125–42.

———. "A Survey of Mutualistic Communities in America." *Iowa Journal of History and Politics* 34:4 (Oct. 1936): 375–444.

Alyea, Paul E., and Blanche Alyea. *Fairhope 1894–1954.* Tuscaloosa: Univ. of Alabama Press, 1956.

Andelson, Jonathan G. "Communalism and Change in the Amana Society, 1855–1932." Ph.D. diss., Univ. of Michigan, 1974.

Arndt, Karl J. R. *George Rapp's Harmony Society, 1785–1847.* Philadelphia: Univ. of Pennsylvania Press, 1965.

———. *George Rapp's Successors and Material Heirs, 1847–1916.* Rutherford, N.J.: Fairleigh Dickinson Univ. Press, 1971.

Arrington, Leonard J., Feramorz Y. Fox, and Dean L. May. *Building the City of God: Community and Cooperation among the Mormons.* Salt Lake City: Deseret Book Co., 1976.

Ayres, William, ed. *A Poor Sort of Heaven, A Good Sort of Earth: The Rose Valley Arts and Crafts Experiment.* Chadds Ford, Pa.: Brandywine River Museum, 1983.

Baer, Hans A. *Recreating Utopia in the Desert: A Sectarian Challenge to Modern Mormonism.* Albany: State Univ. of New York Press, 1988.

Baldwin, Sidney. *Poverty and Politics: The Rise and Decline of the Farm Security Administration.* Chapel Hill: Univ. of North Carolina Press, 1968.

Berry, Brian J. L. *America's Utopian Experiments: Communal Havens from Long-Wave Crises.* Hanover, N.H.: Univ. Press of New England, 1992.

Bestor, Arthur. *Backwoods Utopias: The Sectarian Origins and the Owenite Phase of Communitarian Socialism in America: 1663–1829.* Philadelphia: Univ. of Pennsylvania Press, 2d ed., 1970.

Betterton, Charles, and Linda Guinn. "Stelle: Dawn of a New Age City." *Communities: Journal of Cooperation* no. 63 (summer 1984): 9–13.

Boris, Eileen. *Art and Labor: Ruskin, Morris, and the Craftsman Ideal in America.* Philadelphia: Temple Univ. Press, 1986.

Bradley, Martha Sonntag. *Kidnapped from That Land: The Government Raids on the Short Creek Polygamists.* Salt Lake City: Univ. of Utah Press, 1993.

Brandes, Joseph. *Immigrants to Freedom*. Philadelphia: Univ. of Pennsylvania Press, 1971.

Brown, Margaret Ann. "Not Your Usual Boardinghouse Types: Upton Sinclair's Helicon Home Colony, 1906–1907." Ph.D. diss. George Washington Univ., 1993.

Brundage, W. Fitzhugh. *A Socialist Utopia in the New South: The Ruskin Colonies in Tennessee and Georgia, 1894–1901*. Urbana: Univ. of Illinois Press, 1996.

Bushee, Frederick A. "Communistic Societies in the United States." *Political Science Quarterly* 20 (1905): 625–64.

Carden, Maren Lockwood. *Oneida: Utopian Community to Modern Corporation*. Baltimore: Johns Hopkins Univ. Press, 1969.

Champney, Freeman. *Art and Glory: The Story of Elbert Hubbard*. New York: Crown, 1968.

Cobb, William H. "Commonwealth College: A History." M.A. thesis, Univ. of Arkansas, 1960.

Cohen, David Steven. "The 'Angel Dancers': The Folklore of Religious Communitarianism." *New Jersey History* 95 (spring 1977): 5–20.

Cohen, Joseph J. *In Quest of Heaven: The Story of the Sunrise Co-operative Community*. New York: Sunrise History Publishing Committee, 1957; repr., Philadelphia: Porcupine Press, 1975.

Communities Directory: A Guide to Cooperative Living. Langley, Wash.: Fellowship for Intentional Community, 1995.

Conkin, Paul K. *Tomorrow a New World: The New Deal Community Program*. Ithaca, N.Y.: Cornell Univ. Press, 1959.

———. *Two Paths to Utopia: The Hutterites and the Llano Colony*. Lincoln: Univ. of Nebraska Press, 1964.

Cook, Philip L. *Zion City, Illinois: Twentieth Century Utopia*. Syracuse: Syracuse Univ. Press, 1996.

Crepeau, Richard C. *Melbourne Village: The First Twenty-five Years (1946–1971)*. Orlando: Univ. of Central Florida Press, 1988.

Culmsee, Carlton. *A Modern Moses at West Tintic*. Logan: Utah State Univ. Press, 1967.

Dallas, Jerry W. "The Delta and Providence Farms: A Mississippi Experiment in Cooperative Farming and Racial Cooperation, 1936–1956." *Mississippi Quarterly* 40:3 (summer 1987): 283–308.

Davis, Frances. *A Fearful Innocence*. Kent, Ohio: Kent State Univ. Press, 1981.

Dennon, Jim. *The Oahspe Story*. Seaside, Oreg.: author, 1965.

DePillis, Mario S. "The Development of Mormon Communitarianism, 1826–1846." Ph.D. diss., Yale Univ., 1960.

Dohrman, H. T. *California Cult: The Story of "Mankind United."* Boston: Beacon, 1958.

Duberman, Martin. *Black Mountain: An Experiment in Community*. Garden City, N.Y.: Doubleday/Anchor, 1973.

Dubrovsky, Gertrude Wishnick. *This Land Was Theirs: Jewish Farmers in the Garden State*. Tuscaloosa: Univ. of Alabama Press, 1992.

Eisenberg, Ellen. *Jewish Agricultural Colonies in New Jersey, 1882–1920*. Syracuse: Syracuse Univ. Press, 1995.

Evers, Alf. *Woodstock: History of an American Town*. Woodstock: Overlook Press, 1987.

Fairfield, Richard. *Communes USA: A Personal Tour*. Baltimore: Penguin, 1972.

Fields, Rick. *How the Swans Came to the Lake*. Boulder, Colo.: Shambhala, 1981.

Fogarty, Robert. *All Things New: American Communes and Utopian Movements 1860–1914*. Chicago: Univ. of Chicago Press, 1990.

——. *Dictionary of American Communal and Utopian History*. Westport, Conn.: Greenwood, 1980.

——. *The Righteous Remnant: The House of David*. Kent, Ohio: Kent State Univ. Press, 1981.

Goldberg, Robert A. *Back to the Soil: The Jewish Farmers of Clarion, Utah, and Their World*. Salt Lake City: Univ. of Utah Press, 1986.

Grant, H. Roger. "Missouri's Utopian Communities." *Missouri Historical Review* 66 (Oct. 1971): 20–48.

——. "The New Communitarianism: William H. Bennett and the Home Employment Co-operative Company, 1894–1905." *Bulletin of the Missouri Historical Society* 33 (Oct. 1976): 18–26.

——. "Portrait of a Workers' Utopia: The Labor Exchange and the Freedom, Kan., Colony." *Kansas Historical Quarterly* 43 (spring 1977): 56–66.

——. *Spirit Fruit: A Gentle Utopia*. DeKalb: Northern Illinois Univ. Press, 1988.

Greenberg, Daniel B. "Growing Up in Community: Children and Education within Contemporary U.S. Intentional Communities." Ph.D. diss., Univ. of Minnesota, 1993.

Greenstein, Paul, Nigey Lennon, and Lionel Rolfe. *Bread and Hyacinths: The Rise and Fall of Utopian Los Angeles*. Los Angeles: California Classics Books, 1992.

Greenwalt, Emmett A. *The Point Loma Community in California: 1897–1942—A Theosophical Experiment*. Berkeley: Univ. of California Press, 1955. Rev. ed. published as *California Utopia: Point Loma: 1897–1942*. San Diego: Point Loma Publications, 1978.

Hayden, Dolores. *Seven American Utopias: The Architecture of Communitarian Socialism, 1790–1975*. Cambridge, Mass.: MIT Press, 1976.

Henry, Lyell D. Jr. *Zig-Zag-and-Swirl: Alfred W. Lawson's Quest for Greatness*. Iowa City: Univ. of Iowa Press, 1991.

Herscher, Uri D. *Jewish Agricultural Utopias in America, 1880–1910*. Detroit: Wayne State Univ. Press, 1981.

Hinds, William A. *American Communities and Co-Operative Colonies*. Chicago: Kerr, 3d ed., 1908.

Hine, Robert V. *California's Utopian Colonies*. Berkeley: Univ. of California Press, 1983; originally published in 1953.

Hiss, William Charles. "Shiloh: Frank W. Sandford and the Kingdom, 1893–1948." Ph.D. diss., Tufts Univ., 1978.

Hoagland, Alison K., and Margaret M. Mulrooney. *Norvelt and Penn-Craft, Pennsylvania: Subsistence-Homestead Communities of the 1930s*. Washington, D.C.: Historic American Buildings Survey/Historic American Engineering Record, America's Industrial Heritage Project, National Park Service, 1991.

Holley, Donald. *Uncle Sam's Farmers: The New Deal Communities in the Lower Mississippi Valley*. Champaign: Univ. of Illinois Press, 1975.

Hostetler, John A. *Hutterite Society*. Baltimore: Johns Hopkins Univ. Press, 1974.

Intentional Communities: 1959 Yearbook of the Fellowship of Intentional Communities. Yellow Springs, Ohio: Fellowship of Intentional Communities, 1959.

Jackson, Carl T. *Vedanta for the West: The Ramakrishna Movement in the United States*. Bloomington: Indiana Univ. Press, 1994.

Jackson, David and Neta. *Glimpses of Glory: Thirty Years of Community—The Story of Reba Place Fellowship*. Elgin, Ill.: Brethren Press, 1987.

Kagan, Paul. *New World Utopias: A Photographic History of the Search for Community*. New York: Penguin, 1975.

Kanter, Rosabeth Moss. *Commitment and Community: Communes and Utopias in Sociological Perspective*. Cambridge, Mass.: Harvard Univ. Press, 1972.

Kent, Alexander. "Cooperative Communities in the United States." *Bulletin of the Department of Labor* 6 (July 1901): 563–646.

Kitch, Sally. *Chaste Liberation: Celibacy and Female Cultural Status*. Urbana: Univ. of Illinois Press, 1989.

Klaw, Spencer. *Without Sin: The Life and Death of the Oneida Community*. New York: Penguin, 1993.

Koch, Raymond and Charlotte. *Educational Commune: The Story of Commonwealth College*. New York: Schocken, 1972.

Kramer, Wendell B. "Criteria for the Intentional Community." Ph.D. diss., New York Univ., 1955.

Lee, Dallas. *The Cotton Patch Evidence*. New York: Harper and Row, 1971.

Lee, Lawrence B. "The Little Landers Colony of San Ysidro." *Journal of San Diego History* 21 (1975): 26–51.

Lemieux, Christina M. "The Sunrise Cooperative Farm Community: A Collectivist Utopian Experiment." *Communal Societies* 10 (1990): 39–67.

LeWarne, Charles P. "'And Be Ye Separate': The Lopez Island Colony of Thomas Gourley." *Communal Societies* 1 (1981): 19–35.

———. *Utopias on Puget Sound, 1885–1915*. Seattle: Univ. of Washington Press, 1975.

Lewis, Betty. *Holy City: Riker's Roadside Attraction in the Santa Cruz Mountains*. Santa Cruz: Otter B Books, 1992.

Loomis, Mildred. *Alternative Americas*. New York: Universe Books, 1982.

McKee, Rose L. *"Brother Will" and the Founding of Gould Farm*. Great Barrington, Mass.: William J. Gould Associates, 1963.

Marling, Karal Ann. *Woodstock: An American Art Colony, 1902–1977*. Exhibition catalog, Vassar College Art Gallery, 1977.

Melton, J. Gordon. *Encyclopedia of American Religions*. Detroit: Gale Research, 4th ed., 1994.

———. "Thelemic Magick in America." *Alternatives to American Mainline Churches*. Ed. Joseph H. Fichter. New York: Rose of Sharon Press/Unification Theological Seminary, 1983, pp. 67–87.

Mercer, Duane D. "The Colorado Co-operative Company, 1894–1904." *Colorado Magazine* 44 (fall 1967): 293–306.

Meyer, Pauline. *Keep Your Face to the Sunshine: A Lost Chapter in the History of Woman Suffrage*. Edwardsville, Ill.: Alcott Press, 1980.

Meyers, Mary Ann. *A New World Jerusalem: The Swedenborgian Experience in Community Construction*. Westport, Conn.: Greenwood Press, 1983.

Miller, Ernest I. *Some Tennessee Utopias* (Monograph No. 1, Special Studies in Sociology). Knoxville: Department of Sociology, Univ. of Tennessee, 1942.

Miller, Timothy. *American Communes, 1860–1960: A Bibliography*. New York: Garland, 1990.

———. "Drop City: Historical Notes on the Pioneer Hippie Commune." *Syzygy: Journal of Alternative Religion and Culture* 1:1 (winter 1992): 23–38.

Murphy, James L. *The Reluctant Radicals: Jacob L. Beilhart and the Spirit Fruit Society*. Lanham, Md.: Univ. Press of America, 1989.

Nelson, Shirley. *Fair Clear and Terrible: The Story of Shiloh, Maine*. Latham, N.Y.: British American Publishing, 1989.

Okugawa, Otohiko. "Annotated List of Communal and Utopian Societies, 1787–1919." Published as an appendix to Robert Fogarty, *Dictionary of American Communal and Utopian History,* q.v.

Oliphant, John. *Brother Twelve: The Incredible Story of Canada's False Prophet and His Doomed Cult of Gold, Sex, and Black Magic.* Toronto: McClelland and Stewart, 1991.

Orser, W. Edward. *Searching for a Viable Alternative: The Macedonia Cooperative Community, 1937–1958.* New York: Burt Franklin and Co., 1981.

Oved, Iaacov. *Two Hundred Years of American Communes.* New Brunswick, N.J.: Transaction, 1988.

———. *The Witness of the Brothers: A History of the Bruderhof.* New Brunswick, N.J.: Transaction, 1996.

Pietzner, Cornelius, ed. *A Candle on the Hill: Images of Camphill Life.* Edinburgh, Scotland, and Hudson, N.Y.: Floris Books and Anthroposophic Press, 1990.

Pitts, William L. "Davidians and Branch Davidians: 1929–1987." *Armageddon in Waco: Critical Perspectives on the Branch Davidian Conflict.* Ed. Stuart A. Wright. Chicago: Univ. of Chicago Press, 1995, pp. 20–42.

Richmond, Mary L. *Shaker Literature: A Bibliography.* Hancock, Mass.: Shaker Community, Inc., 1977; 2 vols.

Ross, Joseph E. *Krotona of Old Hollywood.* Montecito, Calif.: El Montecito Oaks Press, 1989.

Sears, Hal D. "Alcander Longley, Missouri Communist: A History of Reunion Community and a Study of the Constitutions of Reunion and Friendship." *Bulletin of the Missouri Historical Society* 25 (Jan. 1969): 123–37.

Shambaugh, Bertha M. H. *Amana: The Community of True Inspiration.* N.p.: State Historical Society of Iowa, 1988 reprint; first published in 1908.

Shankman, Arnold. "Happyville, the Forgotten Colony." *American Jewish Archives* 30 (Apr. 1978): 3–19.

Shepperson, Wilbur S. *Retreat to Nevada: A Socialist Colony of World War I.* Reno: Univ. of Nevada Press, 1966.

Shi, David. *The Simple Life: Plain Living and High Thinking in American Culture.* New York: Oxford Univ. Press, 1985.

Shields, Steven L. *Divergent Paths of the Restoration: A History of the Latter Day Saint Movement.* Bountiful, Utah: author, 3d ed., 1982.

———. *Latter Day Saint Churches: An Annotated Bibliography.* New York: Garland, 1987.

Singer, Richard E. *The American Jew in Agriculture, Past History and Present Condition.* Prize essay, 1941, manuscript at the American Jewish Archives, Cincinnati. Two vols.

Smith, William Lawrence. "Urban Communitarianism in the 1980's: Seven Religious Communes in Chicago." Ph.D. diss., Notre Dame Univ., 1984.

Spence, Clark C. *The Salvation Army Farm Colonies.* Tucson: Univ. of Arizona Press, 1985.

Sperber, Mae T. *Search for Utopia: A Study of Twentieth Century Communes in America.* Middleboro, Mass.: The Country Press, 1976.

Stein, Stephen. *The Shaker Experience in America: A History of the United Society of Believers.* New Haven, Conn.: Yale Univ. Press, 1992.

Swichkow, Louis J. "The Jewish Colony of Arpin, Wisconsin." *American Jewish Historical Quarterly* 54 (1964–65): 82–91.

Tabor, James D., and Eugene V. Gallagher. *Why Waco? Cults and the Battle for Religious Freedom in America.* Berkeley: Univ. of California Press, 1995.

Taylor, R. James. *Mary's City of David.* Benton Harbor, Mich.: Mary's City of David, 1996.

Van Noord, Roger. *King of Beaver Island: The Life and Assassination of James Jesse Strang.* Urbana: Univ. of Illinois Press, 1988.

Veysey, Laurence. *The Communal Experience.* Chicago: Univ. of Chicago Press, 1973.

Watts, Jill. *God, Harlem, U.S.A.: The Father Divine Story.* Berkeley: Univ. of California Press, 1992.

Webber, Everett. *Escape to Utopia: The Communal Movement in America.* New York: Hastings House, 1959.

Weisbrot, Robert. *Father Divine and the Struggle for Racial Equality.* Urbana: Univ. of Illinois Press, 1983.

Wooster, Ernest S. *Communities of the Past and Present.* Newllano, La.: Llano Colonist, 1924.

Wynia, Elly. *The Church of God and Saints of Christ: The Rise of Black Jews.* New York: Garland Publishing, 1994.

Zablocki, Benjamin. *The Joyful Community.* Chicago: Univ. of Chicago Press, 1971.

Index

The Quest for Utopia in Twentieth-Century America was composed in 9.7/13.5 Galliard in QuarkXPress 3.32 on a Macintosh by Kachergis Book Design; printed by sheet-fed offset on 55-pound, acid-free Natural Hi-Bulk, and Smyth-sewn and bound over binder's boards in Arrestox B-grade cloth with dust jackets printed in 2 colors and laminated by Braun-Brumfield; designed by Kachergis Book Design of Pittsboro, North Carolina; published by Syracuse University Press, Syracuse, New York 13244-5160.